First Person Political

First Person Political

Legislative Life and the Meaning of Public Service

Grant Reeher

NEW YORK UNIVERSITY PRESS
New York and London

NEW YORK UNIVERSITY PRESS
New York and London
www.nyupress.org

© 2006 by New York University
All rights reserved

Library of Congress Cataloging-in-Publication Data
Reeher, Grant.
First person political : legislative life and the meaning
of public service / Grant Reeher.
p. cm.
Includes bibliographical references and index.
ISBN–13: 978-0-8147-7575-2 (cloth : alk. paper)
ISBN–10: 0-8147-7575-6 (cloth : alk. paper)
ISBN–13: 978-0-8147-7576-9 (pbk. : alk. paper)
ISBN–10: 0-8147-7576-4 (pbk. : alk. paper)
1. Political participation—United States—Case studies.
2. Legislators—United States—States—Interviews.
3. Responsibility.   I. Title.
JK1764.R44   2005
328.73—dc22   2005024655

New York University Press books are printed on acid-free paper,
and their binding materials are chosen for strength and durability.

Manufactured in the United States of America

c 10 9 8 7 6 5 4 3 2 1
p 10 9 8 7 6 5 4 3 2 1

To the memory of my mother

It was not to be continually loved by all that we—I in the past and you more recently—were chosen. We were elected in the hope that we would do what, according to our knowledge and our convictions, is in the long-term interests of human society as a whole.

—Vaclav Havel, farewell speech to Czech Republic Parliament

I don't like the anger which permeates—it's real easy to touch anger in this job. People in America in general are angry . . . and they get angry at politicians *very* fast. And it's very difficult to deal with.

—Vermont state legislator

Contents

Acknowledgments

I could not have written this book without the support and co-operation of literally hundreds of people who serve the public in a political capacity, either through elected office or staff positions related to the legislature. They are too many to mention individually, and thanking individual legislators would violate anonymity, but I do want to thank them first as a group.

At different stages, the work was supported financially by internal grants at Syracuse University, a grant from the Dirksen Congressional Center, and also indirectly through the Robert Wood Johnson Foundation Scholars in Health Policy Program and the University of Michigan School of Public Health.

David Reeher helped with some of the data gathering. I also benefited from the research assistance of several Syracuse University undergraduate students who worked on the project through the university's Undergraduate Research Program. Four in particular deserve deep and special thanks for providing indispensable assistance at key moments in the project's life course. Early on, Stephen Lisauskas helped to construct a preliminary matrix of the entire population of legislators. Grace Yu provided essential data assistance in the middle stages. Antonio Fargiano and Andrea Jones then supplied sustaining energy, enthusiasm, initiative, and competence as the project wound its way toward final write-up. The book literally might not have been completed without them.

I'm grateful for the administrative support of Syracuse University's Center for Policy Research, and in particular Kelly Bogart's general assistance with the manuscript.

Friends and colleagues of course also helped in different ways. I received advice, encouragement, and helpful criticism from Kristi Andersen, Joe Cammarano, Rick Hall, Glen Halva-Neubauer, and three anonymous reviewers. In the end, the book I produced may not be their favorite one on legislators published during this year, but it is better than it would have been otherwise because of their influence.

My friends and coauthors on other nonlegislative projects, Steve Davis and Larry Elin of Syracuse University's S. I. Newhouse School of Public Communications, have greatly helped me to open up my writing style and have been blessedly tolerant of this book's intrusion on our shared work.

Another friend and colleague in the Center for Policy Research, Doug Wolf, was influential in an unintended way by providing further impetus for the book as it was already taking shape in my head. A few years ago, we had the first of what became an ongoing series of conversations about politics. He remembered then that I had once said earlier, in a seminar, that I liked politicians and found them interesting to talk to. This comment shocked him and stayed with him—how could I feel that way? So many of them seemed to be obviously bereft of competency and civic virtue, and quite a few were downright corrupt.

We shared a mutual surprise, for I was equally flummoxed as to how someone so brilliant and accomplished in his field of demography could hold what seemed to me to be an overly negative view of political actors. That he would advance such a position is a powerful testament to the public alienation with politics that animates this book.

At New York University Press, Ilene Kalish has been the ideal editor. The book is much better because of her. I am also grateful for the excellent work of Salwa Jabado, Despina Papazoglou Gimbel, and Cindy Milstein.

Finally, my spouse, Kathy Sowards, has supported the work and me both emotionally and intellectually, and has encouraged my effort to write in a new vein. She has also inspired me with her own commitment to the public good. Davis Reeher will probably be disappointed to discover that this book, too, is not about airplanes.

1

Introduction
The Sickness Unto Politics

The word *candidate* is very old. Ancient Romans seeking high public office customarily dressed in white togas—hence the Latin *candidatus*, or clothed in white. The candidates' loosely fitted robes made it easy for them to reveal the scars they had earned in battle, while their robes' pure white color, made more intense by rubbing in chalk, demonstrated the purity of their civic purpose in the pursuit of public office.

What today's candidates might reveal about themselves is not hidden by togas; their shrouds are instead woven from the many layers of distance separating most citizens from their political representatives—layers of mediated political information, the absence of politically safe spaces in which to communicate as well as publicly reflect and ruminate, political alienation, and mutual distrust. It is these virtual robes that I attempt to pull back in this book by supplying an insider's view of the political and personal lives of legislators based on their experiences in running for, serving in, and deciding whether to exit from the legislature.

Ultimately, what is revealed in this process is an impression running counter to commonly held ideas about politicians' motivations and the nature of legislative life: that candidates for public office in the United States today actually look a lot like the ancient Roman idealized version. Contrary to what most people think, most candidates pursue office, and once elected serve in office, primarily out of a motivation to advance the public good—and many pay dearly for their efforts.

To uncover these aspects of legislative life, I rely primarily on the extended in-depth interviews that I conducted with 77 legislators serving in the lower houses of Connecticut, New York, and Vermont during the mid-1990s, a time when public respect for and trust in politicians and the political institutions they inhabit reached all-time lows. I also draw on survey responses collected from 233 legislators in the same three states along with data from official records on individual legislators' characteristics and activities, extended personal observations of their behavior, both inside and outside the legislative chamber, and a set of follow-up interviews conducted in 2004 and 2005 with 23 of the original interviewees.

I designed the interviews to give the legislators a chance to talk at length with an understanding stranger, or in some cases a relatively recent acquaintance, about things that were important to them. Our meetings provided a supportive place where they could describe difficult issues, develop points, explain themselves, and register positions, all without concerns about reelection, political standing, or repercussions within the legislative chamber. I believe the discussions yielded honest assessments of legislative life and service, and the legislators' own weaknesses and problems.[1]

Not enough of this has been done. It is strange that for all the attention legislators have attracted in the academic political science literature, so little of it has been focused on them as *people*. There are few direct inquiries into why they do what they do; what attracts them to run and serve; what prompts them to make the transition from active political observer or participant to candidate; and what drives them away from office.[2] Some of the reason for this lack of attention is rooted in certain aspects of academic political science that I will discuss later in this chapter. Political scientists have tended to view these questions as theoretically uninteresting or have inferred the answers based largely on measurements of legislators' behavior while in office. In either case, the questions have not received much direct study. But any valid theory about representation or legislative behavior must ultimately play itself through a process involving people, and thus understanding the people involved is essential to a full understanding of the explanatory work that the theories purport to do.

What result from my inquiry are real stories of the paths taken to the legislature and the experience of serving in it, warts and all, including the effects of chance, strategic planning, and personal gratification. But what also emerges from these stories is a humane and believable portrait of public servants reaching toward the public good—a portrait that should provide some comfort, even perhaps inspiration, for citizens concerned about the state of representative democracy.

The battle scars these legislators carry with them and the civic virtue that informs their purpose are harder to see now, but they are no less real.

Now the scars do not usually result from prior military conflict but rather from the political process itself. The wounds take a variety of forms—private and public, interpersonal and financial. The integrity of the legislators' purposes is reflected in why they seek public office, what they risk and often lose to seek and hold it, and why many ultimately leave. Although the book's focus is on the state legislature, there is good reason to think that the arguments made here extend upward to Congress, outward to other state public offices, and downward to public offices at the municipal level.[3]

The Public, Its Politics, and Its Politicians

Two features about contemporary state politics illustrate the disregard the public has for its politicians. The first is term limits for state legislators. These have exploded onto the political landscape over the past 15 years—they were first enacted in 1990 in California, Colorado, and Oklahoma. Seventeen other states followed suit by 1995. With term limits, voters essentially tie themselves to the mast so that they cannot be tempted by the siren calls of incumbent legislators. The limits were put into effect largely out of a general public frustration with the legislative process, and a more specific belief that the process had become too disconnected from the people and that it was remotely located in the hands of a permanent professional class of politicians. The laws spoke to a desire to return the legislative process to citizen-legislators.

But there is now an active reconsideration of the wisdom of this change, informed by both academic work and journalistic accounts. In particular, the concern is that term limits only eliminate the most senior legislators, who provide needed continuity and knowledge to the legislative process—they function as the institutional memory within the legislature—and that their absence can lead to even greater influence by lobbyists and interest groups. Limiting terms may actually cause some legislators to become even more career conscious and confine their vision of legislative service to a stepping-stone to something else, rather than an end in itself. Indeed, the political process seems to have cooled somewhat on term limits; only Nebraska has introduced them since 1995, and six states have repealed them.[4] Two-thirds of the public, however, still support term limits for members of Congress—the same proportion that would like to see the electoral college replaced by a direct election of the

president.[5] Despite the partial revisionism in thinking about their benefits, limited terms are probably here to stay for a good long while.

The second feature is the growing use in recent years of initiatives and
referendums, procedures through which the public directly votes on legislation. Initiatives were originally a Progressive Era innovation designed
to combat a supposedly corrupt legislative process by vesting more legislative authority directly in the people. Provisions for initiatives and referendums are found mostly in western states, which came of age during
this time period. But during the past 15 years, they have grown in use and
significance. All but two of the term limit laws, for example, were the
products of initiatives and referendums. And a recent survey found that
by over a three-to-two margin, respondents agreed that "the public
should decide issues directly by voting on them" versus "making laws is
a job best left to elected representatives."[6] As with term limits, the political value of initiatives and referendums is being reconsidered, particularly in terms of their vulnerability to manipulation by narrow well-
heeled interests.[7] There is also concern that the policy produced through
the initiative process is too blunt and simplistic, and in combination over
the years, can even become entirely contradictory.

But more important for my purposes here than their shortcomings as
political processes is what term limits, initiatives, and referendums say
about the way the public regards legislators. What is strikingly absent in
these features is the opportunity for extended deliberation in the policymaking process, which for any large-scale political system, requires the
mediation of some representative body with the time and wherewithal to
ponder and decide complicated policy questions, whether that body be a
smaller representative group of ordinary citizens designated for the
task—as has been proposed by some democratic theorists—or a traditional legislature.[8] The public seems reluctant to trust the extension of
that deliberative authority to elected political representatives.

This impression is substantiated by more direct evidence.[9] A recent
survey found that 56 percent of the public agreed with the following
statement: "I don't think public officials care much what people like me
think." Back in 1964, only 36 percent agreed with this statement. During
the same time interval, the proportion believing that government is run
by a "few big interests looking out for themselves" rather than "for the
benefit for all people" doubled, while the level of belief in the honesty of
politicians dropped by half. A similar survey about the relative power to
affect policy decisions by government officials found that 64 percent of

the public responded that interest groups and lobbyists were most influential on these decisions. Twenty-five percent responded that the officials' own sense of the national interest was most influential, while only 7 percent maintained that public opinion was most influential.

Surveys on specific governments and legislative bodies yield similar findings. In 1997, a majority of Florida citizens responded that their state government represented them either poorly or very poorly. Less than a fifth of the U.S. public rate members of Congress or state officeholders as high or very high on honesty and ethics. And in New Jersey, fully a third of the public think that between "half and all" of their state legislators take bribes.

The low esteem in which the public holds elected politicians is disturbing enough in its own right, but even more disturbing is the fact that these opinions seem to be just part of a more general decline in the democratic health of our political system. There is a general turning away from political life by U.S. citizens that manifests itself in both subjective factors—like the declines in levels of trust in politicians and government, sense of personal efficacy in governmental affairs, confidence in the campaign and electoral process, level of trust for other citizens, and optimism about the future—and behavioral factors—like the declines in voting turnout, daily readership of newspapers, and participation in various kinds of politically related activities.[10] Many social and political observers have weighed in on this topic, with a host of diagnoses and prescriptions. One of the most notable accounts in recent years is offered by the political scientist Robert Putnam, who argues in *Bowling Alone* that these statistics of decline are all indicators of a more general decline in something called "social capital," which concerns the stock of interconnectedness and trust among us as citizens. These qualities in turn correlate with our level of civic engagement.

But perhaps more telling than many of the statistics that directly report this political alienation are the anecdotes and quips that illustrate it. Here are three good examples from recent years.[11] Thomas Volgy, whom I will mention again below, reports the following excerpt from a 1993 broadcast of *Larry King Live*: "Politics comes from two words: one is the Greek word *poli*, which means many, and the other word is *ticks*, which means blood sucking insects."[12] John McDonough, whom I will also mention again below, reports the exact same definition of politics, this time coming to him from a constituent. He goes on to quote from Jay Leno: "Politics is show business for ugly people."[13] And a few years ago, I myself came across a campaign button that simply read, "Don't Vote: It Only Encourages Them."

Most disturbing of all is that the problem of political alienation and cynicism seems most concentrated among the nation's youth. It is ironic that in a time when young adults' levels of volunteering and engaging in public service continue to grow beyond those of previous generations, their political alienation also grows, while their political participation declines. Their level of interest in politics, for example, is only about half that of older adults.[14] The level of voting turnout among young adults is also substantially lower than that of older adults, and over the past 30 years it has been dropping at a much faster rate.[15] They have a negative view of politics. When citizens between the ages of 15 and 25 were asked to engage in a word association exercise concerning the word *politics*, "lying" was chosen approximately eight times as often as "responsive," three times as often as "interesting," and twice as often as "public service."[16] Once again, however, it is other qualitative kinds of measures that may be the most telling.

A devastating piece of anecdotal evidence comes from my own city of Syracuse. The Central New York Branch of the National League of American Pen Women holds an annual poetry and art contest for children and adults in the local area. In 2003, first place for poetry in the high school group went to Camille Castro, age 17, for the following piece, titled "Carnival."

> Politics is a carnival
> A fanfare of lights and sounds
> Vibrant flashing colors
> Tricks that deceive the eye
> Vendors selling useless goods
> Five dollars for a ring toss you won't win
> Promises of a prize in the end
> Overpriced cheap stuffed animals
> Sit and watch the show
> Acrobats perform unimaginable tricks
> Human cannons seem unexplainable
> The eye looks where it is guided
> Is it all fun and games?
> Beware of pick-pocketers
> If you look too long the bright lights will blind you

> The roaring crowd will deafen you
> When the last magician has performed his final trick
> Tents will be brought down
> Colors fade
> All that is left behind is a pile of trash

The last line is a democratic heartbreaker. Suffice it to say that to our youth, politics seems corrupt.[17]

As our overall voting turnout for presidential elections hovers around only 50 percent, it is feared—perhaps it is also hoped—that in terms of our political engagement, as a nation we have finally hit rock bottom. Even in the November election immediately following September 11, 2001, when active displays of patriotism were washing in waves across the nation, turnout matched all-time lows for that type of off-year election.[18] The following 2002 midterm congressional election, which did change the party control of the U.S. Senate, nonetheless failed to achieve a significant improvement in terms of turnout. Granted, the presidential election of 2004 returned turnout to a level not seen since 1968, but it remains unclear whether or not this new high-water mark will be repeated and will trickle down to other elections, and whether it reflects an instance of positive political engagement, rather than a moment of extreme divisiveness.

Sources of the Problem

What caused this increase in our political alienation? At first, one might be tempted to respond that it's simply the American way. From our beginnings as a nation, we have always been suspicious of government and government officials relative to our European peers.[19] In policy terms, the evidence for this fact is everywhere: With the exceptions of education, the military, and law enforcement, Americans have waited longer to institute large-scale social programs, and when we have done so, those programs have tended to be less extensive. Our government owns fewer industries, taxes us less, and once it has collected that tax money, uses it less to redistribute incomes among us. Consider, for example, that the United States is still the only advanced Western nation without universally provided health care. These policy differences point to an intensely held sense of individualism in the political thinking of Americans, and a concomitant suspicion of the state, which would in turn naturally lead toward a relatively more negative view of politicians and the institutions of government.

A negative view about how individuals will behave in political matters is also woven into the very swaddling clothes of our government system. While one can hear echoes of the ancient civic republican call for brotherhood in the writings of Thomas Paine, the Declaration of Independence, and the Articles of Confederation, the Constitution crafted by James Madison and his colleagues is all business.[20] In fact, it is in many respects a blueprint for dealing with the evil that men do. No one can be counted on to do the right thing. As Norman Jacobson brilliantly summarizes:

> A crescendo is reached in Article I, Section 8, the crucial enabling section of the Constitution, where the specific powers granted Congress are enumerated. As an expression of political prescience, of the sort of conduct to be expected from strangers and countrymen alike, the words of the authors leave little to the imagination. Pirates and felons are seized, counterfeiters are apprehended, bankrupts are dealt with, militiamen disciplined, captures effected on land and sea, insurrections suppressed, wars fought, invasions repelled. Threats to order were everywhere, and Section 8 takes on the aspect of a demonology of politics, foreign and domestic. Of the functions and powers set down, around two-thirds are devoted to crime and punishment, war, invasion and rebellion. The rest, save a very few, concern taxation and commerce. Beset by dangers, real and fancied, the authors of the Constitution meant their government to be frankly disciplinary and punitive. Today we call such men realists.[21]

Of course, those working *inside* the government could not be trusted either; hence the need for a separation of institutions, because as Madison states in *Federalist #51*, "Ambition must be made to counteract ambition." Again, as Jacobson retells the Constitution:

> In addition to formal checks upon the power of those in positions of responsibility and trust, provision is explicitly made against incursions into the public treasury and into the purses of kings and satraps. No sooner is the plan announced for the selection of representatives of the people and their organization into two Houses, than procedures are established for the punishment of members guilty of disorderly conduct

and the expulsion of troublemakers. And why not? Venality and recalci-
trance are as natural to men as the air they breathe.[22]

The founders thus institutionalized a politics based on "division and mutual hostility."[23] No wonder, then, that subsequent generations of American citizens were similarly suspicious of political institutions and the persons who inhabit them.

Indeed, negative views of politicians are not new. In a commencement
speech several years ago that encouraged new graduates to get involved
in politics, the historian Arthur Schlesinger Jr. reminded his audience of
the storied American tradition of holding politicians in contempt.

> Congress, Mark Twain said a century ago, is the only "distinctly native
> criminal class." "Reader, suppose you were an idiot," he wrote on an-
> other occasion. "And suppose you were a member of Congress. But I re-
> peat myself." "I am not a politician," said Artemus Ward, "and my
> other habits are good, also." A politician, wrote Ambrose Bierce, is "an
> eel in the fundamental mud upon which the superstructure of organized
> society is reared." The basic motto of our democracy has always been
> "throw the rascals out."[24]

To this we might want to add that H. L. Mencken, using imagery similar to Camille Castro's, famously referred to Congress as the "asses' carnival."

But while all of this political background helps to explain how and
why we are different from our peers in the Western world, it does not explain the *change* in our own behavior and views during the last 30 years.
Something significant has shifted in our views of government and politicians. Thirty years ago, many more of us felt pretty good about our government and our elected officials, and more of us voted. The real question
is why that change occurred.

Several culprits have been identified by academic scholars and political
observers, and while some seem remediable with the appropriate public
policy, others appear to run deep in our social structure. They also seem
to be interconnected. The supposed causes include, first, a campaign system that appears to be expensive and relatively unregulated, at least in
comparison with many other Western nations.[25] As the amounts spent in
and around campaigns continue to rise, this system in turn appears increasingly weighted toward the wealthiest individuals, corporations, and

interest groups—and with the sizable increases in economic inequality over the past 30 years, the wealthiest few appear to the rest of us to have become both wealthier and fewer.[26]

The limits on "soft money" contributions to political parties imposed by the Bipartisan Campaign Reform Act of 2002 (BCRA) only scratch at the surface of this problem and have accelerated a new source of growing concern: independent expenditures. Smaller campaign contributions facilitated by the Internet may counteract some of the problem—the returns from election 2004 are promising in this regard—but the overall concern is likely to remain.

Consider, for example, the following data from the realm of "hard money," the direct contributions to candidates, and for which the limits were loosened by the BCRA from $1,000 per candidate per election to $2,000. A recent study by Peter Francia and his colleagues of donations in the 1996 election cycle found that only 4 percent of all congressional campaign contributors and 19 percent of presidential campaign contributors came from families with incomes under $50,000. On the other end of the spectrum, 82 percent of all congressional campaign contributors and 56 percent of presidential campaign contributors came from families with incomes in excess of $100,000.[27] In *Wealth and Democracy*, Kevin Phillips reports that in 1997, only 5 percent of all congressional campaign contributors came from families with incomes under $50,000.[28] And in *The Buying of the President 2004*, Charles Lewis reports that in recent presidential elections, in the year before the primaries, all of the maximum hard money donations to the candidates came from only one-tenth of 1 percent of the population.[29] Note that all of these percentages concern the number of contributors, not the total dollars contributed—the percentages would be even further skewed if that were the case.

Other factors explaining the change include the aforementioned decline in social capital, both as cause and effect, as well as the decline in the relevance of political parties as mechanisms of organizing people versus mechanisms of organizing money. Also thought to contribute to the problem are the changes since Watergate in the way the media cover politics, including a greater emphasis on scandal, corruption, incompetence, and intractable conflict, and a more general shift toward softer news.[30] Accompanying these changes are the attack-and-rant approach taken by an increasing number of media-based political pundits, and the decline of civility on political talk radio. The media developments are of course in addition to the harm brought about by the scandals themselves—Watergate, Iran-Contra, Keating, Whitewater, and Monica Lewinsky, to name a few of the most significant ones. Interwoven through all these changes is another problematic development: the heightened tendency of the branches of government and members of the two political parties, when dealing with each other, to engage in exposure, investigation, litigation, and prosecution. During the Clinton administration, this came to be known as the "criminalization of politics."[31] James Madison's institution of checks and balances is now apparently running amok. Also implicated is the increase in the political candidates' use of negative advertising and more shallow, television-based campaigns, in addition to the fact that many incumbents, not to mention challengers, campaign by running *against* the institution to which they aspire. All of this paints a bleak portrait. Indeed, when viewed in this light, lacking confidence in politics and politicians seems only natural.

What deepens the impact of these changes is that they have taken place at the same time that the issues of governance have become more complicated and difficult to reckon with, due to factors like accelerated technological innovations, increased confrontations with the limits to unrestrained growth, and greater population diversity. Our general stock of political understanding thus requires more nuance and discernment at precisely the moment that our political system seems least able and inclined to supply it.

And academic political science has also played a role. This is in part due to the effects of modern academic intellectual culture operating in the context of the recent political developments just described. It is in the very nature of academics to be skeptical and critical, to take little for granted. In the classroom, professors attempt to teach those same qualities to their students; they want their students to be critically conscious of the world they live in. The line between healthy skepticism and debilitating cynicism is a fine one, however, and oftentimes this line dissolves in the classroom transmission from faculty to student. The basic problem is not new; in Plato's *Republic*, for example, Socrates warns about the dangers of teaching the dialectical method too early out of the fear that youth may then use it indiscriminately to tear apart everything, including worthy institutions.[32] In recent years, though, the potential damaging civic effects of such a culture have intensified.

Political scientists are also implicated more substantively. The way in which they have tended to approach the study of legislatures in recent years exacerbates the negative fallout from the academic culture's generally critical approach. This approach largely began in 1974 with the publication of David Mayhew's provocative and influential *Congress: The Electoral Connection* (note the synchronicity of the publication of his book and the political changes described earlier). Part microeconomics-inspired thought experiment and part empirical observation, Mayhew's book supposes that members of Congress are primarily motivated—as a necessarily more *proximate* goal relative to other and perhaps more deeply held goals—to seek their own reelection. Mayhew then goes on to consider numerous aspects of individual and collective congressional behavior through this lens, producing what another noted congressional scholar calls "a resulting picture, presented in one of the most influential essays in recent years, [that] depicts behavior and institutional practices which are strikingly familiar to Congress-watchers."[33] In an ironic twist to a book that Mayhew himself has described as a "jeremiad," the acknowledgments thank two individual Congressmen by name, as "two members who truly serve in the public interest." One of the two, Frank Thompson Jr., later went on to political ruin and two years in prison as a result of the Abscam scandal.

At least two generations of legislative scholars have now followed Mayhew. Many have applied increasingly sophisticated and narrowly focused microeconomic theories to legislatures in the attempt to understand almost all facets of legislative behavior, rules, and organization.[34] The encompassing guiding assumption is self-interest and rational behavior on the part of legislators, in particular the pursuit of utility maximization. Although political scientists employ this assumption as a lever by which to lift out useful insights concerning patterns in behavior, decision making, and institutional development, it is the assumption itself that often makes the most lasting impression on those listening, whether they be fellow academics, undergraduate students, or the media.[35] This tends to add more bile to the jaundiced understanding of politicians and the political process.

It is now apparently the case that it rarely occurs to academics or members of the media that politicians are primarily acting out of a sense of the public good, or that they are making good-faith efforts to discover that good and what it requires in terms of policy. And this message has not been lost on the public. In addition to the direct and indirect dampening effects such views have on the public's involvement in political affairs, down to the level of voting, the deeper problem here is that taken to their logical conclusion, they make democratic deliberation—which in a large-scale society must necessarily take place through a representative system—almost impossible to achieve. The journalist E. J. Dionne Jr., writing 12 years ago, lamented this kind of political cynicism:

> Senate Republican leader Bob Dole's fight against the stimulus package could not have stemmed, even in part, from principled opposition to government spending. It had to be about Dole's presidential ambitions or his internal problems with Senate Republicans or something else thoroughly selfish. God forbid that we even entertain the possibility that Clinton or Dole might believe in something.
>
> This kind of cynicism judges everything in terms of technique . . . which gets you around having to talk about the merits of . . . programs. . . .
>
> But judging everything by hidden motives and technique leads to mental and civic laziness. It lets us get around ever having to argue publicly about what's really at stake.[36]

As just one example to demonstrate the lasting quality of his point, 10 years later an Associated Press report on Federal Reserve chair Alan Greenspan's pointed criticism of the Bush administration's plan for additional tax cuts included some speculation about his motivations.[37] In trying to tease out what was behind Greenspan's commentary, the AP reporter wondered whether he was no longer concerned about his own future as Federal Reserve chair, no longer wanted to serve as chair, or had learned that Bush was not planning on nominating him for an additional term (the rumor at the time). Nowhere did the piece consider the possibility that Greenspan simply felt deeply that the cuts were the wrong thing to do at the time, based on his knowledge of economics and sense of the public good.

My own home city supplies another powerful example, which I want to discuss at some length because it is indicative of the media messages that most citizens are exposed to concerning politics and politicians, and it is at a more local level. Consider the following stories and editorials found over the course of a year in the city's main newspaper, *The Syracuse Post-Standard*. Around the time that Camille Castro was writing her prizewinning poem, the paper was running an extended feature series, which it called "New York's Tax Challenge," on the different taxes levied by state government. Each story described a different tax and compared it with similar taxes in other states, usually finding that New York's taxes were higher. Rarely was there even mention of the services and goods that the taxes provided, or an extensive comparison of the services and goods in New York with those in other states. The stories were instead focused on the costs and burdens. This went on for months. Finally, at the completion of the series, there was one brief editorial encouraging citizens to consider the services and goods as well as the costs. The overall message, however, had already been well established: The taxpayers were being fleeced by their political representatives.

During roughly the same time period, *The Syracuse Post-Standard* also did a feature story on local elected officials who were not shoveling snow off their sidewalks, and in an editorial mocked the local Democratic Party for not having an early announced candidate to oppose a popular incumbent county executive under the title "A Treasure Waits for a Candidate."[38] On the eve of a local election, the paper ran a story on candidates who had themselves not voted in previous elections.[39] The negative frame is obviously the starting presumption in these stories; they are small-bore but nonetheless telling examples of the increasingly shallow and cynical reporting and commentary style that is put forward as investigative journalism—a style that is popular in part because it is easy and inexpensive to produce. This trend has been noted by many observers of the media.[40]

There are other more significant examples. In late 2003, the paper ran a front-page headline story that was, on its face, about the discrepancy between state legislative leaders' statements that they would freeze spending on their own operations that year and the fact that actual spending had increased by 5 percent.[41] The discrepancy was important and deserved the paper's attention in its role as a public "watchdog." But the story went well beyond providing that information, conveying a more generally critical view of the state legislature. It twice reminded the reader that the spending did not go to state programs but rather to "Senate and Assembly members and their staffs as compensation, as well as to pay for maintenance of their lavish chambers and enormous public relations operations." Note the choice of adjectives here. Different specific categories of spending on legislative operations were described as having "jumped" and "ballooned" in recent years, and the assembly's media facilities, which allow legislators to communicate with citizens—a necessary element in a modern, large-scale representative democracy—were treated as "perks" yielding electoral advantage.[42] The paper followed with a more explicit editorial version of the same piece, which added phrases like "dismal record," "blather and stalemate," "self-glorifying mailings," and "gilded chambers," and ended with a suggestion that the entire legislature be turned out of office.[43]

The photograph accompanying the original story—of a Web site showing the state senate television studio along with text related to a certain Republican senator's position on a proposed expansion of the area's largest shopping mall—was of particular note because it connected with another strand of the paper's criticisms of elected politicians. Simultaneously evoking both Theodore Dreiser and George Orwell, the mall expansion project was christened "Destiny USA." Despite the facts that the expansion's ultimate value to the area was debatable, the track record of the development corporation was spotty, and an artist's rendering of the proposed expansion conjured up the cover art for an H. G. Wells novel, the paper came out hard for the project.

The paper had criticized this state senator in particular when he objected that the tax deals being considered were not wise. His colleagues in the majority party in the senate deferred to his judgment on the local matter, and in the legislative rush at the end of the session, opted not to pass the additional guarantees that the development corporation had lobbied for. In editorials, the paper called the senator a "demagogue," characterized his behavior as "obstinacy and obstructionism," opined that his motivations were solely "to kill the project, to slay a Goliath, to prove he's tough," and ultimately located his behavior in "hatred for the developers."[44] Centered inside one of the editorials was a picture of the senator in the chamber, which captured him leaning back in his chair, eyes closed, bottom lip protruding over the top—an image conveying intransigence. In contrast, a feature story on the developer and his corporation showed the developer smiling in front of a wall of photographs of his grandchildren.

More generally, the paper characterized elected officials deliberating over the tax exemptions for the project as, among other things, not being able "to find their way," and further claimed that given the dire economic straits in the area and across the nation, the political leaders had broken "faith with the people who elected them."[45] A later editorial praising the local congressman for trying to save the project included the following ironic conclusion:

It is a measure of how low public esteem for political leaders has fallen that such a sensible approach to problem solving elicits high praise. It ought to be business as usual. Too often petty rivalry, ego and favoritism for certain interests trump a politician's proper concern for the public good.[46]

Granted, the editorial page is where the paper rightly takes its stand and offers its opinions. Also granted is that the New York State Legislature is in need of reforms to help improve the budget-making process and strengthen committee work, and that the institution has adopted to some degree a "bunker mentality" about certain aspects of the legislative process. In addition, it is important to note that the paper did not frame all of its stories and editorials concerning politicians in a negative light, and engaged in some very good public interest reporting during the year (examples included the use of state "Empire Zone" tax breaks and a canal development project). But on balance, there was a negative tone to its political coverage. The way in which the paper takes its stands and makes its points matters. The problem with the piece on the mall, among many others, is that what should have been portrayed as a reasonable difference in opinion over policy between elected officials and the paper's editorial staff became instead yet another story of political incompetence and civic vice.

In the year just passed, with the twentieth consecutive late state budget (the state has a uniquely early budget deadline of April 1, versus the July 1 date that 46 other states use), the inability of the governor and the legislature to generate a school funding formula in accordance with a state court decision, and the issuance of a lengthy university research center report recommending a set of legislative reforms, criticism of the state government by the media and among the public reached a fever pitch.[47] Again, while certain improvements in the legislative process in New York are clearly needed, the point here is that the tone of the coverage, editorials, and public airwaves commentary was so hostile and aggressive that it largely precluded much in the way of reasoned deliberation. Anger, rather than deliberation, was invited, encouraged, and inspired.

Missing in particular was a recognition that politics is the arena in which claims about what society should collectively aim to accomplish and avoid are negotiated, and that a budget is the principal way in which this is done. New York, a large and diverse state, is rich with competing and conflicting claims, which are divided by a kaleidoscopic array of fault lines depending on people's interests, identities, and situations. Adding to the tension is the fact that the amount of money at stake in the state budget is enormous. Instead, what readers encountered was the message that the correct answers to complicated political questions were readily available, and the legislators were simply incompetent and malicious in not arriving at them and implementing them quickly. To take just two examples, a regularly appearing column at one point described the state of governmental affairs with adjectives such as "revolting," deigned an examination of the governor's State of the State speech "a waste of time," and claimed that the postage on a letter to a legislator "feels like a waste of money," while an editorial on the school funding issue ended by passing the following simple "sentence" on the legislators: "Do your job."[48]

Fortunately, we are now beginning to hear some alternative voices, both in the news media and the entertainment industry, and some, like the show *The West Wing*, are starting to help, but they are relatively few and far between, and still have a long way to go to counter the trend.[49]

The Politicians

Alienation from political life is not limited to private citizens, however. It also appears to extend to elected politicians. Media reports and anecdotally based accounts indicate that legislators are less happy in their jobs than they once were. As a consequence, many legislators leave service in the middle of their careers, while many potential candidates decide not to pursue office at all.[50] In the last 20 years, there have been many high profile "quittings" in the U.S. Congress, in which prominent legislators have left the national chamber out of exhaustion and dissatisfaction with the process, and the costs that public life has exacted on their private lives. They cite declines in collegial comity and trust, the inability to work in good faith on difficult, substantive policy issues, the constant pressure of fund-raising, and the harsh nature of media coverage.[51]

Though state legislatures do not ordinarily get the same level of public scrutiny, a similar disease appears to be growing in virulence there too, prompting concerns about "sick" state legislatures.[52] Despite the fact that over the past 35 years legislatures have modernized and professionalized—meaning that they have increased their institutional independence, become more productive and competent, raised salaries, and provided more and better staff support—and despite the fact that their relative importance as policymaking institutions has increased, many state legislators seem to be unhappy, and it appears that veteran legislators are leaving in greater numbers than before.[53] It is also difficult sometimes to get people to run for the legislature; over a third of state legislative general elections are uncontested.[54]

Possible sources of the problem include some of the by-products of this modernization: a more complicated job, greater demands, being held to higher standards, a heavier workload, and more expensive campaigns. Legislators are also deeply frustrated by the public's lack of respect.[55] Furthermore, some legislative observers have suggested that accompanying those changes has been the decline of internal norms of comity and community, in part as the competition for contested seats has become rougher, as well as the increased penetration into the process by outside forces such as the media and interest groups, which again make it more difficult to work together.[56] Thus, as the nature of the state legislative process continues to change, and perhaps to erode, there is a particular concern over the state legislatures' and the legislators' capacity to function well, and the supply of "good" candidates for office.

Political Dignity

Through this book, I cannot expect to make a positive impact on political participation and the stock of social capital, or the quality of legislative life; indeed, as I suggested earlier, many of the sources of the declines in these areas are long-term and deeply structural. But I do hope to help counteract the particularly negative view toward elected politicians and in that limited sense contribute toward a shift to rehabilitating *the political*. I attempt to accomplish this by relating what I have learned from systematically talking with and watching politicians, and by sharing their real stories and voices.

Of course, I am not the first person to assert the need to counteract the public's negative views toward politicians and to attempt to do so through writing about legislative life. This need has been recognized by many others, often politicians and former politicians themselves. Senator Joseph Lieberman worries about this in his book, *In Praise of Public Life*. Lieberman argues that the central question is the *purpose* that informs public officials' behavior as well as the public's perception of that purpose. His book is both a defense of and a call to action for elected officials. John McDonough, a former Massachusetts state representative and now a health policy professor at Brandeis University, similarly worries about public cynicism toward politics and contends that a principal culprit is the public's lack of a deeper understanding of political dynamics. In *Experiencing Politics*, he tries to apply explanatory theories popular among academics, but little known outside the academy, to his own experiences in the legislature in order to provide some of that deeper understanding in a publicly accessible way. And Thomas Volgy, a longtime University of Arizona political science professor and former mayor of Tucson, is concerned that citizens have lost any sense of *empathy* for public figures, in part because of changes in the way politics is organized and the way the media cover public officials. He wrote *Politics in the Trenches*, which offers an extended annotated account of his political experiences, as an effort to help reinstill that feeling of empathy.

Volgy is on the right track with the notion of empathy, but I think what is more urgently needed, and what this book attempts to provide, is a measure of *respect* for and a sense of the *dignity* of elected office. In this sense, this book may have its roots in my own childhood and my mother. My mother could have been a poster parent for *Bowling Alone*, not only because she always bowled in leagues, but because she was an active member of her church and a local precinct captain for the Republican Party. And she instilled in me my own interest and participation in political life. In 1974, as Richard Nixon prepared to leave office in disgrace, I felt devastated and betrayed—as a boy, I had worked alongside my mother on his election and then again on his reelection. I remember her saying then that we should maintain our respect for the office, despite what Nixon had done. It was cold comfort to me then, in the midst of losing my political innocence, but I think I understand her better now.

The book is also rooted in my previous research on state legislators, in addition to the present research, of course. In an earlier work on state legislators' beliefs about socioeconomic fairness as well as the ways in which these beliefs influence their behavior and decision making, I found that by and large in their legislative work, the legislators sincerely pursued their notions of what was best.[57] Granted, for individual legislators there were a host of other forces limiting their ability to completely realize their beliefs about fairness in their work and decisions. These forces ranged from the need to compromise in order to be effective, to the electoral necessity as well as the desire to be attentive to constituents with whom they disagreed, to the structural constraints of time and information. But on the whole, the legislators were nonetheless trying to do the right thing, as they understood it. In addition, from the beginning of my academic work as a graduate student conducting dissertation research on up to the present, I have continually been impressed by the hard work and dedication of these public officials, and daunted by the demands and expectations placed on them, which I have experienced firsthand as I have trailed after them both in the capitols and their districts.

Caveats and Limitations

I should acknowledge up front that in terms of an elaborate, theoretical treatment, this book largely elides the challenge of normatively defining just how politicians *should* behave and what constitutes corruption, or how they *should not* behave. These are indeed sticky subjects; the controversies surrounding them are as old as politics itself, and are probably no closer to being resolved today than they were in Plato's time. What I have in mind here for the purposes of this book is a commonsense, democratically inspired intuitive notion that the proper normative standard is behavior and institutional structures that advance the democratic purposes of the political office, broadly understood. This standard will inevitably include navigations between general values that reflect fundamental (yet still competing) apprehensions of the public good, and more particular loyalties and concerns.[58] But it bears repeating that the problem with the public's perception of its politicians is not about finer distinctions of what exactly constitutes the public good; it is the widely held and growing sense of gross deficiency that concerns me here.

In anticipation of an obvious criticism of this work—that I set out to find the good in politicians and was thus too selective in my attention—I should point out that this project was not originally undertaken with this theme in mind. Initially, I had planned to conduct a more traditional academic inquiry into the determinants for individual legislators of the level of legislatively oriented activity within the chamber. Interview subjects were chosen to reflect the population of the entire chamber in each state in terms of age, gender, party, seniority, prior legislative service, occupation, education, length of residence in the state, marital and child status, race, and type of district (urban, rural, etc.). In order to get at the topic of legislative activity, I cast a broad net, particularly during the interviews, which treated at length the legislators' experiences and decisions regarding seeking office, their personal experiences of serving, and their decisions about staying and leaving. I was also exposed to and participated in many conversations about these topics in the extensive periods of my observation of individual legislators and the entire legislatures. As I worked more on the project, this set of topics seized my attention and became my primary focus—it thus emerged from the empirical work. I think I have rendered the material fairly, but that is up to the reader to decide and, I would hope, future researchers examining similar topics in similar ways.

And finally, although I want to suggest that the officeholders I encountered are generally an admirable group, are there exceptions to the rule? Of course there are, at all levels of public service.[59] Like in any other occupation, some people are just no damn good, by any reasonable standard. But in elected politics they are relatively few, and perhaps particularly few in comparison with executives in the private corporate world. Furthermore, am I claiming, for those politicians who do indeed evoke in us a feeling of civic hopefulness, that they are motivated *only* by civically pure desires, and at all times? Again, of course they are not. After all, Madison had his finger on something real and timeless. Political behavior is always a complicated mix of self-seeking, self-interest, and broader, higher aims. Indeed, it is ultimately impossible to completely disentangle the two kinds of pursuits, for as E. E. Schattschneider notes, "It is futile to try to determine whether men are stimulated politically by interests or ideas, for people have ideas about interests."[60]

Nor am I claiming in this book that the political system in the United States works especially well. Our political system is shot through with problems, which are located both deep within its structure and at its surface. They have been well identified by political scientists like John Gaventa and Anthony King, political journalists like William Greider and Kevin Phillips, and public interest groups like the Center for Public Integrity.[61] The fact that legislators must deal with these problems is in part the occasion for this book.

But I am writing about the overall tenor of the legislative enterprise. The offices that politicians hold merit our respect, not only because of the democratic importance of the offices themselves, but also because of the dignity of the individuals who occupy them. What I am claiming is that in light of their motivations and experiences, legislators deserve more of our praise and respect, for they are doing a reasonably good job at an exceptionally difficult job—they are navigating exhaustingly difficult terrain in order to discover and produce what they think is good for others.

And they often pay a heavy toll, both professionally and personally, for doing so. In the current political climate, these facts are severely underappreciated.

Overview of the Book

The chapters proceed roughly chronologically through the legislators' service. Chapter 2 tells the stories of their election to the legislature: their backgrounds, motivations, decisions to run, and experiences during the campaign. Chapter 3 follows with a rendition of their experiences inside the legislature: their likes and dislikes, the struggles and challenges that they faced, and their experiences in holding or losing the office. Chapter 4 focuses on their decisions to stay or leave, and further examines some of the costs and benefits of being a legislator. Each of these three chapters closes with a summary of its main points. Chapter 5 is about the weaknesses, both civic and personal, that emerged during the interviews and the observations. These treatments lead to other discussions of leadership along with the benefits and challenges of having a citizen legislature. An appendix follows, which supplies a summary of my methods of analysis and the political contexts of the three state legislatures that I studied.

Although the chapters are broken down by the time line of the legislators' service, and the interview excerpts are meant to illustrate particular points and arguments within each of these chapters, these divisions are imposed and at some level artificial. Thus, the interview material excerpted in one place in a chapter can also illustrate the points made in another place and indeed other chapters. This occurs at the beginning of chapter 2, for instance, in that the three extended excerpts that open that chapter, while they are primarily meant to provide some good overall examples of the paths taken to the legislature as well as the decisions and motivations to run, also suggest important points concerning the tensions between legislative service, family life, and financial well-being, which are explored later in chapter 3. To put it most simply, the arguments and interview material presented in this book should be read in important respects as a cumulative whole.

Brief Notes on Methods and Language

More detail about the methods used for this work can be found in the appendix. For now, note that this study employs all four of the principal methods used to research legislatures: collection of official record data, administration of surveys, engaging in observation, and conducting interviews. By examining legislatures in three different states, it also introduces a comparative perspective. I should make it clear from the beginning, however, that this is for the most part an interview- and observation-based work that relies primarily on qualitative interpretative methods. There are good reasons to employ these methods, given the topic I am pursuing. I have set forward at length those reasons in earlier works using these methods and will not repeat them all here.[62] Instead, I will just observe that I am trying to capture something important about the legislature from *within* that world, rather than from outside it. I am also more engaged in trying to *suggest* something important about that world than in trying to explain it. The ultimate goal is to produce an account that the legislators themselves would recognize as authentic.[63] My methods carry with them certain implications about the way we should evaluate the resulting arguments, which I have stated in a previous work:

> The standards of validity that fit such a project are those of plausibility—of perspectives that "we can imagine or 'feel' as right"—rather than scientific proof, and the evidence that is most persuasive is that of thick description rather than correlation and covariance; the subject does not allow for any more specificity than that.[64]

Regarding the use of language in this book, particularly in the interview transcripts, note that my main concern is to preserve anonymity. I do not name specific political parties, which are often cited by the legislators, unless knowing that party is essential to understanding or appreciating that particular story line. Where possible, I avoid discussing an interview excerpt in a way that identifies the gender of the speaker, unless again, this information is important to understanding the story. In addition, I often enclose a word or phrase in brackets, which indicates that I have substituted a generic equivalent of a more specific phrase or word that could potentially identify the legislator. Sometimes I also use these brackets to condense interview material not necessary to the story line. Note that I do not otherwise "clean" the transcripts. Sentences sometimes stop midway, and the language can be earthy. That is how people talk.

There are two instances where I deliberately suspend the attempt to preserve anonymity. The first is found at the beginning of the next chapter and is an indirect case of identification, in which anyone who is particularly familiar with the politics in that state will have enough information to identify the legislator; the second occurs in chapter 5 and is a direct case of identification, involving Vermont house speaker Ralph Wright. In both instances, I believe the reasons for my decision will be obvious.

The legislative body is known by different names in the three states in which I conducted my interviews. Furthermore, there are informal names that also differ among the states; in Connecticut, for example, the senate is often referred to as "the circle" because the senators' desks are arrayed in a circle on the chamber floor. In order to further preserve anonymity, and for the purposes of convenience, I will refer to the house chamber as the "legislature" or "house," and the senate chamber as the "senate," unless I want to specifically draw the reader's attention to the chamber in a specific state. More important, in the transcriptions of the legislators' comments, I will also substitute "legislature" and "house" for any other words indicating the legislative body or the house chamber, and I will do this without using the brackets that I employ elsewhere.

Finally, after some of the interview excerpts, in particular the longer ones, I will supply a brief summary of the legislator's career since the time of our conversation or the results from recent follow-up interviews, including some excerpts from these interviews. These summaries and follow-up information help place the original interview material in an interesting retrospective context, and further bolster my claims about the legislators' long-term commitments to service in the public good and their dedication to their communities.

2

Arriving

The [incumbent] was appointed to a judgeship 6 weeks before the general election, and there was a hole in [my town]. And I had not been involved in state politics at all, but I was aware of who the opposition was—who was running against her. And it was an insurance claims adjuster, a woman, and a man who was a funeral parlor director as well as—he was the finance manager for [a prominent politician].[1] So he was a big deal in [that] party. I was alarmed to see this hole, and hoping that somebody good in town would fill it, quickly. [The incumbent] had been a low-income advocate, as a lobbyist, before she became a legislator, and issues involving the downtrodden, and women and children, were of particular interest to her....And I couldn't, by going through my mind and looking at the papers, come up with anybody who looked like they would be a viable candidate in town, to fill her shoes. And I was discouraged at the thought that these two people, that I thought were business-as-usual . . . candidates, would be representing [my town].

I had thought my husband might run because he had talked about running a lot of times. But he just can't drop [his business] things that quickly. It was not manageable. . . . He's been a [town council member] and he's been asked to run for mayor but never had. But he's been interested in politics and always thought the state legislature would be a great spot to be. I thought, well maybe this was *his* chance, and he said no, he couldn't do it. It was he who finally said, "Well, why don't *you?*" ...I couldn't find anybody that I felt would be very good. And had there been a longer lead time, I think there would have been plenty of people—I mean, witness the four people that are running against me now....

So I called the papers and told them I was running. I knew if I didn't do something quickly I'd lose my courage completely. I had to commit immediately and publicly, or it would be all over. And then I had to appear before the [party] caucus. . . . There was no time for any sort of primary. . . . I'd never gone to a [party] caucus in my life in [the town], and I needed to persuade them that I was their very best bet. And so I appeared before them, I told them what I believed in, I told them the things I had done, that I had worked on. It ended up being a race between me and one other person, ultimately.... So I was the caucus person.

I might add that I had been in the headlines in the paper for days, saying, would I be on or off the ballot? Because it now involved the attorney general's office making a decision, it involved the secretary of state's office, because no one had ever been so late to get on a printed ballot without a primary, without a duly warned caucus.... Because overnight there was a hole.... Finally, my opponent said, "Oh, please let her run, just let her be on the ballot," because my name recognition was soaring every night, with more headlines about this stuff. I mean, they couldn't buy the free publicity I was getting.... I truly had 6 weeks....And I decided I just couldn't do the stuff politicians do. I couldn't print bumper stickers, I couldn't shake hands and pass out buttons. I just couldn't do that stuff—it wasn't me and it didn't feel comfortable, and I couldn't look at myself in the mirror and continue on.

So I had a quick ad hoc group of people helping me, and between us, they said, "Well, you could do some good stuff and be helpful, besides." One woman worked for a place ... that was recycling stuff, and she was really the genesis of the first idea, which was to recycle magazines. I thought, I could do that and I could spend the money I raised for my campaign trucking away those magazines, and I could make it into a campaign event, but if I lose—and I fully expected I would lose—I can at least say that your money went to recycle magazines, not to proliferate stuff.

Why did you think you were going to lose?

Because I was so late, I figured these other guys had been campaigning [for months].....

And I just felt so humble about the whole thing. I couldn't imagine—the idea of asking people to give money to support a sinking candidate was more than I could stomach to start with, but I thought, if they can at least give money to something that will net positive results for [the town], then they really haven't given money to *me*, and I haven't really lost. It's just been an exercise in, something, but that's OK. So that's why I did these specific causes.... And I really care about recycling, and the idea of just more stuff in people's trash cans as the sum total of my campaign just seemed foolish. And I've never been one to believe that you have to do things a certain way because that's how they've always been done.....

So I had these campaign events. I had the magazine recycling, a coat drive [to provide coats for the poor], and that year I did a gathering of food for [the town's food assistance facility]. I'd worked with low-income people all my life; these were my issues anyway. . . .

At that time, I had quit my job at [a social assistance office] in order to be at home with my kids. And that's when we opened up part of our house as a guesthouse because I needed to make money still, but I wanted to be home. So I had been reincarnated as a small-business person because it was very successful. We bought another house around the corner. . . . So I had social service experience—and that's where my heart was—but I also had successfully run a small business. . . .

The other thing I think that helped me is I decided that, you know, we're all in this together in town. I'm not part of some elite group; I need the help of everyone. . . .

She talks about her campaign poster, which consisted of a photograph of her surrounded by all the people who were working on the three events.

I had people that were very different, working on different pieces for me, and it was a very inclusive campaign. And then when I started gathering the coats, I ended up not only helping but getting people to the voting booth—people who may have in other elections, for all I know, not have voted or have chosen not to vote. On election day, I recognized many of the coats I had collected coming into the polling place. I saw all these coats. I don't know that they voted for me; I just know that I recognized their coats as they tromped up.

This legislator continued to serve in the legislature even as she suffered from a grave illness that ultimately claimed her life. Her colleagues honored her memory through the creation of a charitable fund, and her town honored the legacy of her public commitment by naming a room in the local library after her—she had been actively involved in the library for many years. Her husband completed her term and was elected in his own right in the following election. He is still serving in that seat.

He sold his business after his wife developed her illness in order to spend more time with her and take the vacation trips they had always planned but had put off. The sale of the business largely replaced his previous income from it. Fortunately for the couple, the legislator lived far beyond her prognosis and had a good quality of life for several years. He became more active in politics as she continued to serve through her illness, and before she died he ran, unsuccessfully, for a state senate seat. The race was largely fueled by a desire to counter a statewide backlash against a controversial piece of social legislation that both he and his wife supported. When she died, he sought to be named by the governor to complete her term. The local party committee submitted only his name for the position.

He has "thoroughly enjoyed" his own service in the legislature, where he has a "far more focused constituency" than he would have had in the senate. He also feels like he enjoys the job more than his spouse did because he is more comfortable with the "fact that politics frequently interferes with issues" and even appreciates at times "the elegance of politics when it does rear its ugly head." Serving in the legislature is the only professional activity he currently pursues, aside from volunteer work in the community and the state. He plans to remain in the legislature for several additional terms, assuming he is returned to office by the district. He was unopposed in the last election. He loves going to work: "I just smile all the way over there."

Looking back on his wife's career, he is struck by how much she "grew" through her service in the legislature.

I had been the one with the political interests earlier. When the job came available back in 1990, I came home and said, "I can't run, but why don't you run? You'd be terrific." She responded at first—I think I can quote her exactly—she said, "Who the hell would want *that* job?" And I kept after her that evening . . . and before we went to bed her position had changed to, "What makes you think I could win?"

He describes her first "innovative" campaign in similar ways to how his spouse had described it earlier—he dubs it "the good deeds campaign."

I was the public person, and she was "[my] wife." But over the years, I became "[her] husband." She just blossomed—when she hit that job, she found something she was really good at. And she was able to be of such help to so many people. . . . She just did so much, and when she died, she was headline news in [the papers in the state]. . . . State flags flew at half-mast for a week, and you know, not many of us get that kind of recognition in our life. She was a giant— I was just amazed. . . . I am so enormously proud of the job she did. Not that many people are that purely selfless and really concerned with just helping. And that was the key to her success. . . . I knew she was a good person—I loved her dearly—but I had no idea she had that capability within her. I figure if I can be half as good as she was, I'll be in the top 5 percent.

* * *

I had a family that was interested in the political structure, more out of almost a community service type thing. . . . My mom was on the Republican Committee for years, so I grew up going to political events and doing things like that. . . . My parents were both getting people to the polls, that kind of thing. I majored in political science in college.

He shows a picture of himself at the age of 10, shaking hands with a past governor at a local party event.

The discussions were always there. I had never had any grand designs that the legislature was where I was going to be. . . . My first job was in the school district, in their continuing education program. . . . Then I was hired here in [this] county as county youth director.

The county clerk's job—the guy was retiring, there was no obvious person to take his place. And so at that time, I sort of felt like it was time for a change. And so I threw my hat in. That was an elected position. I did that for [several] years. And then redistricting . . . opened the legislature position up. And it was sort of like, how do I make this decision? I'm not ready to do this yet. But recognize, well, if you're going to do it, that's your opportunity. I have [young] kids. Recognizing the changing schedule, being away, that was a big decision to make, to get into it. . . .

There are a number of people who are in the legislature because they get incensed with things, and that drives them. That's not me as much. Although I get incensed occasionally! . . . But my real motivation for getting in, very honestly—I come out of, with both parents' case, of just the importance of community. Growing up in a small community, feeling really attached, the relationships you have with people. Be their representative and make the state and this community the best it can be. And if I can represent people in a positive way for that, that's what drives me. . . . The reason I got in the [charitable organization] was not so that I could get named as campaign chair but that the money raised is something that really makes the community a better place. . . . [T]hat was very positive, and that helps drive me to say let me be a part of something that's successful. For me that's a personal thing.

This legislator continues to serve in the legislature. The timing and opportunity issues involved in his original run have come up again regarding other offices, but other factors, including redistricting patterns, didn't work out for him to make a run. He also perceives that the longer he has been in the legislature, the immediate connections to his local community, in terms of the focus of his legislative activities, may have weakened somewhat. At the least, the increased tenure has been a double-edged sword. A more closely contested recent election helped to reconnect him.

It's timing and it's always being prepared to quickly make a decision. . . . Some people it falls in their lap and others wait for . . . years and it never happens. You have to have thought about it before because you oftentimes can't make the decision in the time that you're given, because it moves so quickly. . . .

I don't see a lot of opportunities opening up on my part; I'm content and committed to be working [in the legislature] by having more of a responsibility, more of a part of what [my party] is trying to push forward and accomplish. . . .

Naturally, being in the position longer, drawn to some of these statewide issues—you're taken there because of how much time you focus on them, whether they're budgetary issues, or health care or school funding. I have not found it as easy to be connected [to the community] in some ways. . . . It's very difficult to be involved in organizations on a regular committed basis, so that you're able to be real connected. . . . There is some real strength in length of service; there is also some negative in being disassociated more with a community. . . .

Very honestly, I'm in a somewhat safe district, although I'm not sure *any* of them are safe. . . . This year I had a competitive race, and although I wouldn't choose that, there were some real benefits of doing that, of being connected in the community more. Now that takes away from some of the other things you might want to be doing. But that was a revelation to me, having to work through that this year. . . . In that way, I feel I'm a bit better of a legislator today than I was a year ago. I'm not saying that I bought into this totally, but I do think there is a sense of ownership that legislators sometimes get when you are in that position for a period of time.

* * *

I think one major factor in my legislative success was a combination of factors, including luck, that got me elected [for the first time]. Part of it was not luck at all but being part of a small group that got together a few years before high school and clung together, and decided we were going to try and take over the world. And put in an enormous amount of time and energy and planning, and pulled off some—I think in retrospect—rather stunning political accomplishments in a very short period of time, including electing a [young] law student who looked more like he was twelve to the legislature, which was me.

On the other hand, there were some luck factors that made the legislative seat available, with the incumbent leaving to get a job [with a mayor], and if he had left even a year or two earlier, or a year or two later, I might today be making five times as much money as a partner in a law firm. . . .

When I was [a child] I became totally infatuated with John Kennedy running for president. I mean, I was interested in politics and my father had been a [local volunteer], but I don't think that was a major factor. I do believe my being turned on to John Kennedy—I know because I remember the conversations with myself—convinced me that I wanted to be a politician as a career. And then in . . . entering high school . . . I fell in with the debating team and hooked up with a handful of other kids who were also Kennedy freaks, and were similarly determined to be politicians, and we decided we would all do this together. And three of that crew aside from myself, one is [a prominent political adviser], he was my debating team partner, and one is my legislature colleague and now my congressman. . . . And the third fellow is [a prominent lobbyist]. That little crew decided we were going to do this for our lives, and we all got involved in local politics [in my city]. For a couple of years, our main activity was recruiting high school and college students to work in local campaigns, and we had a very substantial impact on local politics doing that. . . .

The big transformation for us occurred in the 1968 McCarthy campaign in which we—at the beginning of that campaign, we were one of the major organizers of a large part of the student forces that went . . . to New Hampshire, and a lot of our whole New Hampshire operation was essentially modeled on a lot of what we had been doing [in the city]. The big transformation in '68 came when we really shifted gears in the McCarthy campaign to concentrating on recruiting neighborhood volunteers for that campaign as opposed to recruiting students from all over the city. And that sort of shift had developed the neighborhood base that became the basis [from which] we in 1969 ran a series of primary campaigns as insurgents to be elected Democratic [local party] leaders—insurgents primarily against incumbent reform Democratic leaders.

Were you coming at them from a particular ideological location? Was this a challenge from the Left?

Somewhat from the Left; I'd say the main themes in our campaign were more that we were more energetic community activists than they were at that point.

For a lot of volunteers, one of the issues was that we very strongly stayed with the McCarthy campaign after Kennedy entered the race, and as almost all the local volunteers and many of the ... elected officials ... went over to support Bobby Kennedy. All of that activity formed the core of ... the leader races we ran and then ... my legislative race....

My predecessor in the legislature—actually we had been planning ... for me to run for that seat because we expected the legislator to run for Congress ... but instead he got appointed to [a state office]. But either way, I had been very assiduously planning the legislative race for two years before I actually ran.... It was the opening of the seat that the focus was on that race.

This legislator continues to serve in the legislature, and has continued to develop expertise and further emerge as a state leader in a particular policy area. The last election went uncontested.

People follow many different trails to get to the legislature. But in coming to the chamber, the legislators I talked with were almost always extending a general path of service that reflected a deeply felt commitment to civic engagement and an organic attachment to their communities, which in their minds necessarily entailed active political participation and leadership. The nature of their previous participation varied dramatically within all three states, from local elected positions on legislatures and school boards as well as spots on party committees, to work on campaigns, both for individuals and causes, to union activity and political protests, to serving on co-op boards and lobbying. The most typical forms of the previous participation were with parties and on local elected bodies. The community attachments were for the most part to their own towns or local areas, but they could also include ethnic groups and geographic regions, socioeconomic classes and more specific occupations, age cohorts and health statuses, and political ideologies. Statistics on the geography of the legislators' lives reveal and also in part explain the local orientation: On average, the legislators had lived 65 percent of their entire lives within their legislative districts, and 80 percent of their lives within their states.[2]

Although each legislator understood in his or her own individual way what it meant to be a public, engaged citizen, they all shared a commitment to be publicly engaged, and all understood that commitment to require the giving of a large portion of their lives to public activities. Thus, before they ever came to the legislature, these legislators were already dramatically *different* from most other citizens; in civic terms, they were already carrying a much larger size bucket of the public's water. At the earliest moments of the legislators' active political involvement, they sometimes seem like ordinary citizens—see, for example, the two stories that began this chapter—but they quickly emerge as qualitatively different by virtue of their long-term commitment to a politically active life, in which they give much of themselves personally.

At times, the contours of the legislators' lives in this regard make them seem almost quaint. Consider the following legislator's comparison of his life with his more cosmopolitan friends, and his general sense of being an outlier by virtue of being so "conventional."

I'm not an idealist. I would consider why I would want to do it—I guess I saw a very strong impression made on me at an early age that politics ... was not by definition a dirty word. This person was ... a state senator, my best friend's dad—I guess my mentor. I worked on my first campaign when I was 7. And I was always—this is what I want to do someday. . . . I just saw, through him, where he was able to make a positive difference in somebody else's life through politics. And my parents sent me to a Jesuit school, where the theme [was] to use your talents to help others. To give service to others. And I was just drawn, I just love politics.

On a state level, you're so close to them that you can make a difference. I was never interested in a local office. I think it was just that the legislature was identified to me at an early age as a place you can go and make a difference, and have a positive influence. It wasn't altruistic. I think just whatever it was, that drew me to it. . . . I think there is a limit in the role of government, what it can and should play in people lives. But it should be there to do some good, maybe a little bit of an equalizer. I find myself sometimes uncomfortable in the middle of a major ideological debate, and I tend to focus more on the pragmatic. What can we do to make a difference? What can we do to help? . . .

My wife needles me because, "Oh god, you're still living in your hometown." And I run into people, college alumni—I've got a friend who has lived in about twenty different places, from Tokyo to five different places in California, to Texas, to Massachusetts, and who has just moved to Atlanta. . . . And I think, here I am so conventional. I truly love this town and I like the connection. . . . So yeah, there is a strong tie to the town, the people, and what it meant growing up.

It's kind of like George Bailey with a policy thrust.

Yeah, it really is! That's one of my favorite movies! But I will also admit one of my other favorite movies is *The Last Hurrah*. I spent last summer reading *The Rascal King*, James Michael Curley's biography.

Looking back on his comments, from the perspective now of being out of the legislature, this former legislator still feels these motivations and the sense of being rooted in the community.

I don't need to live in this town anymore by virtue of having to serve in this district. My office is ... an hour and ten minutes from here. So the commute is long. . . . I have the opportunity to travel a lot more than I used to, but there's still something nice about coming home. I'm lucky to still live in and want to live in my hometown, where I know a lot of people, where I can sneak in and out of the grocery store with a little bit more ease than I used to. . . . Now the only people who yell at me are my own family—there's something refreshing about that.

By the time they reached the house, most legislators were well versed in politics, in one way or another. Fifty-one percent had prior experience in elective office before first serving in the legislature; this percentage was 54 in Connecticut, 44 in New York, and 54 in Vermont.[3] In response to an open-ended survey question about prior involvement in social and political organizations, 53 percent of all the respondents listed three or more of these associations; this percentage was 46 in Connecticut, 63 in New York, and 53 in Vermont.[4] Only 5 percent across all three states failed to list any prior involvement in such associations. And for only 3 of the 77 legislators I interviewed did running for the state legislature constitute the first serious, formal, and extended political activity they had engaged in, but in one of these cases the legislator had worked for many years as a public school teacher—certainly a form of public service, if not political service—while in the other two cases the legislators ran during and immediately following college. Based on the specific responses in the surveys, material culled from official records, and the interview material, it is clear that the most significant variation by state—reflecting the fact that New York has the most professionalized legislature of the three states, and that campaigns there are the most expensive and elaborate—is that the New York legislators' prior political experiences tended to be the most formal.[5] Successful launches into the state legislature in New York require relatively firmer political springboards.

The legislators are united by their civic commitment and sense of duty, but what is almost equally important in completely understanding the story of their elections into the legislature is the individual-level variation that marks their prior political experiences. At the more detailed levels of their experiences, there are simply no one or two "typical" paths into the legislature. As I present below the most important shared themes and patterns, it is critical to remember that in key respects each legislator tells his or her own distinct story.

Roots of Service: Home, Family, Education, Epiphany

Once the future legislators began to become politically active, their levels of commitment and activism increased. The more they participated, the more they understood the importance of civic engagement, the more it got into their blood, and the more they felt attached to where they lived. This phenomenon of activity begetting more activity and attachment has been widely documented at different political levels and for different forms of political activity; indeed, it is a general human trait. But from where did the legislators originally get their political commitment and interest? In about two-thirds of the cases, the legislators to a large extent inherited them from their parents and grandparents as well as their parents' close friends. Also significant were the political activities of more distant relatives and in-laws. This pattern extends uniformly across the three states.

As was the case with the legislators' own prior political experiences, the specific forms of their parents' civic engagement vary widely, but on the whole they far exceed the involvement level of the average citizen. The activities of the parents and relatives range from appointments in presidential and gubernatorial administrations, to service in Congress, state legislatures, and local elected positions, to campaign work, to community activism, protest, and union activity.

I think I [ran] for the same reasons that almost everybody does, whether they're conservatives or liberals or moderates or whatever they are. I mean, it's to make a difference. This is where I can plug into the process and say something that may help. . . . I think with most people there is an agenda on their mind. I'm a reasonable liberal Democrat and that means there are a group of issues about which I care. But I think I was equally attracted and had been reasonably successful with the process. I like the legislative process in theory and a lot of the time in practice. I think the world separates into executive and legislative personalities to a very great degree. . . .

I grew up in a very active political family. My parents: New Deal liberal Democrats. My father: activist [many years] ago. . . . He took me to my first demonstration when I was [a child], and yet, the rest of the family are these Yankee Republicans. . . . My grandfather served in the house, . . . [and] my uncle served in the house. One thing we could always talk about was politics, even though we often disagreed.

* * *

My clearest memory of [early political interest] was the election of 1952. . . . I was attending a small private school in [a suburb]. All Republican, all Christian, except me. . . . I came from school one day wearing an "I Like Ike" button. And my father sat me down on the couch and explained why he was voting for Stevenson. And I've been a Democrat ever since. . . .

My father was a [high-level political appointee]. . . . So I grew up with politics at the dinner table. Not the politics of what's going on inside the legislature; the politics of better and worse, what's better or worse for an individual or a community. And my father knew lots of the important people. One of the reasons I was an American history major and . . . took a bunch of courses in political science was that I was interested in political affairs.

* * *

I've always had the philosophy that it's better to do something than complain. And if you want something done, you should do it. So there's always been that, and this kind of reformist attitude. . . . My parents were not people who just let things slide, and they've always been active. And they've also been very political; . . . our dinner table conversations always involved politics. . . . There were certainly examples of idealism and going for what you believe in.

* * *

Getting into elective politics is something I thought about for years. When I was in college, many, many years ago, someday I wanted to do that. My father was a [city councillor] for 20 years, which is an elective position. So I kind of—it's funny, but I never thought about doing it until I was older and I never did do it until I was older, because my father never did it until he was older. . . .

He'd come home from his meetings and talk to my mother. They were avid readers of the local paper and local political activities. When I was 10 years old or 12, I knew all the members by name of the [city council]. But that was the way the household was: We were a family interested in local politics. It's funny, when I thought about running for something, it was never the [city council].

Often combined with parental influence is the effect of formative experiences that turn a prior political interest and a predisposition to activity into something far more serious and sustained. As the following excerpt indicates, the specific experience can be triggered by chance, and once it occurs, family members again play an important role in prompting the future legislators to run. I will return to both chance and family later in this chapter, but the careful reader of all the excerpts will notice their influence scattered throughout the accounts.

Well, I've always been interested in politics and when I was in college I read this biography of [a prominent woman state politician], so that was kind of fun to do. And my mom was the first woman tenured professor at [a state university] law school. She was there for 30 years and she had a lot of—she was appointed by several governors to different state commissions. . . . Even though she didn't hold elective office, she was very close to folks who were judges or . . . who had elected office, particularly women. She was always interested in the advancement of women, and I always thought that was something challenging for women to be because there weren't a lot of women in politics.

I began to get interested in the legislature when I ran [a statewide candidate's] campaign the first time he ran. . . . I worked for a law firm in [a city]. I heard he was running; I thought he would be a great candidate. So I called him up and asked him how I could help, and one thing led to another and I ended up managing his campaign.

So then I started getting exposure to folks who were in the legislature, and it seemed like an interesting thing to do, and one day I was reading the newspaper and my husband said, "[The incumbent] is retiring." I said, "So?" And he said, "Why don't you run for his seat?" A day later I decided to run for his seat. . . . I primaried for an open seat. I ran my primary and I won by 70 percent of the [party] vote.

...Aside from running [that candidate's statewide] campaign, I really hadn't done anything. I mean, I'd been an intern in my congressman's office and my senator's office, and that kind of thing.

But what about those legislators who come from families that are not particularly active politically? What stimulated them? Two interesting subpatterns emerge from those legislators. First is the political importance of their higher education experience. Although the importance of politically related experiences while in college is sprinkled throughout the interviews, these experiences are particularly salient among this group—and particularly salient within these experiences is the experience of having a politically related internship. Thus, when the legislators' families fail to supply a source for their political activity, that void is often filled by their education. Second, these legislators also tend more than the others to have had some early, poignant, epiphanic experience that spurred them toward a more civic life, and that framed their political beliefs and partisan loyalty. Once again, these experiences vary widely, from attending a political meeting out of interpersonal motivations, to being encouraged and drawn in by a politically active spouse or sibling, to receiving a fellowship, to having a brother killed in war, to being inspired by another political actor to go into politics, to simply observing the political change effected by a turnover in presidential or gubernatorial administrations. The excerpts that follow illustrate this variety of experience, but they also, I believe, speak to the authenticity of these legislators' overarching drive to involve themselves in public service.

Through a fluke I started working—I volunteered my time on a political campaign through a friend and got involved. So it was through my volunteer activity that this bug bit me for politics.

My parents were only involved in politics through a family friend. A family friend, a very close family friend, ran for mayor of [our] city....It was only that correlation, you know how friends support other friends....

I got involved because of a friend of mine who worked in the legislature, out of college....We graduated from [a liberal arts college] together. She was offered a position in the legislature; she pursued it and was employed by the legislature. They were looking for volunteers on a campaign in this community, in [my city]. I knew of the candidate and I knew he was a good candidate....I only volunteered because I was called ... by my friend. I agreed to do it because I thought he was a good candidate and of a party that I would support. That was in '78, it must have been the election in '78. . . . I continued to work. I worked for [a university institute] and then I worked for [a charitable organization]. That candidate lost, by the way, by less than 100 votes; it was very sad. . . .

Two years later another candidate ran, and I didn't get as heavily involved in that campaign as I did the first time, but I was a volunteer again. It was almost like I *had* to go back because we lost by less than 100 votes. That first campaign, it was almost like another part-time job; I really worked very hard. The second time around, I did [too], but I didn't get as emotionally involved. But he won. He won, he took office in January. And in March of that year, he approached me to work in his office. So in 1981, I went to work for a member of the legislature. I left the [charitable organization].

He was in office for about 5 years, but I worked for him for 3 years, and then I went to work for [a leader] of the legislature—I got a promotion. Still working in my community . . . [the office] was in [my city].

. . . Then, about 1990, that's when I decided to run for office. . . . I saw things weren't going the way they should; I didn't think that we were being represented the way we should have been. I thought that with my background now—that's when I thought I was now qualified and that, I guess, I felt that I could do it better than what was being done. . . .

I just felt that the person that was in the district—I now lived in [a nearby smaller city]. . . . I moved [there] in 1985. The person that was representing that district had been there a number of years. And I just didn't feel that he was as effective as he could have been. . . . He had been in office probably at that point over 20 years. Really hadn't done that much for that community. And I just felt that I wanted to take a shot. . . .

Subsequently he ran for [the] senate. . . . He's the state senator now. He decided that when I put my petitions and announced that I was running against him. . . . Our long-term senator had died and the senate seat opened up, and [he] sought to be nominated for that. . . .

So now I'm running for an open seat, of which I lost. . . . And I came back in [the next election], and then it was reapportionment. So now it was a different seat. And now it includes both cities, the cities of [my original city] and [the new city]. So now I ran in an open seat . . . and I won. . . . My most recent election, I ran [for reelection] against the city mayor, a very strong incumbent mayor. And I won.

This legislator continues to serve in the legislature. The reelection campaign referred to immediately above as well as two subsequent campaigns were all "very tough" elections. They have become easier since. Looking back on her original involvement in politics, the legislator still sees the discrete spark as the chance intervention of a friend and the opportunity through her of having an entry into a campaign, but also notes that she had been primed to get involved through her early family experiences and her participation in community and volunteer activities, going back to high school.

Her future plans are to stay in the legislature, primarily because she has gained seniority, worked her way into the leadership, and chairs a committee. She now feels like she is in a better position to have an impact on the institution and has "a voice on major policy decisions." Her plans to stay are also informed by family concerns—possible races for other offices for which her name has been floated would require even more time away from her family.

* * *

I don't think [my interest in politics] happened in my own town, because there was no involvement. I don't think there was even an understanding as to how things work there. I think it grew out of my training in school, which was social studies, government kind of stuff. I was always keenly interested in that. So the interest started early in terms of what I read in books, but in terms of my active understanding as to what went on in the real world I was very limited. I paid a lot of attention to national politics, so I think that's probably how it got started—early years of school and being a student of the national scene. . . .

I left at 18 to go to [college]. At school, I was president of the sophomore class and the junior class. And at school was the first time I'd gotten arrested for sitting in at a lunch counter. . . . So that was probably the beginning. Then after that I left school . . . and I wasn't active in anything, really, because I was working in a liquor store and going to grad school. I can remember being involved in my first political campaign—that was [a large city mayor's race], that was my first political campaign.

. . . After that I went back to [my home state] to teach, and then I got a [fellowship] and had an opportunity to travel across the country for a year. . . . I did an internship with [a congressman] and I took coursework at [a Washington, DC, university]. So that was my exposure to community organization, community activities, apart from what I did in undergrad school. . . .

When that fellowship was over, I came here and started teaching . . . and immediately got involved in community activities because after school I was one of two men at the school, and the only black one, in a black community. . . . And it was from there that I began to see problems, things that needed to be, some sense of how you went about doing it. . . . And I realized from that, that there were a lot of things that weren't happening because people didn't give a shit.

This legislator continues to try to get people concerned about his community's problems through his seat in the legislature.

Here are two other voices that speak to educational experiences and significant personal moments.

[My family] hated politics. I never knew if my parents were Democrats or Republicans. . . . In '56 I was watching the convention, and then I was only [a teenager].

I have no idea how that all works—whether it's ego. I really loved history. I always read about Ben Franklin and the Constitution as a kid. One of the first books I ever read was on Ben Franklin. So history, and doing good and helping out, was always the impulses that I had, and government was a good place to do it. . . .

Even when I was in college I wanted to go to law school in order to get involved in politics. So even then—I was president of the Young Democrats in college. . . . It became more apparent when I went to Washington. I interned in Washington, DC. I was a Capitol Hill intern, a White House internship under Johnson. Then I quit my job when I was [in Washington] after law school to work [on a] campaign. I just quit my job because I wanted to get involved.

* * *

I think as a child I always had that—I always liked being—I would always run for class president or student council or something like that. So I think that it's always been in me. I've always been very active, I've always been an organizer. So I think that was in me.

I think then there was some factors that happened later in life. My brother was killed in Vietnam, and I can remember when that happened I just would say to myself, you know, why are these things happening? And shouldn't we be doing something about it? So I think that that probably really got me thinking more about government and politics.

Ideology and Dissatisfaction

Political ideology and specific policy goals often play a large role in the pursuit of elective office, as suggested by several earlier excerpts, including those that open this chapter.[6] Most of the legislators have strongly held political beliefs and aims, and want to see more done at the state level toward realizing them. They see themselves working toward these ends either by forging legislation, influencing the political agenda and the nature of the political discourse, or raising public awareness, and thereby constructively adding to the policy discussions and arguments that are seriously considered in the state, and that otherwise would remain unvoiced and unheard. Often connected with these aims was a sense of dissatisfaction with the incumbent on these grounds, even if they ultimately decided to wait for an open seat to run. Opposed incumbents were often described as not "doing the right thing" in the legislature or not "representing well."

In an earlier book on legislators and their beliefs about social fairness, I argued that political ideology is a powerful and often underappreciated influence on individual legislative decision making. In addition to political ideology's direct effects on behavior and decision making, which I tracked through a variety of mechanisms, I also considered these beliefs as cognitive and normative filters on the legislators' perceptions of many of the other political forces that act on them. I compared the filtering effect of beliefs to that of the tint on a pair of glasses. As the beliefs become stronger and more deeply held, the tint becomes darker, filtering out or coloring an increasing number of objects. The filtering effect can both enhance and diminish the independent effects of other political forces, depending on how those forces interact with the tint.[7] We might consider beliefs and ideology as having a similar effect here, in the legislators' desire for elected office. Beliefs and ideology have a direct effect on this desire, but they also can influence other important factors, like the perceptions of electoral vulnerability of opponents as well as the expected personal costs and benefits of making a run. The seat appears more winnable and service seems more doable where there is a perceived large ideological disconnect between the incumbent and the challenger.

[I feel] a need to present a point of view, educate, conscious raise, on issues that are important, both to you as a person and you as a legislator, and that may or may not be the things that people either in your constituency or your fellow legislators are aware of. That is to me maybe one of the most important and exciting aspects. It may not be exactly what people think of in terms of what the job is.... [A] commitment and obligation to social justice, when you distill everything out.

* * *

I started getting involved in electoral politics directly after I came back from England, and . . . I worked on [a congressman's] first congressional campaign, when he was sort of the upstart challenger. Had the fortunate experience of actually being involved in a campaign that was a winning campaign. And then I had the experience in law school of working for [another congressman] at the Capitol, which was something that I just stumbled onto, and we're best of friends right now. I enjoyed that experience of working at the Capitol immensely, and then some good friends . . . ran for governor.

. . . I always sort of had my eye on [the legislature] a little bit. . . . The guy who was the incumbent Republican at the point was—everyone just figured, well, he's going to be pretty tough to beat, and so it was, for a Democrat, it was kind of like up for grabs for anyone who really had the stomach for trying to take on this incumbent guy who had beaten a fairly well-established Democrat in town twice, pretty handily.

So they weren't ready for me yet at that point because, again, I had the experience of working at [a congressman's] grassroots progressive coalition type of campaign, and [a statewide candidate] had put together the same type of things, and they had never seen anything like that out here, so . . . we brought in [a citizens' lobby] organization. . . . We just really took this town by storm. I mean, it was a fun campaign; it was just the best campaign ever of the four races, by far, because, again, they were pretty confident that they had the seat— pretty much a lock on it, and we just kept pouring it on, and then we beat them by 500 votes on election day. It was considered a bit of an upset locally.

. . . I certainly went in there pretty charged up and [loaded for] bear. Again, the [congressional race] was a fairly tumultuous thing, which brought together a lot of progressive liberal forces. There was this view when we went in there that year, it was this real kind of watershed sort of change that was going on there.

. . . [There's] the basic story line of the legislative experience, and what it does to people who come in from the outside with a philosophical or ideological bent. There's just no question that at some point you're going to get shaped and formed a little bit by the institution, and it's going to soften some of the edges and change your behavior a little bit in terms of what your politics are. I mean, I really do think it has that effect—I don't think it's a horrible thing.

* * *

I just felt on issues that were affecting towns that the gentleman who was in the office wasn't a leader, enough of a leader for me—even though he talked about . . . that he was interested in tax reform, he wasn't doing anything about it, and I thought that was the defining issue for [the state's] future.

. . . I think [there] is an abysmal level of political debate currently. . . . I think it's built around trying to play on people's economic anxieties. It's trying to pit people against each other in hopes of either short-term political gain, in terms of controlling Congress or getting a political majority here in [the state]. But it's only successful when somebody triumphs over somebody else. It talks a lot about denying welfare benefits, taking away benefits from people to kind of appease the working class, who are losing their standard of living. It manifests itself in giving more corporate tax benefits. In creating a better business climate in the state instead of trying to understand what kinds of job skills businesses in this state are looking for. . . . I think that just sucks. I think it tears at the heart of a democracy. I believe that the new political agenda should be built around the concepts of community in a civil society, and that talks about going back to a civil political discourse.

. . . And that by economic segregation we are breaking down and losing what I call "social capital."[8] You know, when social capital is built up from the ability of people to have relationships across economic class lines, outside of work. And the result is the ability to trust people to lead. And so as we become more economically segregated and we lose that social capital, and we pit each other more against each other, we lose the confidence in institutions and in the ability of people to be able to lead.

. . . I see some harmony between my progressive politics and the process that I think is necessary because if I change the process then those politics are more likely to happen. . . . Right now, I think that I'm more and more concerned with the process of politics. . . . I'm a great believer in unusual partnerships, looking for common ground between people who don't think they have it. And using a different process in trying to get them to recognize that the common ground is there, and to get people to work together, where they hadn't traditionally. And that's all part of trying to change the political dialogue, by using process. I think I'm talking a little in circles, but it may be because they are—

the lines are still a little blurred as to how to exactly talk about them yet. That's exactly what I'm working on, trying to write right now.

. . . If you're going to lead and you're going to govern, I think you need to do it from a point of view. I think you need to do it from a direction that you think differentiates you from the other party.

. . . I think of public service as a personal commitment to being an active participant in the political process and understanding that it is a responsibility rather than an opportunity. . . . I think it's a responsibility to lead. I think it's a responsibility to try and mold political thought. I mean to do that constructively, to not do that driven just by partisan politics. . . . I may come at it from the Left, but I don't think that it's that much different than somebody coming from the Right who may believe in public service. I see it as an activist role.

. . . I don't want to use—I don't want to say "elitist" view of what your social responsibility is. But it is, somewhat. I mean that's the way I was brought up, that you give back. I just bring a more active political agenda to the—that melds in with the other things that I was talking about.

I don't want to be cheeky here, but it sounds like "public service, improved by ideology."

Oh, yeah, it is. I'll agree with that. But I guess for me it's a—as I listen to myself say it, it's very easy to throw darts at it. I mean, I can just see it. I mean, "Who is this foolish guy to think he's so pure or whatever, that he's motivated by these things?" But I honestly think that it's a genuine, very strong core belief of mine. And to me that's an important community value. . . . These are very interesting questions to listen to myself answer and make sure that I'm not full of shit.

This legislator served several additional terms and became a leader among progressives within his chamber before deciding to leave the legislature.

* * *

I ran for the school board . . . when a new school opened. It had a planning committee, and they had planned a very modern school, [a] very ultramodern, liberal policy for the school. It was to be all open classrooms, no traditional rooms or walls. Anything, the sky was the limit, any subject was allowed. There was no discipline. That school opened, and there were about 5 or 6 of us that said, "No way is it going to stay like this." . . . The first year that there was an election, I ran for the school board because of this experience. . . . And we ran that school ragged. . . . We were unhappy and we just got organized, and we organized a whole bunch. I tell you, we turned that place upside-down. I was on the school board for [4 years].

[The incumbent in the legislature] was giving it up. And I said, "Well, maybe I'll run for that." . . . [We] had all the same philosophy. . . . [He] was a very conservative Democrat, but that didn't make any difference. . . . So I ran and sure enough I got elected.

Being Held and Being Pushed: The Influence of Others and Circumstances

Being seriously interested and involved in politics is one thing; actually putting oneself forward for office is another. What about the specific decision to enter a race for the state legislature? The excerpts above have attested in many ways to the central role often played by close family members in the decision to seek a seat in the legislature, in addition to their role as fundamental roots of the legislators' more general commitment to political life. Family members—especially spouses—give critical support, and often supply the catalyst prompting their mates to take their active political interest and involvement to a higher level, of pursuing for themselves a state legislative position.[9] Family members are also key campaign staffers. Close friends can fill the same roles, and are frequently the ones who originally introduce a future legislator to more formal political activities.

Recruitment by local and state party leaders is also an important independent factor, decisively so for a few legislators, but it was not a prominent feature in most of the legislators' paths to legislative service, and it by no means matched the influence of family and friends. Perhaps paradoxically, it emerged as a more significant factor in Vermont, which has the least professionalized legislature of the three states. This fact was largely due to the efforts of Ralph Wright, the Speaker of the House at that time, who took it upon himself, with the assistance of a deputy, to recruit and train potential candidates during the off-season leading up to the campaigns. Many of the speaker's colleagues saw this behavior as motivated as much or more by the desire to generate loyalties among the newly elected legislators for the subsequent election within the chamber to choose a speaker, and for later floor votes in which the speaker wanted to take the caucus in a direction different from where it might go otherwise, as it was by the desire to increase the number of Democrats within the house. I will return to Wright in the final chapter of this book.

I had worked on one of our [state] senator's campaigns. I ended up working on his first campaign. Just behind the scenes really because I didn't have a lot of time to do stuff. That was kind of fun. I have a degree in political science. . . . And then this district was looking for a Republican candidate, and [the senator] had gone to our [local party] meeting apparently. . . . He came to me and said—first his wife came to me and said, "Would you be interested?" I just laughed and said, "You've got to be kidding." And then a few hours later [he] said, "Is this something you would consider?" And I don't think he expected me to say yes, and I said, "I would consider it." And I laughed and I said, "Who is going to vote for a [young] freckle-faced kid?"

I talked to my folks, and [my dad] said, "Just be prepared to lose." And I said, "Thanks a lot dad." And he said, "No, just mentally, you need to be prepared that that's an option and that might be what happens. You also should be prepared to run twice, whether you win or lose. This is a commitment that you should make to the people who are willing to work hard this time to support you."

. . . I was very timid about the whole thing. It was the worst roller coaster ride I had ever been on. Every week I thought, oh my god, what am I doing? And the next week, it would be like, oh this is going to be great. It just went like that the whole [time].

. . . And there wasn't really a lot I could do prior to filing my papers, other than introducing myself around. Fortunately, one of the former legislators was a golfing buddy of my granddad's, and he wrote a fund-raising letter, and solicited money for me. It was very—I had a very small organization—my family and just some friends.

Another singularly important factor is the state of the individual legislator's or the legislator's family's financial and professional situation. Legislators often spoke of the decision to pursue a seat in the legislature being ultimately determined by whether or not their personal financial situation could accommodate their campaign and service, or whether either their own professional life or that of their spouses—or both—was in the right place in order to run and serve. Situations conducive for a run could take the form of important things being in place—having plenty of money in the bank or reaching a certain level of accomplishment in one's career, for example—but they could also take the form of things *not* being in place—

having a business or a career that was at a slow point, no longer having children living in the home, or no longer being in a marriage due to divorce or death. In different ways, these "favorable" circumstances all reduce the difficult trade-offs constantly faced by legislators when they commit to this level of civic involvement; the chapter following this one relates their experience of those trade-offs in greater detail.

[I did] not run for office until my kids were grown and out of the house. I don't know how anyone who lives any distance could do this with young kids at home, with a clear conscience. I don't mean to judge anyone else's conscientiousness as a parent, but I know for myself, I could not have done this if my kids were at home. It *is* difficult. My wife is amazingly resilient and adjustable, and basically, she sees that I'm a much happier person doing this than I was practicing law and therefore I'm less miserable with her. She sees it as an investment in her own happiness. It has from time to time put strains on it.

This legislator served a few additional terms before retiring from the legislature. The follow-up interview happened to catch him at a moment when he was reflecting critically on his original decision to wait to pursue the legislature and wondering, "in hindsight, whether it was a mistake." A younger, close former colleague of his in the legislature had recently been elected to Congress. He concluded, "If your goals are higher than the legislature, then you must start earlier."

* * *

I was on the school board in my town for three years. Then I was pretty much focused on my own business, which I ran. Then, I ran a friend's campaign for the senate in '88. She won. And then I decided to run, myself, for the house. . . . I sold my business in 1986—did some other stuff, ran [my friend's] campaign in '88. I had the time. I had a job, but I wasn't really into it; it wasn't working out. I had the time, I had some money in the bank. So I could do it.

While all legislators face at least some of these trade-offs some of the time, it is the women legislators who confront them most vividly.[10] This is in part due to lingering traditional notions of the female role in a family, held by their spouses and themselves, and by the occupational and salary structure that accompanies and reinforces those notions. Thus, even though they are just as likely to win once they run, women come to the legislature at different times in their lives than men—often at times when the trade-offs are not as severe.[11] Consequently, they are often older when they serve. Women legislators serving in the three states were on average 3 years older (52) than their male counterparts (49).[12] And this difference in age is not driven by women staying longer in the legislature; in fact, the average number of terms served for men is 3.1 versus 2.3 for women.[13] Note also that the age distribution curves for men and women legislators are similar—both are normal distributions, with the peak for women occurring at a later age. We will see these gender-based differences again in chapters 3 and 4, when the legislators discuss their experiences in the legislature and their decisions about leaving it.

The more severe trade-offs are of course also partially reflected in the lower overall percentage of women who serve in state legislatures across the nation (currently 22.5 percent) and the likely fact that other things being equal (particularly local political culture), in states with more professionalized legislatures, the higher levels of competition for seats (whether at the party nomination stage or the general election) work against the success of historically disadvantaged groups, including women.[14] That was indeed the pattern here: Women in Vermont constituted 33 percent of the chamber's membership versus 27 percent in Connecticut and 21 percent in New York.

It's not a part-time legislature; it's a full-time job. I was very fortunate—my husband and I own a small business, which I've been involved in for many years. I was very fortunate—I could kind of go if I needed to, in the business. . . .

I think the timing was right for me. My children were—my youngest was in high school, I had two in college. Our family life could handle this, but you could feel it changing. And it was something my husband and I really enjoyed together—being that my husband was very supportive, my children were very supportive, although they weren't too involved. But there was a certain sense that your time was mortgaged.

* * *

I think how I actually ended up in the legislature was just by pure circumstance really. It wasn't something that I planned; it was just something that happened. I had one child. Everyone else was at home having their second and third. That wasn't happening for me. . . . My son was off to school, and I had nobody there. So I became pretty active in the community, and one of the places I found myself was with the League of Women Voters. . . . The League of Women Voters—

that was the organization. It was definitely through the league that my real interest and my opportunity to become involved—it was through the league that that was really generated, and nurtured, and made possible.

* * *

Both of my girls were in high school or I would never have done it. Never, absolutely. I would never have taken the time from my family or jeopardized my family as a result of the time that's required to spend in this job because I think your family suffers, if you're doing the job properly. Thank god I have an understanding husband, who is interested in what I do and is supportive of what I do. And he himself is politically involved. If it wasn't for that, he and I would probably have problems. Because I don't get home nights—when we're in session, he hardly sees me. We're like ships passing. And you know, he's very understanding about it.

Calculating Rationally

Of course, by the time they were ready to launch a bid for the legislature, the vast majority of the legislators were no longer political neophytes; they were attuned to the need to think strategically about their timing and choose their moment wisely. Like any student of American politics, they understood that incumbents are usually pretty difficult to beat. They thus considered the broader political context in which they would be running, often waited for open seats to emerge, took advantage of the drawing of new political districts, and carefully gauged the strength of potential opponents. This waiting process was particularly apparent in New York, where campaigns are more expensive and elaborate, and where the political system is more structured. Across all three states, these strategic calculations were more prevalent among more seasoned political officeholders and political actors.[15] Even when the incumbent appeared to be strong, these challengers often had their own information indicating that they could win, as in the case of the legislator who spoke earlier in this chapter about bringing a grassroots coalition into his campaign and taking the incumbent by storm.

Well, it became an open seat—the fellow who had it, had it for 12 years. . . . I was considering running for it whether he retired or not, just because I felt personally, in my personal life, that it was a good time to run. And I do feel strongly that you should have choices and debate, and there hadn't been a whole lot of that going on in this district. And I knew that it would be a difficult seat to capture if I ran against an incumbent. I hadn't made a decision whether I would run for it if it was not an open seat. It became an open seat and that made it easier.

* * *

I had served on the board of education for 5 years and had always done very well at the polls. My first time out I did very well at the polls. After that I alternated spots with my husband, first or second, as top vote getter.... My husband was town councillor. I served as mayor of [my town].... And [the woman] who held the seat before I did died unexpectedly. And Republicans wanted to hold onto the seat and wanted somebody who had a strong vote-getting ability to run. Because of the special election, people just don't turn out to run. So I was approached, and yes, I said I would be interested.

... I had [thought about running before] and felt that at some point in time I would like [to be in the state legislature]. So it was a matter of waiting and biding my time until the timing was right.

In Vermont, this process could take an interesting twist, as many of the legislative districts have multiple members and candidates for office below the state level run without a party label. The distribution of the party identification of the voters in the district, the number of candidates running from each party, and their relative individual-level, nonparty-based appeal to the voters could produce situations in which, for example, a Democrat might actually be *advantaged* by having an especially strong Republican opponent in the race. Such an opponent would increase the Democrat's chances of finishing second, but also ahead of all other Republicans and Democrats, and thus winning a seat. In the interviews, a number of Vermont legislators sketched out these complicated calculations, which varied with the individual characteristics of each legislative district.

Long-standing political ambitions combined in complicated ways with short-term strategic calculations and personal circumstances. The right equation looks somewhat different for each legislator. The following excerpt from a legislator who is still serving reflects the individual-level complexity of the mix of these factors.

I beat an incumbent. . . . My reason for deciding to run at that point—I mean, I had always aspired to be a state legislator because I had worked in state government for so many years. But because of where I lived, and because of the numbers, it was almost impossible to think that you could do it.

. . . [The seat] was held by a very popular incumbent who is now a state senator from the district, and so there was no chance of going after him and really being successful, and everybody knew that. I would never ask people to invest in me if I thought it was going to be a losing campaign. And as a matter of fact, the seat did open up two years prior and they asked me to run. At the time, I was actually running [a party] campaign committee for these people here. So I just felt too committed to—I had taken on that responsibility. I just felt I couldn't leave them in the extreme, so I said no to the legislative seat which I had waited for for so long.

Two years later, it became apparent to me that the candidate who won was a very weak candidate. Certainly not an articulate spokesperson for the area. He had disappointed a lot of people. His stands on a lot of issues, particularly in the areas of education, were really contrary to the way people feel about education, you know, where I live. So I saw him as being vulnerable. It was a presidential year. There was a possibility that more [of my party] might be registering to vote, so it was the right time.

But what the previous excerpts as a group illustrate, and what bears repeating from the first chapter, is that these calculations are not the primary force behind the decision to seek office. Much of the recent literature in political science has tended to overlook this fact; instead, it often appears that the world political scientists see is made up only of people who simply *want* a seat in the legislature, and who are making rational, self-interested decisions in order to make that happen. At the specific moment of throwing one's hat in the ring, this view might correctly model much of their decision making and yield some accurate predictions about their behavior as candidates, but it does not begin to understand what brings the legislators to that moment in time, nor does it really get at everything that is in their heads when making the decision. And once again, it contributes to the prejudice that they are stepping into the political arena simply to satisfy their own narrowly defined preference orderings. Such a limited view not only detracts from our civic knowledge; it also damages our competency and efficacy as citizens.

Serendipity and Synchronicity

On top of all these factors I have described, sometimes things just happen to these people, and *for* them. Their personal and political stars come into proper alignment, making a run possible, and then an unplanned, external force intervenes to make the final difference in their decisions or successes. They happen to be in the right place at the right time, or talk to the right person, or be in the right mood on the right day. The importance of these kinds of events is no greater in politics than in any other professional field, particularly those in which the funnel leading into the profession has a fairly narrow spout. One often needs a bit of chance. Also embedded in these stories of chance are the factors previously described: professional and personal circumstances, family support, dissatisfaction with the status quo, recruitment by other political actors, and strategic timing. I include several excerpts here because they reinforce the significance of these other factors, but in each case illustrate an element of chance that deserves separate appreciation. Yet as the excerpts also suggest, even for the legislators upon whose faces god smiles, it is still the case that the deeper currents transporting them to the legislature remain similar to those of the legislators without the benefits of chance—a combination of commitments to service, desires to do better, deeply held political and policy beliefs, and intensely felt connections to their communities.

This is a fun story, I think. I went down and voted in the primary, and looked at the list of people that there were to choose from. No Democrats; five Republicans, who would have been damn close to faceless or straight right-wing loudmouths. I came home and said to my wife, jokingly, "I'm sick of voting for these guys; I'm going to run. What do you think? What do you think about me running?"

We joked about it the next day. We went to a friend's and joked about it. The primaries were on Tuesday, that was Wednesday. Thursday, maybe somewhere along there, me and my wife had a serious talk about it. I said, "This is really on my mind." She was just beginning graduate school. . . . The timing was not great. But it was doable.

She said yes; I said yes. At the end of the school day, 4 p.m., I called the state Democratic Party. I'd never had any involvement in party politics. Ronald Reagan certainly took me nowhere I wanted to go. And I called and I'm pretty sure a [state legislative leader] was on the other end. He said, "If you're serious, we have about a half-hour to get a letter in the mail. There is some process where a district caucus can put your name on a ballot because nobody ran in the primary. But the deadline for filing that letter is 4:30 p.m. today."

Yeah, I'm serious—that's how I ended up getting on the ballot, that way. . . . So from there, I have a friend that's a printer and a neighbor that's a writer. They looked things over and helped me package it. I didn't spend a lot of money. I had brochures printed up and hit the road. . . . In this district, that was something new. The party hadn't been involved with me and I'm sure it had—they didn't have any feeling that I had a chance in hell. This was a very Republican area. . . . I did go to every door. People knew I was serious about it.

* * *

I got involved in politics because my mother was a newspaper reporter, and when I got out of the service, she called and said she hadn't seen me in a while. "Do you think your wife would mind if you come down and sit with me at this meeting, a local tax board meeting?" That's how I got involved in politics: I said, "Oh, OK."

I was listening to what was going on to some degree and took a few notes, and we were chitchatting about various things. I began to listen to what was going on in this meeting. . . . I can't believe this is how they treat people. I guess I know I can do better than this. . . . They had the police chief there. He asked for three patrol cars or something like this. They said, "Oh, come on chief, what are you going to do with three patrol cars?" He said, "Well, I guess I could live with two." So they browbeat him some more and now he's down to one. I thought, this is no way to do business. The man comes in and tells you what he needs, you discuss the issue and you say you can't afford it. What are the other options? You talk about them. This is the best we can do, and everyone goes home and the person still has their respect. Not being belittled for 2 or 3 hours about things. That was wrong.

. . . A political bug bit me after I went to that meeting. I wanted to get involved. . . . At some point in the future, I would get on the town committee and I was elected to the tax board, which is the board I sat at that first time, when I listened to the raking of the chief of police.

* * *

It's really bizarre how I'm here today, as the legislator. What I wanted to be, or what I originally started out to be, was sheriff. . . . A lot of people were prodding me to run for sheriff. And so I did the preliminary thing where you call all the committee meetings and send out the letters, and you do this and you do that—politic within the [party] committee. And it came down to what they call an executive committee vote, and I lost by 1 or 2 votes. . . . I said, "That's not bad, against a [longtime] incumbent. So let's take it to the full committee, let's see what happens." So we did, and started all over again. And again I lost. . . . He called in a lot of favors. I got my doors blown off. OK, that's the end of it.

. . . [A week later, a] senator passed away. And [my legislator] was going to go up for the seat. It was 10 o'clock at night—never forget it—sitting there, getting ready to go to work at midnight, watching television. Phone rang—it was [the legislator] calling me from [the capitol]. He was talking to me about my support—because I was still a committeeman—for the senate. I said, "You got my support."

He said, "That's not really the reason I'm calling you. We'd like you to run for the legislature." He said, "We think that you'd make a great candidate for the state legislature." I said, "I couldn't even get the goddamn sheriff's nomination, you think I'm going to get the legislature nomination?" He said, "That was a whole different story. Everybody likes the way you conducted yourself, and contacting people to run for sheriff, the campaign you put on, you put a committee together, you really worked. And when you lost, you just went away and you didn't cause any problems. And they think that you're the type of person, the caliber of person, that would make a good legislator."

I said, "This is crazy." If [he] hadn't called me, I would have never thought about it.

For the legislator in the next excerpt, an unexpected visitor, showing up at the eleventh hour of a campaign, secured the outcome.

When I ran the first time, I ran against an incumbent Democrat who was the star light of the Democratic Party in [my town]. I was this young wet-behind-the-ears guy just out of college who had just come back from touring Europe for a year, and the Republicans needed a candidate and were like, "Yeah, *you* run." . . . They had nobody that wanted to run. . . . My mother was on the party committee. . . . The only other guy had run for the seat and lost four times. And he didn't want to run again. . . . They didn't want him to run again because they knew he would have run and lost for the fifth time.

So you had been interested in politics?

Oh yeah, I majored in political science. I interned up at the capitol my last term. So I was interested in the process and I thought this would be fun someday to do. So it was always an interest of mine. And I didn't expect it to come together so quickly after graduating. . . .

That was the Reagan year. [The incumbent] took a look at me—"phfft"— and she looked at me like that and didn't take me seriously until the very end of the campaign when she started going out to meet the voters, and I had been doing that since July. So I was hitting doors twice and she started maybe in mid-September, and people would say, "[He's] been here twice." And she started to panic, but then it was too late to play catch-up. . . . And then Ronald Reagan came to town [right] before the election. . . .

She was jumping around about this opening of a park that she was getting the governor to come in for that Saturday. My campaign manager went up to her and whispered in her ear that he had just heard that Ronald Reagan was coming to town on Monday. . . . It was so close to the election it wasn't even funny. And she just went white. . . .

I was on the podium, I got my picture taken with him. It was unbelievable. It was like—I was like, I can't believe this is happening to me. Who runs for office the first time and gets the president of the United States to come to his district, and gets to stand on the podium next to him and shake his hand in front of 20,000 people in the town . . . ?

If I were trying to get a handle on what was driving you, what was your purpose— what was the thing that was motivating you? Was it being involved in the process?

It was helping people. . . . It was more I wanted to get in and help people, and I enjoyed working with people.

The Honor of the Town

Finally, there are some legislators, particularly in Vermont and some parts of Connecticut, who run for the legislature as the last political thing they do, the state-level end point in a long string of more locally focused civic activities. They are often retired or near retirement in their professional careers. In some cases, it seems like their communities are recognizing and rewarding them for their life of service—with prestige rather than money—by literally placing on them the title of "honorable" and sending them off to the capital. In other cases, the communities or parties are filling needed spots with seasoned and locally known public servants.

I think you have some people who are in the legislature who have—near retirement—or have made their mark in their professional careers and are the kind of person—"You know, you ought to think about running for the legislature." And well, OK, they go up there after completely establishing themselves, who they were. . . . If you look at some of the ones that are close to retired, some of the older members, their level of involvement might not be as much. They're going to go up and make their contribution, do their thing, put in a term, a couple terms, and leave.

These legislators are usually not the most active ones from the standpoint of pushing legislation and setting the agenda. Based on my observations and interviews, they are nonetheless driven by a sense of duty and civic commitment, and are for the most part conscientious and dutiful committee members who are also attentive to constituent service. It is also probably the case that as a group, they bring with them a valuable wisdom accumulated through their political, professional, and life experiences.

In the interviews, these legislators emphasized the formal aspects of their jobs, and even the formal aspects of the outside-the-session parts of their jobs, rather than the proactive development of legislative initiatives, and networking and other informal work among colleagues, the media, and the governor's office in order to get policy ideas moving through the system. They focused their discussions on attending committee meetings and receptions, meeting groups of constituents at the capitol, and other more ceremonial activities. Their specific reasons for involvement in politics are similar to the other legislators, usually minus the strong political ideology motivations, and the specific decisions they make regarding when to run for office are also similar to the others, but the legislature has a somewhat different place in their political careers.

[I had] just a personal belief that if you weren't satisfied with the way things are being—instead of complaining about it, you ought to try to get involved. . . . [T]he reason I was then involved in the town is because, well, I don't know—I just feel kind of a sense of duty. . . . I used to have a theory that, well, I think it used to disgust me to have people that wouldn't even bother to go to town meeting or wouldn't bother to vote, complaining about what was going on. . . . I was always involved. . . .

I was selectman, school director, board of civil authority, justice of the peace, and on the development corporation. I served on the zoning board . . . and most of the town offices. And I had stated at one point . . . when I was still farming—not in a position where I felt I could run—that I was going to [run]. When [another town resident], he's now [in the executive branch]—he was elected four terms—and before he ran he came to see me because we decided we weren't going to run against each other in the primary. He came down and it was the year that I had gone in the [dairy] buyout, '86. . . . I went in the buyout, when I sold my cows, went out of farming. . . . [T]hat was quite an experience, selling off your cattle in the program, and so I wasn't ready to run, and I told [him] to go ahead. Well, he was appointed to [an executive position]. . . . I was appointed my first term. . . . And so that's how I ended up the first term I was down there. Then I would never had been satisfied, so I ran, which I did 2 years ago and I won the election for 2 more years.

* * *

Believe it or not, I didn't even want to go to the legislature. Three times [the party] asked, and I said no. Finally, they said, "You have to go." I didn't have any desire for the legislature. . . . They said, "We need you, we want you to help." And I thought, OK, I'll go to help. . . . I sacrificed income to do this.

But some of these legislators' younger, more active colleagues did criticize them—in Vermont, they were often called the "faceless 40"—on the grounds that they were not as active and informed in committee meetings and on the floor as they should have been in order to be responsible legislators. But the critics also usually acknowledged that these legislators might be oriented toward constituent work and more active in their districts.

There are definitely members there who are in . . . the inert family. And it's maybe because they've been there long enough and now they've got to that plateau we talked about. . . . They just reach a level and they plateau, but not necessarily because of an inability on their part. . . . But for whatever reason, they are not accomplishing.

Are there just some people who arrive inert and stay inert?

Not many, but there are. . . . Wonder how in the world they ever got elected . . . but they do. . . . Older . . . I'd say male.

* * *

You have some old animals.... I guess the gray hairs that sit up in the back and have seen a lot, and they aren't very vocal. But when they talk, they say an awful lot.... They are basically backbenchers ... probably good legislators paying attention to what is going on.

The era of these "honorables" may be quickly passing, however, even in rural Vermont.[16] During the interviews, one house leader compared the present to an earlier time when one "stood" for a legislative position rather than actively ran for it. His prime example of the change was a woman from a nearby town who had lived in her district for "only" 3 years and was actively pursuing a seat. In my more recent follow-up interviews with the Vermont legislators, several keen observers of the chamber and its history noted that these "faceless" legislators were becoming more scarce.

Summary

The stories of the legislators' pursuit of office reflect an overall concern with the public good, interpreted of course in competing ways, which should provide some comfort to those who either worry or assume that most political figures are driven by personal ambitions for power and fame. To be sure, the legislators are an ambitious lot, which is to be expected, and which is necessary for the system to work and replenish itself—I will return to ambition in chapter 4. But their motivations are primarily civic in nature.

More specifically:

- As a group, legislators report a variety of motives for their pursuit of office. Woven through these, however, is a commitment to public service. In many instances, legislators were reluctant to run and often needed outside prodding.
- Most legislators have deep roots in their community and state. They feel an organic attachment and run as an extension of prior service to their community.
- The vast majority of them have significant prior involvement in social and political organizations; for a little more than half, this in-

volvement includes prior elective office. This background is most pronounced in the most professionalized legislature, New York.

- Their political interest and activity are often inherited from parents, extended family, or close friends.
- Family members and close friends were also often the suppliers of the final push to run for the legislature; equally important was the favorable alignment of personal and professional circumstances.
- When political interest is not inherited, it is usually developed through formal education experiences, often further fueled by internship experiences and set to flame by revelatory personal experiences.
- Although strategic calculations are important in the decision to seek office—most legislators did not simply throw themselves into the first electoral breach they saw—these calculations are not the primary way to understand their overall decision making.
- On top of and running through the above factors is the role of chance.
- There is a subset of older legislators whose service constitutes the closing act of a political career. As legislatures continue to professionalize, this group may become extinct.

3

Serving

I'm a pretty sensitive guy. I have deep emotions about things. I used to leave here with a lump in my throat, because you get just so into it and it's just such an all-encompassing experience. I guess it does something for me emotionally. You talk about motivation, but I hope it's in a good sense that what I'm getting back from it, I'm also giving out in some ways. . . . I always thought that was weird that—how can I care about this so much that I get a lump in my throat when I leave this place? There are guys that are just trying to cut my head off and stick pins in me.

. . . Because it's just—it's the commitment that people have and feel. And they work so hard to make things—they're involved in it, and you can't not be involved when you're there and you're working that hard on something. But they aren't doing it for themselves; I mean they're looking out at the constituencies and their families. They are looking at their heritage and they are looking at their futures, and they are trying to do the best that they possibly can.

. . . I never shared that with anyone. I think it's important because it's very instructive as to what makes people tick. Sometimes the tick goes beyond getting a higher office, or to this or that. Sometimes it's just public service, you know? And trying to do the best they can and trying to have responsibility, and trying to fulfill it.

This legislator is still serving in the legislature, now as chair of a high-profile committee. The qualities he described then still continue to motivate and move him emotionally. Some of the controversial issues that the legislature has addressed in the intervening years and the electoral price that some of his colleagues have paid for their decisions only strengthen this feeling. The one "proviso" that he would offer now, as an observer of the process generally rather than about his own experience, concerns the influence of money in the campaign system, which he sees "creeping in" and ex-

erting a pressure to "change allegiances" in some instances from the constituency to more special interests.

I love the job and get great satisfaction from the job. . . . Our [dealing with those controversial issues] is an illustration of the quality of the people who served in that legislature. . . . I think some people voted because it was the right thing to do. They upheld their oath to do what they were supposed to do, without fear or favor of any person, and they did that. And we lost a number of people because they were profiles in courage. But they did what they thought was right. And I guess that's why I can continue to marvel at the people and how they operate—that they are citizens there to do a job and to do the job the best way that they can do it. So to me, it's truly amazing.

* * *

I think that getting the people to feel that their government is responsive is probably what I would think is the foremost job that, at least in my 10 years, I did. Coupled with the fact that I did spend a lot of time helping draft legislation and being a part of the process.

I think the thing about constituent service is that when you're a freshman legislator, nobody really cares too much about what you think up at [the capitol]. I mean, they may ask your opinion, but as far as you sitting down and rewriting a . . . bill or really having impact in a committee, you're kidding yourself if when you're first elected, you think you're going up there with that kind of influence. But constituent service is the kind of thing that from day one, you can really sink your teeth into, be effective and influential. What I was able to do was continue that, get my staff used to doing that, so that when I built up seniority and became the ranking member of [a committee] and then sunk my teeth into things, . . . the constituents didn't feel that I dropped them and left them by the wayside in order to become more effective in the process. . . . I kept that in the forefront of my mind—that if I did that I would be doing a disservice.

. . . In the beginning, I would take a lot of personal time and do the casework myself, return the phone calls, visit the household myself, actually do the return letter myself. As I became more important in the process, I would have my intern and my staff concentrate on the follow-up and letter, and I would have a meeting maybe once or twice a week, where I would get updates on how Mrs. Jones's case was doing.

... I mean, there was only so many hours—amounts of hours in the day, and when I'm expected to read all the insurance bills and be the one that is going to argue them on the floor. It's either reading Mrs. Jones's letter myself, calling her back myself, and drafting a letter, or knowing when that bill came to the floor what was in the bill and not looking like a fool on the floor of the legislature. . . .

By my fifth term, I was instrumental in negotiating [a significant insurance reform] bill. The membership knew that I knew the issues of the insurance so they would come to me on other issues like uncompensated care and the Medigap insurance.

. . . I have a lot of personal reward from getting somebody's social security check or whatever. I mean, we had some very touchy cases: women who were being beaten by their husbands, rape cases called up, I mean really personal stuff. I remember a grandmother calling me up once because her grandson needed drug rehabilitation—we got him into a clinic. So you get a lot of personal reward that way. The legislative stuff was intellectually stimulating, and gave me a lot of intellectual reward and challenge. So it was on two different planes, the kinds of benefits I received, and I can't really say, "Well, the constituent work was much more rewarding." It was a different kind of reward.

. . . The majority of my staff [time] was spent with constituent service because I had a lot. . . . I really made myself accessible to the district. Refrigerator magnets, billboards—call me if you have a problem. . . . And they took advantage of it. Even now that I'm retired, they are still calling me.

What do you do with that?

It depends. One woman called up—89 years old, blind. I'm going to say, "Call [the current legislator]?" She calls me her *son*. I'm going to say, "Sorry, I'm out of office now?" So I helped her, you know?

. . . I was a very good legislator. I mean, I don't want to be modest—it's not the time to be modest. But I was a very good legislator. I knew the issues, I knew what I was voting on, I was one that other legislators came to and asked how they should vote on specific legislation and on major issues where I was in the minority voting. . . . The fact that I would be returned to office between—in the end, it was anywhere between 70 to 80 percent of the vote. I think that attests to the fact that the district thought I was a good representative also. . . . I was able to give it my full effort because I treated it like a full-time job.

...I loved what I did. ... I loved the issues that I studied. I loved dealing with the public. I loved being involved with the process and affecting the process. I loved the floor debates. Overall, I really liked what I did.

I hated campaigning. I hated it.

Why? Some people like it.

Well, some people like it; I hated it. In my district, where the Democrats liked me as a rule, the Republicans like me, the independents like me—members of the Democratic town committee would quietly tell me that they were going to vote for me—there weren't issues that they could run when they ran against me, so it became a very personal, very vicious all-the-time campaign. So they weren't even fun and challenging as far as you know, "Let's discuss the issues." I mean, I got involved in a primary campaign once and [my opponent] found that there were no issues, so it became a whisper campaign about—because he was a blue blood and I was [ethnic] ... and it was like, "We don't want one of his kind to be representing." ... He said I was on the take from the trial lawyers, and that became a joke. I was like, "And I have my million dollar house in Aruba that I'm waiting to fly to. I just live in a three-room apartment because I like it."

...I had one year where there was token opposition. John Blank actually was his name. And it was funny because I would go door-to-door and they would ask who was running against me. I would say, "John Blank." They would say, "OK, you don't have to tell us his last name if you don't want to." I'd say, "No, that's *really* his last name." Because he was a candidate that was like—he didn't show, he didn't do door-to-door, he didn't do any mailings, and it was humorous. So that was my one year of token opposition.

This legislator had just retired from the legislature when I spoke with him. A few years later, he returned to elected office at the local level as mayor of a small to midsize city. In that office, he "stepped into a minefield" of difficult issues, including the imminent lowering of a bond rating, the building of three schools and the closing of another, the need to raise taxes, difficult contract negotiations with a public employees union, and shady external servicing arrangements with the same employees, all of which he actively addressed. His subsequent reelection effort, a rematch with the person he had defeated, was "really ugly," and featured a smear campaign against him by some of the public employees that employed a Web site, an airplane banner, innuendo about his sexual orientation, and personal attacks on his family. "It just got uglier, and uglier, and uglier."

After his defeat, he came out as gay and went full-time into the private sector. He then relocated to another state, in an area where being openly gay is not an imped-iment to political success. After the move, he immediately set about making politics a career, and now serves on a county human rights board and directs government af-fairs for a quasi-public transit authority. He also switched party affiliations when he made the move because of the difference in the ideological centers of weight within each party in the two locations and the heavy electoral influence of one party over the other in his new location.

Even though his move was occasioned by the negative experiences in the reelec-tion campaign, he carries with him "a lot of good memories" and satisfaction about his term as mayor. The town had many problems that had not been properly ad-dressed in recent years, and he could list many accomplishments regarding them in his short tenure, including school constructions, facilities management improvements, better constituent service, downtown revitalization, and an important contract to build a rail station.

His future political plans include running for a legislature again someday.

I wanted a brand-new start. I wasn't running away—I don't want it to sound like I ran. But I wanted to go somewhere where I could start all over. Just to give you an example, before I left I had a fender bender. And it was front page of the local newspaper. And this was after I was out of office. I'm like, "I don't need this any longer."

. . . I was not out [as gay] when I was in office. Given the age I was—you know the jokes—given the age I was, I didn't have two heads, I dressed well, I loved to cook, people had always inferred or wondered. It got to the point where I would get letters, and then on the Web page, just ugly stuff.

He tells a story about a particularly crude and hurtful communication sent to his nephew.

It was so ugly. . . . The problem is, it's systemic in politics today. I'm sidestepping a bit here, but given what we pay our elected officials and then for them to go through with this shit, the caliber of people that are willing to go in is going to become less and less.

. . . But I don't want to leave it at that. . . . When [a] school, when the mold there had become an issue, the board of education wanted to reha-bilitate the school. I said no. I closed the school and built them a new school. And to this day, those parents, they took a picture of me and it hangs in the entryway.

... [The mayor] who held the position 6 years prior to me publicly stated many times that the town had never had so many issues on its plate and nobody had ever dealt with them successfully the way I did. So the reward I got out of that—I have a lot of good memories.

... I have politics in my blood. That's why one of the first things I did when I got here, I really started networking. . . . I wanted to get involved.

* * *

The . . . low was really the abuse I got for the income tax.[1] It was so bad that one time I broke out in a case of hives. My blood pressure went way up—I just stopped taking it. Is the name [of a former state senator and then political advocate] familiar to you? It wasn't so much attack from my constituents . . . but the pressure from people outside my district, phoning and writing. [He] targeted me, as 1 of 13 legislators that he targeted. So he had his people attacking me. One person was calling me—I think the earliest he called was 5:00 in the morning—he said, "This is your wake-up call, have a taxing day." So I got an answering machine. And I thought that what I was supposed to do was . . . listen politely no matter what was said. You can't believe how bad it could be. And I thought I was supposed to listen and be polite. And if you could have a conversation, I would try to have a polite conversation. And then it would disintegrate and I felt, I can't hang up, I have to be nice. So then I'd hang up and feel upset.

Some other people, they have more sense. They get this kind of tone and they just say, "I'm not talking to you." So it really was quite stressful.

And then . . . I got shot at. That was probably the ultimate. I was home; my husband and our son, [we] were all in the back of the house watching TV. And we heard this crack [slaps her hands]! And I thought it sounded like a rifle shot, and [my husband] thought it was backfire—we had that kind of conversation. So he and [my son] went out and circled the house, and didn't see anything. The next day I was going to [a town]—my district encompasses a portion of [that town]. I was going to the [town] road race. It was a couple days after this noise. I went into the front living room and I thought there was a leaf plastered on the door. This was the door from the hall—it's an old saltbox, and the door from the hall to the front living room was open against the wall. And I closed the door and there was a bigger mark on the back of it—it was broken through. And then I looked under the window and there was plaster missing. And then I went outside the house and just below the window there was this little hole. Tracing that through the door to the hall, there was a bullet in the stair in the rise of one step, [and] casing in the next. So if I had been walking into that hall, I could have gotten "kneed," let us say. . . .

I think a bunch of guys stopped off for a few beers after work. Some people who felt very strongly about the income tax had a few beers and decided to give me a hard time.

So a few people called up—and I thought they were being sympathetic—and they said, "We're sorry they missed." I suppose that was the hardest time.

. . . I got the big hit from outside because [the advocate] targeted me. You see, I was running against a conservative Republican. So he was helping some of the Republican candidates by sending out a letter saying that these bad people, that I was running a *viscuous*—he misspelled the word vicious, and that amused us all—he actually named 13 [candidates], and little old me. . . . So he generated a lot of action outside my district. Within my district the feeling was pretty evenhanded. I felt I could honestly say, if I was listening to my constituents, I was left free to make my own decision because I could go in any direction and demonstrate support for it.

This legislator, older than the average, voluntarily retired from the legislature following the term I observed, but not before she could find someone from the community to sponsor as her successor who she thought would do a good job in her place. Her successor still serves in the legislature. Like the legislator in the previous excerpt, she later came out of political retirement to serve in a local elected office, and still serves there.

Despite the harrowing stories in these interview excerpts, there is much to like in legislative service, particularly for anyone with an active mind and a healthy ego. Knowing that they are engaged in something that they find important and think to be essentially good generates a lot of job satisfaction. The process can be exciting and is at the center of much media attention. It matters tremendously to the life of one's community and state. Legislative life thus offers the potential for a great sense of personal efficacy as well as the ego gratification of fame. In addition, the intricacies and puzzles of the actual pieces of legislation, the policies that they ultimately yield, and the complicated processes by which they are made, all draw and hold many of the legislators' intellectual curiosity.

Legislators described these kinds of attractions during the interviews when offering or responding to my prompting of what they liked about their service. They liked feeling effective and being important in people's lives, both individually through constituent service and collectively through legislative activities. Many talked about the intellectual and psychological gratification that came from engaging in an interesting and complicated job, including the challenges of figuring out the technical and political puzzles of crafting and passing legislation and of helping individuals with complicated governmentally related problems. They were also gratified by the feeling that they had effectively contributed to raising awareness on important political issues that were of particular concern to them, not only in the legislature itself, but also in the larger political system and among the public. I described this ideologically oriented sense of purpose in the previous chapter. Another source of satisfaction was simply connecting in a personal way with a tradition of legislative service in the state, as manifested in the grand surroundings of the capitol along with the spirit of history that the building and process embodied. And finally, although the job demands much from them—and as will become clear later in this chapter, they often feel like their lives are not their own—they also appreciate that in some fundamental respects their job is of their own creation. There is no set, given legislative job description to which they must conform; their ultimate performance evaluation comes every two years in the form of reelection or defeat. Beyond that, they set their own standards. As the excerpts that began this chapter indicate and again as we will see later, that fact is both a blessing and a curse.

The following excerpts relate the various attractions of legislative service I have just described. I will then explore two in greater detail: efficacy and friendship.

If something came in that was at all complicated, the chairman would look at me and say, "You're reporting this bill." And so in fact, I did all the major pieces and it was—it felt good. I had a very good relationship with my chairman. I developed a rapport on the house floor. People actually liked me.... Because of my experience as a teacher, I was able to take some very complicated bills, break it down and take out the stuff that was extra and is not really important, and then put it fairly and squarely in an intelligible way, and usually with some humor. And my bills passed. You know, it was fun. It felt real good, about my role in that regard.

* * *

[The legislature] gives me a lot of the things I need, except that I can't make a living at it. I like the work; it makes me feel worthwhile. I feel like I'm doing something useful. I feel like I belong. It gives me a lot of the personal things that I look for in a job.

* * *

The reality of the situation was that the academic experience to me, at that particular time, wasn't real. . . . In the legislature, you could actually do something. You could do the same research, essentially, and you could actually accomplish something. You could touch people's lives. . . . It takes everything I've got some days not to get through the day, but to figure out the day and be challenged by it to the highest degree. And I want to get up the next morning and get into it again. And if you got that, you're where you should be.

* * *

To me that's the puzzle of the legislature: I've never had a job where I didn't have a job description and a supervisor, or a board of directors, or something. In this job, the only strings are that if you do really badly you're not re-elected. . . . No one notices if you're there or not, if you're paying attention or not, if you're cheating in some sort of way. All of that is up to your own discretion. So I've made my own job description.

. . . For me, the sense of history, and just working in the building, is really critical. I've always worked for antipoverty agencies or no-profit agencies, and the structures I've worked in and the circumstances in the buildings have all been real low-rent, ugly, unattractive, no amenities. And it isn't really the amenities, it's the reality that I'm in this beautiful building where all these people have been before me and all these people will go after me, and for some tiny slice of time, I am one of them. And that's just thrilling to me.

The findings from the survey I administered are consistent with the picture painted by these excerpts. The survey included several questions that are related in various ways to satisfaction with the legislative job, but one in particular concerns it directly: "How would you rate your experience of being a legislator from a personal standpoint?" The respondents located themselves on a 9-point scale from "extremely unpleasant" to "extremely pleasant." Although it is just a single, simple question, it is a good measure of the basic concept of personal satisfaction with the job, as indicated by the fact that the responses to this question are positively and significantly associated with responses to other questions that tap similar subjective experiences.[2]

The findings from my survey are consistent with one of the few notable existing studies on legislative job satisfaction, which examined satisfaction among county legislators. Drawing on work in industrial and organizational psychology, that study argued that overall job satisfaction in the county legislature was high because "legislative positions offer a variety of intrinsic job rewards that are generally sought by people in all lines of work and that are strongly associated with high levels of job satisfaction," in particular the rewards of "variety, autonomy, and task significance."[3] Among my survey respondents, 50 percent selected either an 8 or a 9 on the 9-point scale; 91 percent selected 6 or above. Furthermore, there were no statistically significant differences in the responses to this question based on age, sex, seniority, party, or family income—a fact suggesting that liking the legislative job resides in qualities about the job itself rather than specific aspects about themselves that legislators bring to the job.[4]

Political ideology, however, did appear to matter for satisfaction. Both reporting oneself to be more liberal than one's colleagues in the house and being in fact more distant from the ideological center of the self-reports of the entire house were independently associated with lower levels of satisfaction.[5] If ideology were to be a significant factor in job satisfaction, my original hypothesis was that its influence would be driven by the difference between one's own views and those of the median member of the majority party in the house. I reasoned that frustrations with the job based on ideology would most likely be due to alienation from the median ideological position of the party better able to get its programs through the chamber. The distance between one's own ideological location and that of the median member of the majority party in one's house, however, was not a substantial or significant factor in predicting job satisfaction.

In terms of state, New York had the most satisfied legislators, followed by Connecticut and then Vermont. Sixty-seven percent of the New York respondents selected either an 8 or a 9 on the scale; this figure was 50 percent in Connecticut and 39 percent in Vermont.[6] Vermont also had the highest concentration of the respondents selecting the lowest points on the scale, or in other words, those who were the least satisfied. Two-thirds of the bottom 10 percent of the respondents across all three states were from Vermont. These results are consistent with the material from my interviews and observations, indicating that many of the professional and career-related struggles experienced by the legislators are particularly concentrated in Vermont and Connecticut. I will turn to those struggles later in this chapter, and also in the next one.

The Joy of Mattering

Although it is clearly woven through the legislators' general discussion of the sources of satisfaction with their job, efficacy is such a central component of this satisfaction that it warrants a separate treatment. Having a firmly held belief, reinforced by poignant experiences, that what they do is important, that it really matters to people's actual lives, and that they are effectively serving the public, is a powerful source of legislators' gratification. This sense of efficacy can take a variety of forms, and some legislators emphasize one particular kind over another while others draw on all of them. The focus can be on producing specific policies of importance to the state or their district, tackling a vexing political or policy issue, helping individuals and groups with pressing problems and needs, or raising awareness on certain matters and influencing the political debate in ways that reflect their deepest beliefs. The feeling of mattering is bolstered by the media attention they receive as well as the supportive communications that come back to them from interest groups, organizations, and individual members of the public. Finally, to top it off, there is for the successful incumbent the exhilaration of being reelected in an anonymous vote of one's fellow citizens. Indeed, few other occupations offer similar levels of those kinds of positive reinforcement.

Running through all this and anchoring it geographically is the organic connection that the legislators feel with their communities and state. This connection was a key factor in their original political involvement and pursuit of elected office, so it is no surprise that it also helps to sustain them once they are inside the legislature.

This is a public service that I'm doing and it's very important. Public policy is not only very important but also very interesting to me; how we organize ourselves as a society to take care of the people who are having a tough time, to mobilize resources to where we need to build those resources. . . . The country was founded on the principle . . . that all people are created equal. And obviously people aren't all created equal. That principle is—will sum up what's important to me in life, is that some people have more than others. That doesn't necessarily mean more money but more ability to move around, get around through life. And you can use that just to take care of yourself or you can use that to help people who are having a difficult time, and maybe they have skills in other areas. So to me I think that's important. I think that I have a skill in this public policy area and the more I think about social issues. . . . I'm not interested in just writing ideas and getting from point A to point B. I'm interested in moving issues.

. . . You know, an individual can make a tremendous difference. . . . I think it depends on the individual personalities, different agendas. What's mine? I think that what I said earlier—I think it's about injustice and wanting things to work. I care about the state. I grew up here, I think of it as my home, and I want things to work.

When this legislator looked back on the remainder of his legislative career, which extended for two additional terms after we first spoke, these motivations continued to be primary. There was also a sense of satisfaction in what specifically was accomplished regarding them, but the focus necessary to do that came with a price.

I knew that to do what I did—not that I did it, but I did a lot of it—required that I not do other things. The legislature can just kind of eat you up, in terms of there's so many issues that are so compelling. It's very hard to focus, and without focus you can't be a leader on an issue. . . . To do that, you can't be working on a lot of different things; you have to be really kind of narrow in your focus.

* * *

The more you're there [in the legislature], it's easy to see new opportunities and new things you could do, and you amass a sense of being able to set your sights on something and doing it. . . . Feeling that I have the ability to change, to what somebody else might be small things, but to me are big things in the system. . . . When you work on something and you see that it's going to happen. I set myself some personal goals at the start of last year and I achieved all I could do on all my personal goals. . . . And if I hadn't done them, they wouldn't have happened. I truly believe that. I feel like I set this up for me to do, and against great odds, I did them. And I feel good about that.

* * *

I think the sense of having felt that I've made a difference in people's lives, which is something that at different points along the way I have had resonate deeply, meeting with people or from letters received—that to me is probably the most important because that's one of the reasons why I ran, because I do believe that government can be a force for good things in people's lives. It can be a force for bad things too, but the fact is it can be a positive force to improve people's circumstances. And doing those things where you can see for real people, it's made a difference. That sort of reinforces my belief that the system can work and that it does matter that *I'm* here, instead of that other guy who was.

This legislator, who is still in office, continues to be gratified by her sense of efficacy, but has also had moments when it seems like "chucking it all is the more sensible thing to do." Part of that feeling is from the "pounding" that she's taken over time, in part due to being a woman legislator and in part due to her district encompassing her core urban base along with wealthier, more vocal suburbs. Added to that is her growing level of seniority and responsibility in the chamber, which has led her to take on more visible tasks and positions, thereby attracting sharper interest group attacks and well-funded electoral mobilizations against her. The 2004 election was the most difficult for her in many respects, particularly because "the whole atmosphere was just ugly."

It's hard for her to imagine running again in 2 years given the 2004 experience, but she observes that she is already making decisions about attendance at functions with that in mind. With more seniority and a greater feeling of power and effectiveness to accomplish things that she believes make people's lives better, she feels more deeply committed to additional terms and more heavily invested in the institution, primarily out of a felt sense of responsibility to those who have elected her as well as those she believes need to be spoken for and represented at the capitol.

I do reflect on the fact that we've been able to help people and to make a difference in both a macro and a micro sense. If I weren't here, would there be another woman in this seat? Would there be another [person of my party] in this seat?

. . . I make the decision every two years—if I feel engaged, doing challenging work, as well as making a difference for people. The work is intellectually challenging. Individual legislators can make the work as challenging or as not challenging as they choose to, I guess. I've been fortunate in that the leader of my house has recognized my ability to be helpful in dealing with very complex and difficult issues.

...As long as I feel like I still have the energy to make a difference and to make that contribution, it's not fraudulent, it's not inappropriate for me to run again. The fact that I have some successes in making a difference in people's lives is a very rewarding feeling that's hard to express. That certainly factors into the decision about running again. There's no question that the seniority, that the longer that you're there, both in terms of the mastering of the issues, your knowledge of the players and the process, make it more likely to accomplish some things.

* * *

I, along with two other [colleagues], have had an inordinate impact. And I've heard that from the chair of the appropriations committee—he said it specifically. We lose more fights than we win in appropriations. And I said something in my frustration to him, and he said, "Listen, you guys have more of an impact than you can imagine." Because they know when they're cutting that there's going to be a group . . . who are going to raise hell. . . . We'll raise the contradictions. . . . What we've effected is that we put out another position in an articulate manner. . . . We articulated positions which would not have had a hearing were we not there.

As the excerpts indicate, some of the legislators' renderings of what they most liked and found most gratifying about their jobs are centered in particular aspects of the work. The survey results supply some additional information related to understanding what parts of the process legislators tend to focus on. One survey question asked the legislators to choose, among the following five alternatives, which is the "most important thing" they should do "as a legislator": "get bills passed," "work on committees," "provide constituent service," "try to cause the house/assembly to move in a particular direction," and "other" (with a request to specify the activity). Across all three states, the most popular response was moving the chamber, followed closely by constituent service, and then more distantly by committee work, "other," and bill passage. There were no consistent significant differences in these choices based on party or sex. The lack of a difference based on party is interesting, as minority party members are generally less included in the passage of legislation, particularly in New York.

There was a clear and significant difference, however, based on state. Legislators in Connecticut and New York most often chose constituent

TABLE 3.1

Choice of most important legislative task, by state (percent)

Most important task	State			
	Connecticut	New York	Vermont	Total
Bill passage	10.6	3.4	6.7	7.0
Committee work	12.1	1.7	24.7	14.6
Constituent service	37.9	46.6	21.3	33.3
Influence on chamber	28.8	41.4	38.2	36.2
Other	10.6	6.9	9.1	8.9
Total	100.0	100.0	100.0	100.0

Note: N = 213; Pearson chi-square = 24.71; Sig. < .01.

service, while in Vermont moving the chamber was the most frequent choice. Relative to legislators in Connecticut and Vermont, proportionately fewer legislators in New York emphasized bill passage and committee work—indeed, committee work was selected by only 1 legislator there. Vermont stands out from the other two states primarily in the frequency with which committee work was chosen, and the comparatively less frequent choice of constituent service. In the final chapter, I will return to committee work in Vermont. Table 3.1 shows the percentages of choices in each state.

The Social Aspects of Service

By spending such a large amount of time in close working proximity with one another and being involved in close working relationships on a day-to-day basis, legislators get to know many of their colleagues very well. And they bond with many of them, particularly because of the political nature of their jobs. Within each party, legislators are involved in a collective enterprise, a shoulder-to-shoulder political battle that is in turn rooted in a shared normative vision of how their world should be constructed. The social rewards of serving are woven through these shared experiences, and reinforced by the intellectual rewards of dealing with challenging legislative puzzles and learning about public policy. As legislators more generally, beyond party and ideology, they are united by their shared public service, and the stresses and difficulties that they must face, including the shared gauntlet-running experience of the campaign. In addition, for many of them the capital is at a significant distance from their homes, which adds to the sense of camaraderie and shared experience while in session. According to many social observers, these kinds of interpersonal bonds are increasingly rare in our society, and increasingly precious. Indeed, for some of the legislators, these bonds become an important sustaining factor in their legislative service. And for most of them, these relationships and bonds are key elements of the job's most significant attractions.

One of the greatest joys of the job is the camaraderie. It's bipartisan. It doesn't matter which side of the aisle you're on. It's something that I had not done before.... I'm a pretty friendly guy, but never felt a sense of oneness the way I feel with the people in the [legislature]. By and large they're a good bunch of people, well-intentioned. Some brighter than others, but why not? We represent the people—a perfect mirror image! It's a joy to me to, at the end of the day, be able to go to dinner with 10 or 12 of my colleagues, and sit around and just listen to the stories of the old-timers. I love that.

* * *

On a personal level, it's a fun place. It's very social; you meet a lot of people.... You're meeting people and you learn, I think, a tremendous amount from your experience about things that you never really ever thought about or spent much time in, and that I think is an incredible benefit to anybody who goes in to that place.

Again, there was a social aspect of it, which when I was single in my first term, I probably spent a little more time in there, going to dinner and just meeting a lot of people, and all that stuff. You do build up relationships with people that you probably would never come across otherwise than there.

...And I like politics.... [A] former state [party] chairman used to say, "It's a noncontact sport for middle-aged people." And to some degree it is. There's a competitive, sportslike thing about it that keeps you into it.

What was a joy could become a sorrow, however, when the competing visions of the public good ran up against the bonds of friendship.

Sometimes [friendships] get in the way of the process . . . if there is a contentious issue and it splits 2 of your colleagues, and you want to maintain your relationship with both of them. Most often, even if there is a split on an issue, it's not so emotional that they can't understand that whatever your position, we're going to remain friends—most of them do. On occasion, they become so invested in the issue, and so emotionally involved in the issue, that if you oppose them, you're not their friend anymore.

This legislator served several additional terms before retiring, both politically and professionally. He then reentered public life as an attorney for his city. Looking back on the later years of his service, he believed that the friendship across party lines diminished in the face of a "growing wall of partisanship" and a sense of isolation within state government among members of his party.

Another social aspect of service that the longer-serving legislators found rewarding was the experience of acting as a political mentor to younger colleagues. This experience was mostly recognized and discussed in the follow-up interviews, when the legislators and former legislators evaluated their work from a longer-term perspective. The mentoring experience gave them both a sense of a lasting impact on the institution and resonated with their goals of public service. Several former legislators also spoke of a "responsibility" to act as a mentor, and if they were voluntarily leaving the legislature, to find and guide a suitable replacement. Note that such mentoring would necessarily be curtailed, if not lost, through a system of term limits.

I've got some institutional memory here, and I'm pretty good at helping people understand where things are lined up and where the movement is, and what's real in making things happen and what's fluff. I'm fairly useful at that.

* * *

I just had this experience—I went to the capitol for the opening day of the session this year for the first time since I was defeated, to see [a legislator become a leader]. I'd mentored [the legislator] through this whole thing.... [The legislator] is a reluctant leader.... I've been with [the legislator] all through this process.

...This year, we also elected a very good person from my district and defeated [the legislator] who defeated me—which is kind of sweet in some ways. I'd finally been able to find somebody who I thought could win.... I talked to [the new legislator] a year ago, ... but I'd known [the person] for years.

* * *

I enjoy watching my successor. . . . In my '92 campaign, a 10-year-old kid came into my headquarters wanting to work on my campaign. He was really interested in politics—his father brought him in. He became a fixture in my campaigns and then went away to college. . . . He became my state representative—he ran and is now serving in his first term of office. And he got elected a year younger than I was when I was first there. . . . I was, I guess, his gateway into politics.

Lead Linings in the Silver Cloud of Service

So aside from the interpersonal tensions that arise from time to time, what is the problem with the job, then? Why did I argue in the introduction that the legislators had become *scarred* by their service? The most evident scars come from personal and psychological trials, which I will describe later, but in this first cut I will concentrate on the reverse mirror images of the very things that the legislators identified as sources of satisfaction. For all the efficacy, sense of importance, tradition, fascination with the process, and intellectual challenge that resides in the job, there are also feelings of being pressured, powerlessness over the inability to achieve desired goals, frustration over partisanship, and pique due to repetitive speeches and predictable political dynamics. In addition, the workload is extremely heavy, particularly in comparison with the light pay.

Although the job is largely self-defining, not all the decisions about what they can effectively focus on come from the legislators themselves; some are in effect given to them, particularly for those legislators in the minority party, as they are usually far less included in the process of lawmaking than those in the majority.[7] That feature is especially strong in New York, which has a political tradition and a legislature that emphasize party governance (but as the survey results reported earlier indicate, that fact does not keep them from trying, relative to other states).[8] Legislators there and in the other two states who expressed dissatisfaction with this aspect of the process, and with whom I followed up more recently, tended to think that the level of partisanship had either remained the same or had grown more intense over the years. And in all three states, at least some legislators experienced dissatisfaction over their relationships with leadership, either in committee or the party. Chairs and leaders were thought not to be sufficiently inclusive or effective. I will return to one particularly salient example of this problem in chapter 5.

Of course, the negative feelings are made all the more intense by the fact that high stakes are involved in legislative service. These aspects of their jobs are not just personal annoyances for the legislators; to them they are pressing problems threatening the public good. They cut deeper.

When I started [in the legislature] my blood pressure was 125 over 75. Before I went on vacation it was 160 over 110. My doctor has told me, "You have got to chill out." But the problem is if you're—I'm an Italian and when you have that emotional part of you, I go home and I can't sleep. There's just things that gnaw at me because I know there are things that we should do that would ultimately benefit all of the people in [the state]. But I can't do it because when you don't have power, when you're powerless, it's so frustrating to know what is in your heart is right and you have nobody listen to you. And because they have a few more votes than you've got, it just doesn't matter how much you care. It doesn't matter.

* * *

I resent it when I see some good amendments that go down the drain on a party-line vote because the Democrats have determined that there will be no amendments, without even knowing what they are. . . . I have a problem with that because I think we've lost some good ideas and ways of making something better, because of that kind of attitude.

* * *

It was the inability of [the committee chair] to get the committee to work, in part because she doesn't trust anyone, so she does all the work herself, doesn't delegate well at all. It makes people feel like, why even bother coming, or why bother talking, or why bother? So the committee just dissolved, and she would continue charging on, all by herself, almost oblivious to the process around her. When you think about the fact that everyone there has worked very hard in their town to be elected to come and to do something. They get there—one of the better committees to get on is our committee. They get on this committee and then there's nothing for them to do given the style of the chair of the committee. . . . Trying to grapple with that problem was a big low point in this year.

* * *

The longer you spent there, the more you were in meetings where you sort of heard the same stuff over and over again, and there were people that you ... had to listen to in caucus get up and whine, and you saw a lot of unreasonableness up there, both in the body and outside the body, in terms of demands that get made. And again, definitely, just the feeling of being pulled in a million different directions time wise.

Legislators openly accept the heavy workload that comes with being a public officeholder. The magnitude of that workload, however, still needs to be recognized, both physically and emotionally. The hours are long. There is much travel, and most of it is nonglamorous. And legislators are always "on call," both to their constituents and the media. A recent survey-based examination of state legislators in five states—Maryland, Minnesota, Ohio, Vermont, and Washington—found that during the session, 75 percent of them reported working 50 hours per week or more.[9]

Although most legislators relish working hard, it can take its toll. This becomes particularly true in psychological terms, when legislators consider their own personal investment in the job relative to what they are paid. While legislators are paid a solid, midmanagement-level salary in New York—$57,500 at the time of the interviews, plus extra compensation for leadership and committee duties—they earn far less in Connecticut ($16,760) and Vermont, where the legislature is considered to be a part-time job; indeed, in Vermont the pay is so low—approximately $8,000 for the regular session at the time of the interviews—that legislators are almost donating their time to their constituents.[10] Nevertheless, legislators' salaries and their other office-related "perks" continue to grab the media's attention and capture the focus of much public ire. To return to my hometown newspaper, *The Syracuse Post-Standard*, for an example, a recurring story in a state political column is how much the legislators "cost" the taxpayers through their individual district office operations. Again, the tone of the stories is consistently negative.[11]

I've put my entire soul into it. It's a 7-day-a-week job. It's like 20 hours a day. I'm out of my house at 8:00 in the morning, and I'm back around 10:30, 11:00, if not later, and it's constantly going. I carry a change of clothes in my car now, if I go to a morning function and then something in the evening. And I come dragging in; I've been doing that for a while.... I enjoy it. I never complain about it. I look at it as part of the job....This is all I do. It's not a well-paid full-time job because I put so many hours into it—it works out to be, like, $4 an hour.

* * *

I think in fairness, for somebody to do their job adequately, if you factor out the whole year, the extra hours to count when you're in session, campaigning, responding, you're really getting paid half-time for a full-time job. And the commute is a difficulty. We have legislators that have to go—I think the farthest is 90 miles—180 miles round-trip to go to work is ridiculous. To do the job adequately takes full time. I just don't think people recognize that. I think I was the only person up there who got a raise in salary when I got up there because I wasn't working full-time. I bet I'm the only person for whom that was the biggest salary they ever got in their lives.

* * *

We're supposed to be a part-time legislature. With the special sessions and depending on what's on the platter, we can end up in session from January to November, as we did the year of the income tax. But we don't make that great [an] amount of money, so that it really can eat into your livelihood substantially. In addition, it doesn't end with just [the capital].There's many many meetings locally—people will want you to come, attend this meeting, attend that meeting. You can be out almost every night of the week. Before the session, there's every group that has a breakfast to try to sell their agenda to you. And receptions for this, receptions for that. I mean, it gets to be ridiculous.

Personal Challenges and the Problem of Time

The most frequently cited and intractable problems were more personal in nature. To begin with, as several of the excerpts above suggest, there are the problems of being spread too thin, being pulled in too many directions at once, and never having enough time to do the job the way the legislators think it should be done. Though ultimately each individual legislator has control over the parameters of his or her job—at least for as long as he or she can keep it—the outside demands on the legislators are intense, and in day-to-day terms they often feel like they are constantly answering to others' requests. True, they actively sought out this situation, but it can nonetheless be wearing. Here is a typical example of the problem, stated in detail.

I don't like the lack of control of my time and my schedule. For example, on a typical day at [the capitol] it's probably the worst, but on any typical Monday . . . I'll have five receptions that I'm supposed to go to that night, and I don't usually want to go to them, but I'm supposed to go, and so it's always that constant struggle between work that I want to do—I could be making phone calls back to the district about one thing or another, or I could go to these receptions, which I don't particularly want to. I have committee meetings and then sandwiched in with the committee meetings are appointments, mostly with constituents, but not only constituents, and so I'll be booked from 8:30 in the morning right through 5:30 or 6:00, dealing with a different issue every half an hour. And that's very hard to stay focused and to be really at your best when it's changing that many times.

And I never know, someone else controls my schedule. I mean, well yes, I can say, "Don't schedule anything for thus and such a time," whenever someone says to me, even if it's a personal friend, "Can you have dinner with so-and-so, and so-and-so, on this night?" I never know, just because of the magnitude of the demands that are made, and it's important that I try to—I think it's important for me to go to as many things in the community as I can, so that people do have that sense their government is there for them when they want it to be there.

I don't go to everything by any stretch. I don't think anybody can go to everything that we get invited to, but it is in some ways overwhelming. Particularly during the first 3 months of a legislative year when I'm back here [in the district]. I'm in [the capital] usually Monday, Tuesday, sometimes Monday, Tuesday, Wednesday—I get back Wednesday night usually having something I'm supposed to do Wednesday night as soon as I get back. And since I'm only here 2 days, a whole bunch of things scheduled for Thursday and Friday, usually including legislative breakfasts or lunch, with different groups that lobby us about one thing or another, and then we'll have things scheduled for most of the day Saturday.

Do you just feel kind of overworked?

Not overworked but I sometimes feel—how I term it is overwhelmed. It's like I get home on Saturday night and there's a dinner that I'm supposed to go to, and I say I just can't do it. I cannot make myself get into the shower and re-make myself to go to this event. There's one particular legislative event we have every year that is a Sunday morning from 8:00 until noon, and that particular weekend always depresses me because it's like my Sunday is—usually I head back to [the capital] on Sunday afternoon or the evening.

. . . So that schedule is what I hate the most. I also always say, wearing lip-stick, because I never wore lipstick until I ran for office. People told me I had to do it because on television my mouth disappears. . . . I think the physical de-mands of traveling back and forth and the schedule is something that people who haven't experienced it, can't really appreciate.

This legislator is still making the treks, filling her schedule with legislative tasks, and wearing lipstick. Looking back on these comments now, she still sometimes feels over-whelmed, in particular regarding all the requests that are made of her during a typ-ical day—requests that she wants to respond to, but that are also sometimes acci-dentally "dropped." Yet she has also found that with increasing seniority, she is more comfortable declining certain event invitations. And over time, she has been able to develop a deeper base of expertise on the issues that most concern her and the com-mittee that she now chairs, such that she can more quickly become familiar with a particular issue. But the overall tension remains.

I'm more up to speed on more issues, but it is still a challenge to carve out the time to be able to devote to a policy matter that you would like to move for-ward. For example, now I chair [a committee] which has the oversight of [a complicated state policy], among other things. The policy is a huge system and it's a disaster in many different ways. The politics of trying to do changes there are enormous. But just trying to be able to hold the world back so you could think about how to make the system better, separate from looking at who's proposed what—I mean in the abstract, as a policy matter, what would you do—is really difficult.

Another deeper set of personal problems involves the impact of legislative service on one's family. The demands of the job create multiple tensions in family life. First, there is the sheer amount of time spent away from home. Second, there is the emotional attention demanded by the work. If, as Joseph Story famously remarked, the law is a jealous mistress, then leg-islative service is more like a dominatrix. Third and by no means ex-haustive of these kinds of problems, family members must live through the invectives and attacks that legislators receive, while at the same time having little or no means to respond to them. Two of the excerpts contain explicit references to the serious marital problems that can result from these tensions. Marital problems were noted by many other legislators, and in my follow-up conversations, a few observed that these problems had intensified in recent years.

Legislators constantly agonize over the family-oriented trade-offs inherent in their service. In the next chapter, we will see that favoring the family in these trade-offs leads many legislators to leave the legislature sooner than they otherwise might have wanted, but it can also cause them to forgo pursuing more authority and responsibility within the chamber while they are there, due to the additional time commitments that such positions usually entail.

I think my children aren't so sad to see it end and will be a factor if I decide to run [again]. . . . I think politics is very difficult on a family. A candidate can make up their mind to want to know what the downside is. A family only sees all the work you do—it's very hard for them to understand the criticism, especially when it gets very personal.

* * *

I think some of the newer members . . . who are younger, who have recently married, are feeling it. I've heard complaints when we're kept there for extended budget deliberations, or when the session goes beyond the closing date, or it interferes with a vacation or a family function. I've heard complaints. "How am I going to explain this to my kids?" That type of thing. . . . And constituents don't often understand that that's a sacrifice that a lot of members make.

* * *

Personally, I will have a decision to make at some point, of, do I want to spend pretty much my kids' entire school days where I'm gone [most of] the week and talk to them by phone, whatever. I'm probably getting, after this next term, in a position of just saying to myself—then it will have to be a conscious decision on my part. . . . I am still trying to convince myself and some other people that you can have a strong family commitment and be a successful legislator. . . . I think if you're honest, it is a struggle.

. . . There's lots of families and marriages that are ruined because—so part of my determination too is, do you want to take part in those meetings or responsibilities that are going to keep you there longer? You can go and vote, and do your things and make your focus more district oriented. Or you can—you can't be in real leadership positions without extra commitment and involvement in [the capital]. And to this point, I have not sought the other out. But that part of me that always ascends to something, starts to draw me to saying, "If only I was doing this and that."

This legislator still serves in the legislature. Looking back, he observed that he didn't originally plan to stay in this long. Over the years, he has moved into leadership positions and has had more policy influence, which has increased his investment in the institution. The trade-offs he described have continued, and he has seen others face them as well and come to different decisions from his.

When I was making a decision whether to run for my fourth term, my kids were [adolescents], and I can remember sitting down with them and my wife, and talking about whether or not it was a good idea for me to continue. Interestingly, they, at that point and their ability to do that, ended up being very encouraging. . . . It did end up working out well. I would say my wife has never loved the leaving and whatever. But, for instance, I had a choice of whether to go [to the capitol] last night or this morning. That's been one of the things— how do you squeeze a little family time out of it and still make it work. I missed a school board meeting [in a city] because I was at my [child's] swim meet and my other [child's] track meet. It is a trade-off, but we continue to make it work.

. . . My two best friends both left the legislature—one's a county judge and one went into private business—and both of them started their families when they were in the legislature. And either of them could have easily been the leader or run for something else at some point. But they made conscious decisions to both pull back. For me, it's been more of a balance.

* * *

I've known a lot of people to get divorced while they were in. Given the legislative stuff and the [outside] job, that leaves very little for family. There are people up there that don't see their kids grow up, including myself.

* * *

I'm single, so the time I'm away, and be away at night, doesn't affect anybody but me.... I know some of [the legislators] that take a real ratchet on the home front because of being away when we get into these long sessions—at budget time, at the end of the session—not being home. They got a life, they've got a family to take care of. Sometimes the electorate loses touch with that fact. We're just people, doing a job.

... [Legislators] have to juggle ... decide whether they're going to go march in a parade or go see their kid play little league baseball—your kid only grows up once. But then people want to see you in the parade. "Ah, the son-of-a-gun didn't show up in the parade." And they forget you've got a family. I think the hardest thing about being in politics or being a politician—or an elected official—is people think they *own* you. You know, "I pay your salary, you're *mine*."

Just as family concerns had a differential impact on women legislators when they were contemplating seeking office, these same family concerns regarding legislative service, while weighing on all of the legislators, are more deeply felt by women. This gender-based pattern of difference may change in the not-too-distant future, as gender-based patterns in the distribution of family responsibilities and domestic labor continue to change, but for now the relative difference in experience is clearly heard in the interview responses. That difference is reflected in the fact, as reported in the previous chapter, that the average length of service for women in the three legislatures was 2.3 terms versus 3.1 for men.[12] It is also reflected in the fact that 42 percent of the women legislators had outside occupations compared with 58 percent of the men.[13]

It's hard because I'm a mother, I'm a lawyer, I'm a legislator, and when I find it particularly difficult is when I'm campaigning and trying to do all those three things. So as a matter of fact when I'm—last summer, when I was running for reelection, I had a 7-month-old, [I was] trying to run my campaign, I was trying to be a legislator, and trying to be a lawyer. I was in the office trying to do all those three things—I knew I couldn't do any of them the way I wanted to do them, so I decided to quit practicing law.

... I may go back to doing that. But right now it's hard with having little kids. But I expect to go back to practicing law because I think it's important. I think it's particularly important for women in the legislature because a lot of the women who are in the legislature do that as their only occupation. I mean, there are some folks who are nurses and who actually do other things outside, but there are also a significant amount of women who, you know, do their volunteer work, run around a bit, and somehow came to the legislature, and that's not the route that I came from. . . . One of the things that I think that I can contribute to the legislature is the perspective of a young woman who has a career, has young children, and is in the legislature.

* * *

I see the legislature as a real challenge, especially if you have a family, in trying to figure out how much a part of your life do you want to make it. I've made a conscious choice that if it ever comes to the legislature or my family, the legislature's going in a flash. And I really limit the time I spend there and the amount of time I put into it, consciously, because it could consume you.[14]

Juggling Outside Careers and Making Money

Related to the concerns over family life are the problems associated with trying to maintain any kind of momentum and continuity in one's previous professional career while serving in the legislature, and with earning enough money. For younger legislators at the beginning stages of their careers, there is the additional concern that extended periods of public service will permanently cripple them professionally—that they will lose ground early on that they will never be able to make up. These tensions are not felt as deeply by legislators near the end of their professional careers or those who are already retired, but a "citizen legislature," in which the members do not consider themselves to be professional politicians, should not necessarily mean a "retired legislature."

These concerns run rampant in Connecticut and Vermont, where legislative salaries are low. Relative to the legislators in those two states, New York legislators tend to consider themselves to be completely full-time legislators, meaning that they engage in legislature-related work to the exclusion of other professional pursuits throughout the year. Sometimes, they view their service as a long-term sabbatical from another career, or conversely, see themselves as being committed to a lifelong formalized career in politics. It bears repeating, however, that almost all the legislators in all three states view their legislative work as their primary occupation, for which in Connecticut and Vermont, they are paid a part-time or secondary wage. They are in essence putting in overtime in order to pursue their other careers. Like legislators in most other states, most of the legislators in Connecticut and Vermont held outside occupations—67 percent in Connecticut and 73 percent in Vermont. In New York, by contrast, only 30 percent had an outside occupation.[15] In Vermont, where the salaries are particularly low, legislative service takes a heavy toll on the careers of the younger legislators, and as we will see in the next chapter, ultimately causes many to leave. That dynamic is reflected in the fact that the average age of a legislator in Vermont, at 53, is greater than the average of 46 in Connecticut and 49 in New York.[16] Illustrating the dynamic at the individual level is the following note one of the survey respondents in Vermont felt compelled to add at the end of the form: "I won a contested election and two uncontested elections. I am a retired teacher, aged 67. I would like to be replaced by a young working woman or man. This is unlikely due to financial loss incurred by serving in the house. I might be willing to serve a fourth term if circumstances warrant."

Many legislators in Connecticut and Vermont also expressed more general concerns that the financial and professional tensions created by the legislative salary kept many good potential candidates from entering legislative service.

We get paid $16,000 something and we get $3,500 for expenses. So it's a great part-time job. And what I think happens here is because of the pressures of it, I think there are a lot of wonderfully qualified people in Connecticut who just for economic reasons can't do it—who I think should be here. And many of them would be certainly more qualified than I am to do this job. I mean, you really almost have to have some kind of a super passion.

One of the questions in the survey asked the respondents to locate yearly family income within a set of ranges. In New York, 42 percent of the legislators lived in families with incomes between $66,000 and $95,000, and 38 percent lived in families with incomes above $95,000. In Connecticut, incomes were not as heavily tilted toward the top end: 46 percent of the legislators lived in families with incomes between $66,000 and $95,000, and 20 percent lived in families with incomes above $95,000. In both New York and Connecticut, the most frequently selected specific income range was $66,000 to $80,000 (25 percent of all the respondents in New York and 26 percent in Connecticut).

In Vermont, however, the picture is dramatically different. There, only 18 percent of the legislators lived in families with incomes between $66,000 and $95,000, and only 8 percent of legislators lived in families with incomes above $95,000. New York thus had almost five times as many legislators in the top income level than did Vermont. Even more telling, the most frequently selected specific income range in Vermont was not $66,000 to $80,000 but rather $21,000 to $35,000; 28 percent of the Vermont legislators placed their families' incomes in that range.

In terms of family income, the notion of a genuinely representative "citizen legislature" is much more of a reality in Vermont than in the other two states, and indeed, the distribution of legislative family incomes parallels the levels of professionalization in the three legislatures. The legislative family income in Vermont seems to be roughly in step with the median Vermont household, which had a yearly income of approximately $36,000 during the same time period. By the same token, the legislative family income in Connecticut is at least within distant earshot of the state's median household, which had a yearly income of approximately $41,000. It is New York's legislators, 80 percent of whom lived in families with incomes above $65,000, who enjoy a much greater income than their state's median household, which had a yearly income of approximately $32,000.[17]

While these figures indicate that the individual legislators in all three states are far from starving in the street, bear in mind that they often include a significant spousal income or retirement package, and of course the outside jobs of the legislators themselves, when they have them. In Connecticut and Vermont, the legislators are usually scrambling to put these family incomes together. Also note that the incomes I cite here are probably skewed toward the higher end of the distribution, due to selective nonreporting.

The following excerpts bring these figures and the professional struggles to life.

We do have a pretty good cross section, [but] you don't have many people like me. I work for a large, large company. . . . There's not many people that come from big business, and that has been a problem.

. . . When I first went to the [legislature] . . . I had a very responsible job. . . . I had at one point in time over 300 people working for me back then. . . . Then . . . I did a 180-degree career change. . . . They came to me and said they would like me to go to the facilities . . . to implement all these things you've been putting together for the past 2 or 3 years. . . . I said to them, "I'm in the legislature. The only way I'll think about doing this is if you let me pick the section chiefs." . . . So they told me I could pick anybody I want.

...That worked until ... [my party was] back in charge of the [legislature] and I was [in the leadership], and that entailed quite a bit more work.... I was traveling a lot to other plants.... I was traveling a lot and got in a big hassle with my boss. He told me I had to stay down there. I told him I had to be back for the legislature. So we had a terrible hassle, and then he transferred out.

...I think I've always made time for the legislature, whatever it took, whatever it took. I do have to tell you that the first 2 years I was in the legislature, there were so few [of my party] that I was on four committees. So I ran myself ragged to the point that I got pneumonia the last week of the session. I felt so bad.... I lost 40 pounds. I was out of work for like 3 months. So from that, I found that you have to pick and choose what you're going to do, other than the real process. I have over the years just to some degree curtailed—I mean, I get invitations like you wouldn't believe, everywhere known to man.

This legislator, still serving and now retired from his outside professional career, looked back on the tension between the two jobs and thought that he had indeed probably given up some chances to further move up in his company because of his legislative career. He is currently wrestling with the question of whether he is finally ready to retire completely or run for a state senate seat should it open up, which it is likely to do.

Who knows where I might have been if I didn't go to the legislature—let's put it that way. Because things were good for me [at the company]. But I always had this bug about being involved in public service and the political world.

* * *

I'm part of a 2-person marriage and my husband's working. But if he weren't, I don't think I could do it. Because of the business I was doing before I moved into the legislature, I've been able to juggle stuff. Certain jobs work well with the legislature, and I was able to have one of those. But I think for a lot of people it's a never-ending struggle. And that's one of those issues that can get your dander up because I think people who aren't in the legislature look at the amount you make [while you're in session] and think, well, how can you complain? ...What they neglect to see is all the meetings and obligations for the rest of the months, and how almost impossible it is to hold down lots of normal jobs.... I think most people need to earn a living and are having a hard time.

Are you interviewing [a farmer-legislator] by any chance? ... He would often be up at 5:00 in the morning spreading manure on his fields before he got to the legislature, with a coat and tie on.

It turned out that I did indeed interview the legislator she had referred to. Here is what he had to say on the topic.

It's a tough balancing act. Quite frankly, I'm in a position where I'm [middle-aged], I'm not sure I can continue a whole lot longer getting up at 4:30 in the morning, working here for an hour and a half, coming in, showering, changing, and going an hour and 15 minutes to [the capital] and spending in many cases 10, 12, 13 hours down there, then running back home. ... By Friday, I'm wiped out.

The problem that I have is that while you work the process, as you go up the ladder, if you are successful in [state] politics it's through the legislative process. At [my legislative salary], you have to have a real job that pays the bills and keeps a roof over your head. And for me, that's been the farm business. I could go to work [in education], I could get a teaching job, could do any number of things. My problem is that I'd go to my prospective employer and say, "The problem is that I won't be around [for several months]."

I like the legislature, but it's been difficult. At some point in time I'm going to have to choose between business or politics. The choice is already made: Somehow, some way, I'm going to afford to stay in politics. I've said to people jokingly all along, if I didn't have to work for a living, I'd do what I do in politics for free because I like it, I love it.

He talks in detail about how he anticipates having to sell most of his farm if he stays in politics, and about how he has given up time with his immediate and extended family.

I know a lot of people who really struggle. [A colleague]—he's got to be an excellent teacher, a top-of-the-line teacher. It's a real wrench for him to be out of the classroom as long as he is and to turn his class over to a substitute for as many months as he does. [Another colleague], a teacher at [a small town] high school, same situation. People with law practices.

I'm learning how to say no. I'm going to have to say no. I used to be a serious skier—I haven't skied since 1987. All because of the time constraints.

The financial trade-offs continued while this legislator stayed in service in the legisla-
ture. He ultimately sold his livestock on the farm when he took another full-time gov-
ernment position—a position that also required him to leave the legislature.

Many other voices echoed similar concerns and professional struggles.

I'm a manufacturer's rep in [a construction-related] business. I cover [the state
and part of another state], and ... we sell products to wholesale and retail accounts.... I have to go see my customers and take orders, and solve their problem when they don't get billed right or when the stuff doesn't show up. And so
I have seen my people probably 60 percent less than I did before.... My wholesale business is off 60 percent because the construction industry is going
nowhere.... So from that standpoint I looked at it and said, if you make a determination of whether you think the market will turn around I should be
doing my regular job. If the market is not going to turn around even if I go and
see my customer, he can't buy anything anyhow.

... [F]inancially it's a terrible struggle because I do think—I do know that a
number of my competitors have used it against me to tell my people that he
don't care about you because he's too busy doing *that* stuff.... You know I'll
work Saturdays now when I'm not here to go call a couple because a lot of my
customers are open Saturdays. So you begin to see that there's other pressures of when you finally leave this, that you're doing your regular job on the
weekends, that you just don't have any time to kick back.

... And what's concerned me because I've never had—of course, I'm [mid-
dle-aged], I'm some 20 pounds overweight. So all those issues come into play
as well. It's the stress, it's the lack of exercise.

* * *

I don't work full time in the emergency room. Close, but not full time. I work
32 hours a week, which is 4 days. And of course, in that profession you do every
other weekend, so that I am off several days during the week. I try to schedule
things when I'm not in session during my time when I'm off.

And when we are in session, it depends on what one's committee assignment is. The committee assignment I carried this last session was horrendous.
I found that I was in [the capital] right off the bat, Monday through Friday. And
that normally doesn't happen, based on your committee assignments, ... until
midway into the session.

...What I start off doing is cutting my time [at the hospital] back. And I will work Monday days and weekends. Then I will end up working just weekends and then I take a leave of absence. And I have to say they've been fantastic.

Some of my colleagues don't do anything else. Others are teachers and have to finagle time off. Others are attorneys or CPAs and have their own firms or business, and have the flexibility of taking the time off. But it has to eat into their profits. I think the job should pay more than it does. People have no idea the amount of time that is required to spend at this process.... If you take the job seriously and you do the job right.

This legislator has continued to juggle her profession and legislative service. But in reflecting on the challenge in the follow-up interview, she also noted that it has been a double-edged sword for her legislative service. On the one hand, it is harder to do each job well, but on the other, her outside occupation has helped to inform her legislative work and enhance her impact on basic positions taken by her party.

Prying Open Emotional Vulnerability

The family worries and harsh professional trade-offs create a lot of stress for the legislators. But in an even more personal sense, running and serving can be an emotionally raw experience. Legislators place themselves on a stage of maximum personal exposure, appearing before a public and media with almost no limits on their assumptions of what they are entitled to know and investigate. Legislators are publicly judged without an opportunity to judge in return. They must ask for support and money from people they do not know. They encounter difficult and irascible people, whom they must not only tolerate, but must try to win over. When things turn sour, as they inevitably do at times, the legislators cannot help but feel like they are being treated unfairly, and this aspect makes the experience all the more difficult to cope with. And when legislators lose, either in pursuit of reelection or some important goal in the legislature—and sometimes this feeling of loss comes simply from how long it can take to make progress on significant issues—their egos take yet another hit. At the least, it all takes a thick skin.

There was no obvious pattern among the legislators in discussing this aspect of their jobs, except that women legislators were somewhat more open about it, on the whole.

Somebody said the other day that the difference between community service and public office is just tremendous, and the difference really lies in finally reaching a stage in your life where you're strong enough personally that you can risk being rejected. I think it was an evolutionary thing.... I have to be very honest about that—I'm not as courageous as I like to think I am. The first step of the ladders I've climbed in public life, the first step has usually been given to me—either appointed to fill a vacancy or being tapped on the shoulder by [my legislative district predecessor], who says, "I don't want to run for the legislature again. The [party] desperately wants you to. Will you? They'll run your campaign for you and probably make it so that nobody opposes you."

In later years, this legislator ran in several races that weren't as "given" to her as the ones described here. In retrospect, it seemed to her that as time went on, things got "easier" in terms of ego, but she also observed that politics had generally become "meaner and uglier" in the state, due primarily to fallout from the controversy surrounding two particular policy issues. Her dislike of campaigning never went away, even though she was never defeated in an election. She recently retired from legislative service.

In reflecting back on her service, she also observed that this challenge of ego was more pronounced for women, given lingering social norms and prejudices, and the ways in which they are embedded in the presuppositions of women themselves. She thought this factor contributed to why women often come to the legislature later in their lives, because they need to build up their confidence more gradually. In her mind, it also accounted for the observation that women, relative to men, were generally more serious students of policy as opposed to the politics of an issue or their districts. This observation was echoed by several others, both men and women, in different legislatures.

Women have walked slowly up a ladder, gained the confidence by the school boards, by the select boards, by the library chairs, or whatever. And that gives them at least the confidence to put their name out there. It does take a lot of courage.

But the basic problem was shared across the sexes. Here are several other voices.

It's tough. I've been here 4 years. My work on [an issue] was focused on for about 16 months, maybe less. And we lost. It went nowhere, I mean, no legislation. How many times can you go back to the well, summon the energy, take on a big one, create good public policy that really addresses the issue in a sustainable way, and then lose, and do it again?

... I don't like running for reelection every two years. It feels very much like a personal judgment. Obviously, that's not a personal judgment, but it really feels like it is. It's hard for me to separate that. Do I like you? Don't I like you? Are you doing a good job? Are you a good guy? That kind of thing.

... It's the running for it. It's the constantly trying to ingratiate yourself with people so that they'll vote for you. You're constantly putting yourself out there on the block and saying look at me, a [middle-aged] male, how much? It's *that*, that's so difficult.

And I've always felt that my races are going to be tight and I guess they always have been pretty tight. ... I would be delighted if there simply was a referendum on what [I] stand for, what [my] values are, what he's done and not done in the time that he's been in office. If that were knowable and people could say, yes, we'll give him 2 more years, or no, we won't give him 2 more years. ... So the process of election, I find, is very stressful. I know it makes my stomach turn somersaults; I get anxious about it. Is this person going to vote for me? Did this person vote for me? Are you still going to vote for me? ...

My first term, I voted differently than I really in my heart wanted to on the social welfare reform bill. There were only 7 people who voted against it. I wanted to vote against it. But I was scared to. I'd won by [a handful of] votes the first time, I was staring reelection in the face. I know everybody wanted that bill. ... So I went along. But I voted against it last year and the year before.

This legislator was narrowly defeated in a later election. It took him a year and a half after that to realize "just how filled with conflict" his life had become while in the legislature. The psychological dynamic that he described earlier about the campaign process had become more of a year-round condition—the worrying over saying hello to enough people at public events, having to constantly be "on" in any public setting. Because of his work on a controversial issue, he was conscious of "a sense of anger toward me just when I was walking down the street—at least that's how it felt."

But after his service, he observed, "I could just relax and be myself." He also came to realize how exhausted he had been after commuting back and forth to the capitol and working the long hours there, and how much better the lives of his family and his own personal life were when he wasn't doing that anymore.

He also noted that in later terms, he cast no other votes like the one he described on the social welfare reform bill in his first term. He voted incorrectly in several instances, meaning that he would have voted differently now based on what he subse-

quently learned about the issue, but there were no other votes that he cast specifically not to lose electoral support.

Here's a nice little metaphor about all this [campaign process]. I have an [old sports car]. It's the only car I've ever owned that everybody smiles at. . . . Normally during the winter, I drive a [newer European car]. So in odd-numbered years, I would have my legislative plates on [the European car]. And then sometime after the session ended in even-numbered years, I would take those plates off [the European car] and put them on my old pickup truck, and I'd avoid driving the [old sports car] throughout the campaign season. The metaphor is that I—that *I*—just couldn't be myself. Because what I thought was being appropriate for a person in my district at that time wasn't a person tooling around in expensive cars.

Once I got out of office, I began to realize just how great—I remark on it frequently even now—just how nice it is . . . to just be a regular guy again. Frankly, I think these people—and I don't care whether they're [a United States Senator] in a big job or [me] in a little job—it's hard to imagine that they don't lose a good bit of themselves.

Negative experiences with campaigns and the media are a large part of the emotionally bruising aspects of legislative service. They are usually two sides of the same coin. One legislator, for example, had recently gone through a difficult campaign for mayor—both in the primary and general elections—an office he had pursued in the off-year between legislative elections. He described how he had been completely turned off to politics by that experience, though he still professed to love the job of legislating, and was not planning to step down from the legislature or leave political life any time in the near future. But he would remain haunted politically by the experience. After our interview, he went on to lose his reelection bid, in part because of the negative fallout from the nasty campaign for mayor.

I wanted to get involved. I wanted to make [politics] my career. Working with people—I love people. And I loved politics. Now, I love my career and I love working with people, but I hate the political aspect of it. Politics has gone into the gutter lately. Do I believe in the good of the people? Yeah. Do I believe for the most part the people can realize the good? Yeah, but I also can see how nasty and vicious it can be.

People don't want to run for office anymore. Why do you want to run for office if your personal life is destroyed? Why the hell would you want to run for office if you were married and had 2 kids, and maybe had an affair on your wife 20 years ago? No matter what you can contribute, why would you want to run? Give me one good reason, given what happens nowadays. There isn't one.

People talk about mediocrity and voting, and mediocrity and candidates. Well, you can blame the system for it. And you can blame those who cover the system for it also because they run that crap. They run it either on television or in the news media.

Plato once said that the greatest profession of all is the art of public service, you know. That was it. . . . It's just the worst, worst—I am living proof—of the worst side of working in the political system, when you go through what I went through last year. I had a woman come up to me. I was in [a local department store]. . . . She said, "I will never vote again after what happened to you." I said, "Well, I'm sorry if I offended you." She said, "It's not what you did. It's what *they* did to *you*. . . . That was the most repulsive, disgusting thing I have ever seen in my life. I'll never vote again." . . .

I looked her right in the eyes, and I took her hands and I said, "I want you to know one thing. I'm very much at peace with myself and I'm not bitter because I believe in the Lord. . . . Don't be bitter, because I'm not. . . . I would hope that what happened to me is an example for people to understand what can happen under the worst conditions." . . .

It's wrong. We're ruining the level of government in this country. We're taking it down. . . . And the people that condemn the negative campaigns cover them more than anybody else. Did you ever see a newspaper, or a television, or a radio station refuse money for an ad that's a negative ad?

After his reelection defeat, this former legislator remained in public service for a few more years, through an appointed office in a mayoral administration. He is currently a lobbyist and political consultant. Informally, he has provided campaign and general political advice to selected Democrats and Republicans who have asked. Despite his sense that the bad aspects of political life, including polarization, have only become worse in the intervening years, he still misses much about it and is reconsidering the pursuit of an elected office. In fact, he feels compelled to reenter the fray.

One of the things about being away for the years I've been is to find out, really, the disdain that people have for political people. They've come to accept the fact—and they say it with a joke—"Well, what do you expect? He's not going to tell the truth, he's going to say what he has to do to get elected." So that is still a bit of a disillusionment with me.

Do I miss it? I probably miss it a lot more today than I did maybe 4 years ago. I miss being part of problem solving. . . . I must tell you—and my friends are telling [me] they see it in me all the time—they tell me I'm like the prize-fighter who's got to come out and answer the bell one more time. I was out to dinner the other night and there were 5 other couples, and 2 of them said, "When are you going to do it again?"

. . . I didn't think I'd run for a long time, or ever run again. I think now, there's times when I wake up in the morning when I think, maybe I should get back into this business. . . . In the past few years I would not even consider doing it, but in the last year or so—let's put it this way, I don't dismiss it outright anymore. Because I do believe it is the noblest of all professions, and I do believe there are certain people that can do it well. . . . There are certain people who are meant to be in public service, there are certain people that communicate, there are certain people that can work with people to solve problems. One of the things I've been blessed with is to have some of those skills. I happen to believe that there's people like myself out there—we have a responsibility.

Obviously, however, and as suggested by the previous excerpt, most legislators cannot dislike these aspects of the job so much that they don't pursue office or reelection. And for most of the legislators, most of the time, the prospect of actually losing a reelection bid is rather remote, assuming they run a good, hard campaign. As a factual matter, this has been documented by numerous studies of state legislatures and Congress.[18] Whether the legislators actually believe this fact or, more to the point, believe *in* it is another matter, however. And by "running scared" for reelection, they may help to create the high rate of return. But during the interviews, the legislators, and in particular the Vermont legislators, often spoke of the expectation that if they were conscientious in their jobs, they could expect to be returned to office. There is evidence from the surveys that this is a view more generally held among all the legislators.

One of the survey questions concerned the legislators' sense of their own electoral vulnerability and asked them to choose among the following four descriptions of the electoral safeness of their own seat: "relatively safe—barring any unusual circumstances, incumbents are reelected"; "somewhat competitive—incumbents are usually reelected, but sometimes lose"; "very competitive—incumbents are just as likely to lose as to be reelected"; and an open-ended "other" category. Half of the respondents selected the "relatively safe" description of their districts, while another third selected the "somewhat competitive" one. Only 12 percent selected "very competitive," leaving the remaining 7 percent in the residual "other" category, which they described in various ways. These results were quite consistent across the three states.[19]

At the very least, most legislators have a well-developed coping ability for the difficulties of the campaign process. And although many legislators do not like the campaign, in particular fund-raising, many others actually enjoy the interpersonal aspects of campaigning, as frequently reflected in the stories in chapter 2 about the legislators' paths to the legislature.

Enduring Criticism and Attack

As suggested earlier in the discussion of campaigning and media treatment, and graphically related by some of the interview excerpts, the legislators withstood a lot of attacks during their service, ranging from occasional potshots to sustained broadsides, and coming from opponents, potential opponents, colleagues, the media, and constituents. While these attacks rarely matched the extremes described at the beginning of this chapter by the legislator whose house was shot and the legislator whose sexual orientation was scandalized, the general tone of disrespect and disregard that they labored under was not out of the ordinary. Prior studies, as well as my interviews and surveys, indicate that the legislators' experience and awareness of the low esteem in which the public holds them is a significant component of their frustration with their jobs, combined with the limitations on their ability to communicate effectively with the public about their jobs and the issues.

In listening to the legislators talk about their experiences, it was clear that the criticism took its toll on them emotionally. Of course, some legislators seemed better than others at letting the torrent run off their backs. They found refuge from the abuse in different places—many in the work itself or their families, but others in less obvious places. One legislator, for example, spoke of a particularly difficult period in her time of service, during which she took respite every night by losing herself in the complicated ethical dilemmas of the *Star Trek* episodes that she had recorded on her VCR earlier in the day.

Frustrations of this sort are certainly not new in legislatures. In *Profiles in Courage*, John F. Kennedy relates a story from 1934 of California Congressman John Steven McGroarty, who dealt with the criticisms of a constituent by firing back the following response.[20]

> One of the countless drawbacks of being in Congress is that I am compelled to receive impertinent letters from a jackass like you in which you say I promised to have the Sierra Madre mountains reforested and I have been in Congress two months and haven't done it. Will you please take two running jumps and go to hell.

Nevertheless, as I have set forward in the first chapter, in recent years the views have become more negative, and the drumbeat of criticism from the public, the media, and political groups more regular as well as more harshly framed. It follows, in turn, that the emotional wounds are now deeper.

In the course of my more recent interviews, one legislator who had been defeated in a close election after we first spoke mailed me a constituent letter he had received following the election, and that he had saved because it was so harsh. He kept the letter to remind him of the downside of his service. In two and a half pages of single-space type, the letter gloated over his defeat, criticized his management of public committee hearings—which the writer characterized as "obscene"—and hypothesized that his constituents found him "disgusting." Other adjectives used to describe either him or his behavior included "petulant," "dogmatic," "mean-spirited," "vengeance driven," and "envy driven." The writer had copied his letter to the governor. Two additional points are relevant here. First, regarding the content of the disagreement between the constituent and the legislator's positions, the main point of contention seemed to concern the legislator's work on a controversial law involving tax structures. Second, I had had the opportunity to watch this legislator and his colleagues work in this policy area on several occasions during my periods of observation, including once during the off-session, and what I consistently observed was hard work, thoughtfulness, and wrestling with a complex issue.

At the time of our original interview, the legislator described the problem more generally.

I don't like the anger which permeates—it's real easy to touch anger in this job. People in America in general are angry. I think anger is not far below the surface. I'm not sure how much of it has to do with our parents, how much of it has to do with the economy, how much it has to do with environment, chemicals. . . . People are angry, and they get angry at politicians *very* fast. And it's very difficult to deal with. I think dealing with anger, have a hard time with—I know I certainly find it very difficult. My preference is to try to deal with it in a way to try to get as clear as possible what is the source of the anger. What, if anything, is my role as regards to that. . . . I'm talking about an editorial, or a letter to the editor, or a constituent, an opponent, that kind of stuff.

The emotional challenge inherent in political life is not a new topic of academic interest, but curiously, for many years the obvious relation between cause and effect was reversed. A theory prominent in the 1950s and 1960s about serious and sustained political activity actually asserted that in some fundamental respects, political activity was the *product* of psychological ill-health. For many politicians, political activity was compensatory—a public response to the basic psychological conflicts that afflict us all, but that have damaged them more deeply. As the political scientist Harold Lasswell claimed in 1948: "All men are born politicians, and some never outgrow it."[21] The research supporting this view was often based on case studies, ranging from historical political figures and people receiving psychiatric care to actively serving judges and politicians. One study, for instance, examined political activity within an Illinois mental health institution and found that paranoid individuals were more likely to be selected as leaders in democratic settings; their sensitivity to negative communications apparently led them to attempt to control their social situations through exercising political leadership.[22] In addition, a classic, often-cited study of first-term state legislators in Connecticut published in 1965 argued that while the best, most effective legislators possessed high self-esteem, most were engaged in one fashion or another in compensatory behavior for low self-esteem.[23]

Most evidence, however, points away from psychological damage as the primary source of political activity. Although the interpersonal behavior of some individual high-profile political leaders—like Richard Nixon, Lyndon Johnson, or Bill Clinton—might invite such inquiries, on the whole it is much more likely that the actions and qualities required of today's politicians are fundamentally at odds with deep psychological insecurities and dysfunctions. The political histories of the legislators I interviewed certainly suggest this—they *must* have had fairly thick skins and strong emotional structures to have gone through what they did.

Before the legislators can get to the point of receiving the kinds of attacks recounted below, they must first endure the emotional challenge of standing for election. As described earlier in this chapter by a legislator discussing his campaign experience, putting yourself before an anonymous vote of your fellow citizens is psychologically daunting. The election result is not based on an objective measure of concrete achievement over which a candidate has direct control. Moreover, the rendered judgment is simply up or down, elected or defeated. When a candidate loses, the defeat cannot help but feel to some degree like a personal negative judgment. And after that, of course, there are the attacks waiting for the winner.

I think I was a victim of talk radio.... I'm from the city, in what is essentially a rural district....The radio station here—there's three other radio stations [in my district]—the station in this setting chose to, just as I was leaving the board of education, they chose to go to a negative radio format. The day after I was elected [to the legislature], soon after this radio format started, the comment was made, and never let up, "She spent so much money as the chairman of the board of education, and now we're sending her to [the capital] to spend more money?" ...The good things I did, the changes in policy I made, were lost in the quest for ratings. This station still continues; it's still very negative. Any time I tried to answer it, I felt it was taken out of context, it wasn't treated fairly.... And I think that is the main reason that I did lose [reelection]. There are many people who *still* think that I'm the chairman of the board of education, and I haven't been the chairman for 3 years....

I campaigned very hard [in the first election]....I had a lot of name recognition in my hometown, which is what carried me. I came out of my town with a 1,200 vote plurality, won by 600 votes, because all the small towns did not know me. But that changed. The second election, I won my small towns and I lost my hometown. So I think it's the negative radio, negative campaign.

* * *

I'm getting much better about this, but when constituents are critical or when editorial writers are critical of me—if they know my position and they're critical that's OK with me. I guess it's when they don't want to hear anything, when it isn't a balanced—when there's no give-and-take allowed, or whatever. I think that's hard.... I've come to realize that the more you do things, the more open you are to criticism, and maybe it's a sign of being effective that you get criticized. . . . But in the beginning, I'd be pretty wounded when I'd see really awful stuff.

* * *

We got beat up pretty bad this year for the public perception that we weren't effective. They forget that we passed [a number of significant and helpful bills]. They forget what would have been a busy, good agenda in any year, [but] we didn't pass [two high-profile bills]. The house passed what I thought was a good, tight package. On [one bill], the senate never had any intention of passing that package. [The other bill] probably shouldn't have been passed, though it was for different reasons. Those were the two things that didn't happen. . . .

Knowing what I went through and what we went through to try to give birth to those bills, and to get those bills through the process and to the senate, and then to take the rap that we were ineffective. . . . The sad thing I learned about politics, and it didn't take me long to learn it: When you're in the legislature and you're concerned about the issues, you eat, sleep, and breath the issues, the people—you think that everybody out there on the street has the same level of understanding and cares as much as you do. The fact of the matter is they don't know and they could care less. And that becomes frustrating. Until it gets to the point where the press feeds what they fed on this year, all the negatives that went on, then that's when the average Joe gets all the sound bites, and then, bam, it comes back to you and you're continually explaining yourself. That part for me is frustrating.

* * *

When I first ran, I was always shocked by when I went door-to-door [that] people would say, "Oh, you know, I really don't know why you want this job. One person can't make a difference—it's nice that you want to try, but, you know, good luck. I'll vote for you, you want to try to do something—that's great." But I think that people have this fundamental lack of confidence in their elected officials. I think that people don't believe that people who hold elective office are honest or have integrity, intelligence.

So my goal in holding elective office is to try to reinvigorate people's confidence in their elected officials. So one of the things that I do is that every month I have office hours so people can come and talk to me—and I alternate between my three towns. . . . So people can have the sense that if they want to come see me face-to-face that they can do that. And also when I campaign, I've now been to every street in the district something like six times. So people on every block—I have made friends everywhere.

... I think that one of my personal priorities for any particular day is making sure my constituent stuff is done. I call people back. I let them know that I'm working on their problem immediately. Obviously, I do that out of self-interest and I want to get reelected, but again, it sort of goes hand in hand with the theme we were just talking about. People ought to know that their representatives are responsive, and that they care and that they are going to try to help folks out. So that is part of my—is one of my priorities.

A New Income Tax

Among the three states during the extended time period surrounding the interviews, the criticisms and attacks reached a crescendo in Connecticut, as a result of the institution of a statewide income tax in 1992. Connecticut was one of only eleven states at the time without an income tax. Up until then, the question of whether or not the state needed an income tax had been a perennial political issue, and the prospect of instituting one had always generated deep and visceral responses from citizens as well as lobbying groups.[24] In 1971 the legislature, reacting to a budget crisis, actually passed an income tax, only to repeal it just 6 weeks later amid a hail of protest. Thereafter, at least up until 1992, a publicly stated stand against an income tax had been almost a requirement for election in many districts in the state. This stand came to be known simply as "the pledge."

But during much of the 1980s, state legislatures across the nation were forced to respond to changes in the spending and taxing priorities of the national government that left them with less funds (a situation that recently returned with a vengeance). This slack in resources was complicated by greater demands on public support networks during the same period. For Connecticut, which was undergoing dramatic economic growth during much of this period, the adjustment was initially not that difficult; however, as the Northeast underwent a deep recession in the late 1980s, the financial situation got much tougher. In 1990, a new budget crisis and a new governor, independent Lowell Weicker, brought an income tax to the front of the legislature's agenda in Connecticut, and in the summer of 1991, an income tax was finally pushed through the legislature by the slimmest of margins after a protracted deadlock.[25]

Legislators on both sides of the aisle who supported the income tax were pilloried by members of the public, various members of the media, lobbyists, and even some of their colleagues. The story at the start of this chapter, while more extreme in form, vividly illustrates the problems with the public and lobbyists that resulted from supporting the change. The following story indicates the problems that some legislators encountered with their own colleagues.

I need something to build back my confidence that was destroyed after the income tax vote. As I said, it's beginning to come back. Yes, I had served as a ranking member of a committee, which was a plus. And I've managed to handle it well, but my confidence level is not where it was before.

I was a leader.... I was moving up the ladder. And all of a sudden to have the ladder pulled right out from underneath you and have to try to work back to that point. I always have had the belief that you can do anything you set your mind to doing. If you want something bad enough you can attain it, but you just have to believe in yourself, and have a goal and go forward.

...When I had the ladder pulled out from underneath me, I lost a lot of that kind of confidence that I had. I used to be able to sit and talk to myself, and walk into a room and handle any situation. And I lost some of that as a result of this whole thing. When I had people that I thought were my friends, that were political acquaintances—associates ... who would hang onto the political position as opposed to the friendship that I thought was there, that's devastating to me. I put a great deal of value on a relationship with a person—the political business is beyond secondary to me. Once I find that I am moving back to the level of where [I was] or beyond, and that I am accepted by these people, supported by these same people, I will have back the confidence that I had before.

This legislator has continued to serve and has moved into a party leadership position. Fully getting back the "confidence level" has been a struggle, however. The fallout from the tax still echoes in the treatment by the party leadership, the likely prospects for future upward movement in the chamber, and the legislator's own memory.

It is scarring experiences like these, in addition to the accumulated effects of the difficulties I have traced throughout this chapter, that lead many legislators to leave the legislature. That decision—to stay or leave—is the focus of the next chapter.

Summary

Considering what legislators go through to get and then keep their jobs, in addition to some of the things they must endure while working at them, it is striking that they enjoy them as much as they do. Certainly, drawing loosely on the notion of "revealed preference," legislators *must* get great satisfaction of some kind from the experience; otherwise, they wouldn't pursue it. But the interviews and the survey findings provide a more direct account of the legislators' love of legislative service. That being said, the negative experiences run deep and the costs of service, in several dimensions, can be quite high.

More specifically:

- Legislators' levels of job satisfaction do not seem to be related to different aspects about the legislators themselves, including age, gender, seniority, party, or income. Political ideology, however, does appear to play a role, with more liberal legislators being less satisfied. Satisfaction also appears to mirror the level of legislative professionalization.
- A powerful source of satisfaction is the sense of personal efficacy the job can bring, which takes a variety of forms including legislative accomplishments, constituent work, and puzzle solving. The concentrations of the legislators' attention vary with the state, rather than with the party or gender.
- Friendship and camaraderie are also significant sources of satisfaction, but they appear to be in decline, at least across party lines.
- On the downside of service, legislators can experience seemingly overwhelming time demands and find themselves overextended—an experience made more distressing by the importance they and others attach to what they are trying to do. Family life is strained and often suffers.
- The strain is also deeply personal. Few other persons are as publicly examined, evaluated, judged, and criticized as legislators. Campaigns are especially difficult in this regard, and the attacks exact a psychological toll.

4

Staying and Going

Actually, I made my decision [to leave] when I ran last time. At the time, I was renting a farm over in [the next town] and in the process of buying it. Sixty cows—it was a lot of work. I had to hire a person through the session. When you have that much invested, it made me nervous, and 6 years is long enough in many ways.

Then, just after the session started, my wife left, which put me in a very different place. And I was a little nervous that as much as I like the legislature, it was very easy to, you know, totally throw yourself into that work to avoid facing other aspects of life.... But I think it's a better decision to put myself out in the world and face the music....

Especially next January, when the session starts up again, I'll miss it a lot. So nothing negative about it. I just—I certainly wouldn't rule out doing it again sometime....

If I were still a teacher, I probably wouldn't have had felt the same compulsion to leave. It was as much deciding, well, at the time—it's like having a family all 6 years—if you're going to do the job right, you have to put in a lot of time, at least during the session. So I had—even before I had the farm, I had animals here, so I'd get home and I'd get out and do chores, and it was 10:30, quite often, by the time I'd be in to say hello to my wife. That didn't work out real well....

I think it's difficult for many people to do. I mean, you're putting other aspects of your life, if not on hold, then on some sort of greatly reduced participation level for a minimum of [several] months.... I think ... for anyone who's working for someone else, or self-employed and involved in a relationship, or have children, or whatever else, it's extremely difficult.... [Y]ou have to invest your time.... It isn't a place, as you know, that we can just have some momentary thought on the way down [to the capital], and hand it to some staff person three offices down from our big desk and say, "Here, take this."

Under what circumstances would you run and serve again? What's the future scenario for you going back into politics? Can you sketch that out for me?

I don't know. It would certainly be to have lived life outside of that world for a while. Worked full-time for somebody; ideally, have established a life with more than myself, my dogs, and my heifers. And *not* be happy with the kind of representation I had.

This legislator did indeed leave. After his service, he became deeply involved with environmental protection and outdoor recreation initiatives, and currently directs a project related to these fields for a private nonprofit organization. He did return to elected office as a school board member, but has since stepped down from that position. He does not consider himself to be particularly civically active since then, but he recruited friends to follow him into his legislative seat, so he has managed to still feel connected with the process, at least informally.

He also missed being in the legislature, particularly in the first few years of being out. He missed "the day-to-day fray of things" and the "stimulation" the work brought. He had worked extensively on a significant issue while in the legislature, which finally came to pass after he left, "and it would have been nice to have seen that through."

He sometimes wonders—not particularly seriously—about pursuing the state legislature again, but one factor that makes the possibility even more remote in his case is the change over the years toward greater campaign expense and the need for a more organized campaign.

* * *

I was in 8 years, and the first term . . . was when [the state] was in very strong economic shape and the stress on the state legislature—I mean comparatively speaking, in hindsight, looks almost barely on the radar screen. There was such—again, in comparison to what it became—a very relaxed, collegial type of schedule and atmosphere that it was a very manageable type of situation. I was also single, had no kids, and as a lawyer you're always somewhat more flexible with your time, I think. . . .

Beginning in my second term is when the economy of the state began to deteriorate rapidly. And the legislature became much more of a lightning rod for problems, beginning of course with the obvious, which is the budget. The deficits really started almost immediately upon taking office the second time. But also, you know all the concurrent problems—the caseloads going up higher and I think just the societal stresses. I mean, I think that place just really changed a lot from when I was first there.

I was also appointed committee chairman . . . my second term, which also was a place where these problems of a bad economy started to really create much higher levels of argument. You know, literally the 6 or 8 years prior to that term it was really a question of how to spend the surplus, . . . and from that point on . . . it's been how do you respond to the deficit and, again, all the other problems. And again, [my committee] was a fairly nasty place to be. I enjoyed it; I loved every minute of it.

I did two terms as chair of that committee, and between the Medicaid budget, which is obviously one of the big hemorrhagers in all states, and trying to deal with that, plus all the [other] issues . . . it was a pretty intense place. And then I switched over to [another] committee, the chairman for my last term.

I left with mixed feelings. I mean, it's a fun place in a lot of respects—I love public policy work and campaigning is not a real problem, but in the meantime I'd gotten married, got two kids, and the pressure again in this office in terms of the economy. You could really see our [legal] office taking the hit here. And the time away just really started to obviously become a problem here, and I'm not independently wealthy. The pay in there doesn't do it, for any kind of family income. I just sort of hit the wall personally in terms of the time and money issues.

When we did the income tax, we were virtually in session from January to December, and they were exciting times. I'll never forget it for the rest of my life and I enjoyed all of it. I felt like I was certainly not hounded out of office— I won by a fairly healthy margin my last race even having voted for the income tax, and I think I went out on a fairly high note politically in town and also in the building there, so it was not like I felt pressured out of the place on that score.

Yeah, I mean the place has become much more intense, much more demanding, and again, if you're a part-timer in there in terms of trying to carry on another life—and also the family situation was the last straw in terms of just making it. I couldn't juggle the three balls at once.

Having been out it for a year now . . . I do see how I was probably getting a little whupped by the place.

This legislator found his absence from the legislature "refreshing" in that he was able to broaden his interests and thinking, but also went through some "tough withdrawal" as well. The withdrawal apparently got the better of him; since his retirement from the legislature, he has been a candidate for statewide office and Congress.

Legislators decide to stay or go for many reasons. This chapter attempts to assemble from their stories some of the principal factors in those decisions; however, it does *not* treat those legislators for whom the decision to stay and stand for reelection was an easy one. Indeed, for many legislators this decision was almost automatic. Those legislators might well have been included, as they help to advance part of the central argument of this book. They like legislative service, believe they are having an important and positive impact on the state and their district, have found a way to make it work for them time wise and financially, and are reasonably confident that they will be returned to office. Theirs are stories of "successful" representation. But because of this book's overarching concerns—the health of the political process, the more challenging and difficult experiences of the legislators, and the public's low regard for elected officials—I am more interested here in those legislators who have struggled in some important respects with the decision to stay or have decided to leave. Also note that I do not examine in detail electoral defeat, though the legislators' observations and experiences regarding that are sprinkled throughout this book. Again, my focus here is on the legislators' *decisions* to stay or leave.

At the simplest level, those who are most satisfied with their legislative jobs are the most likely to want the jobs to continue and to choose to run again. This fact is borne out by the findings from my survey, which included a question about an intention to seek additional terms of service. My examination of the relation between the responses concerning job satisfaction (described in chapter 3) and the intention to pursue additional terms is limited to first-term legislators in order to avoid the effect of more senior legislators being satisfied, but also getting to the end of their natural legislative careers and thus responding that they planned not to run again. Not surprisingly, the most satisfied legislators were far more likely to state an intention to pursue additional terms relative to the others: 68 percent of the 31 most satisfied first-term legislators indicated an intention to pursue two or more additional terms, while only 34 percent of the 38 other first-termers indicated the same intention (see the discussion of the satisfaction scale in the previous chapter).[1] These findings are also consistent with other similar inquiries conducted by political scientists.[2] By looking at actual terms served and including the more senior legislators, it also appears that the legislators make good on these stated intentions: The average number of terms served for the most satisfied legislators is 3.5, while the average number of terms served for the others is 2.9.[3]

During the interviews, the typical story of exit was that of a convergence of several related personal, professional, and political factors—it was rare to find a legislator who focused on just one factor in explaining his or her decision to leave. Evidence for this tendency toward convergence is found again and again in the excerpts appearing below as well as the two stories that introduced this chapter.

The modal story of voluntary exit related by the legislators centered on two separate but related factors: first, declining opportunities for moving up within the body, either because the legislators have reached a plateau, like ranking member, committee chair, or a higher position, or because they have been passed over several times; and second, a felt sense that they had completed their biggest achievements and were beginning to experience staleness or burnout. Often added to these was a third factor, which changed the decision from simply retiring from the legislature to running again, but this time for a different office: the sense of a "natural progression," as many phrased it, to a different and usually higher office after a period of service in the house that was thought to be sufficient. For any given legislator choosing not to run again for the legislature, any one or two of these three factors could be primary, but it was usually the case that either the first two or all three were described together as a package. It is interesting to note that in the interviews, the legislators observed more burnout among their colleagues than they admitted for themselves. It is also interesting to note that in New York, with its tradition of relatively stronger party-based politics, expressed plans about staying and leaving were more contingent on potential changes (or an expected lack of changes) in the party makeup of the legislature or the governorship.[4]

Essential to forming the context for this decision were the accumulated effects of the more personal joys, frustrations, and negative experiences of service that were described in the previous chapter. And in some cases, these experiences were the primary factors keeping the legislators in or driving them away from the chamber, over and above the political factors.

Struggles with family, professional, and financial concerns constituted the second most prominent overall theme, and indeed, these concerns were key elements of the decision context for most of the legislators who contemplated not standing for reelection. But in terms of actually being the most proximate set of forces driving the legislators out of the legislature, these concerns were somewhat less prevalent than the three politically related factors.[5] Consistent with the state-based patterns that have emerged in the previous chapters, personally oriented struggles were more prominent in Vermont, followed by Connecticut, and then more distantly by New York, with its highly professionalized and relatively well-paid chamber. The average turnover in recent years in the three states bears out this pattern: In Vermont, close to a third of the house members are newly elected each term, while in Connecticut about a fifth are newly elected. In New York, by contrast, only about a tenth are new.[6]

The final introductory point, which emerges in particular from the follow-up interviews and the brief epilogues at the end of some of the excerpts, is that it is often quite hard for the legislators to predict accurately what their own futures hold politically. When the legislators make some fairly specific point predictions about their own futures, including how long they will continue to serve, they are often wrong. Their collective inaccuracy reflects the fact that their ultimate exit from politics, just like their original entrance into it, is heavily influenced by context and a variety of external factors, which can change.

Hard Choices to Stay

Let us start by considering the difficult choices to stay. As the interview excerpts indicate, these decisions are in many respects reverse mirror images of the decisions to leave. Similar personal, professional, and political needs constitute the fulcrum for the decision, but given their particular situations the balance tips in favor of pursuing reelection. Consequently, these legislators seemed close to deciding not to run, and the decision to stay did not come easily. Borrowing from the language of public health, we might say that these legislators remain "at high risk" of retiring.

So what tips them toward staying? Foremost among a set of leading factors is a sense of investment in the legislature, and either a concomitant belief that they are poised to move up in the legislature, or a desire to reap the policy and political benefits of a recently achieved move upward. These legislators feel committed to legislative service, despite its drawbacks, and they want to exert influence on the institution, and expand that influence if possible. Often alongside these feelings and desires is the attraction of the excitement of both the legislative process and politics.

At the same time that they experience these attractions, however, they do not see their service as a permanent occupation. Most of them believe that their service thwarts other important professional and personal goals in their lives—hence the tension inherent in their service and the constant "risk" of exit.

I'm not going to stay in this job forever, but I'm at the point now where I've achieved a level of seniority that I'm happy with because I'm on the cusp of really moving now within the body. I would like to get a chairmanship in January that's rewarding. I don't expect to get [the] ways and means [committee], but at least a meaningful standing committee. Whether I get that or not is no longer questionable because of seniority. . . . I'd like to stay in enough terms to reach what I think is probably the highest I will get, and that is chairman of a major committee. . . . I'd like to leave some good retirement time. I'd like to travel. I'd like to spend some time on my boat, which I rarely get to do. I've got a married son, so sooner or later I expect to see grandchildren. You know, there's life beyond the legislature.

This legislator soon achieved the chairmanship he spoke of, then lost it in a struggle for power within his party. Later, he assumed the chair of a different committee before retiring from the legislature.

* * *

Well, I don't think—I guess my own personal belief is that you don't do this forever. I'm not planning a career out of being in the legislature. I think that I'd like to—I would probably like one more term after this. I think 6 years is enough. It may be—and I'll have to consider—a lot will depend perhaps on [my spouse]. Just as I see it, our situation is like—my daughter, she's just incredible to be exposed to somebody involved in all this, and I have this wonderful husband, but it is a pain to a family. This is year-round—forget what they say about a citizen legislature. But I don't really know.

I have moments when I think I would like to run for the senate, and I just don't know whether, at this stage of my life, whether I want to go at it with the same energy that I feel like I want to do this job. . . . Will I have something to offer, really, at that level, and what would be my focus? I guess a lot would have to do with where the focus is, but I thoroughly enjoy this, and I discovered that

I really want a political opponent. There is no doubt about that. I like it and I love competition. I really eat it up. There's just nothing I enjoy more than a battle.

After serving an additional term in the house, this legislator was named by the governor to fill a vacant seat in the senate.

* * *

I don't know why I'm a leader, quite frankly. My talents are overblown by everybody but me. Probably because I'm not—I enjoy being there. It's sort of my element when I'm there, and I'm just as happy not to be there. I'm not a terribly ambitious politician. So I'm somebody who's in the thick of it and doesn't have a grand plan.

You see every 4 years or so a really big turnover in the legislature. And if you look at what is turning over, it's the people who have been there 6 or 8 years. By and large they just finally said, "Wait, this is just too much time." And if they're chairman of appropriations or something, there's probably enough extra glory that they'll stick it out. But most people aren't intending to be governor. . . . And so people sort of go in headstrong and then they start to slow down a little bit. Then they just say, "I'm not accomplishing anything, I shouldn't be here." And then you have people like me who have kids heading to college and say, "How long can I do this? What should I do when I grow up? Shouldn't I really be working for a job that pays, and has a pension and benefits?"

This legislator stayed in the legislature for one additional term and moved into a different position of leadership before leaving. The legislator then held several better-paying positions in the executive administration, including agency head, before becoming a senior administrator at a private secondary school.

Other legislators spoke more specifically about other possible plans, and how those plans fit with their broader political ambitions, professional goals, and personal needs. The actual path taken can deviate from the predicted one, but can be better understood in that light. The follow-up interviews are particularly enlightening as to how things ultimately fit together.

I seriously considered running for the senate this year. . . . I actually don't think I want to be in the senate. I mean, I thought seriously that I did, but I really don't want to be in the senate. . . . I don't have a problem imagining running for statewide offices at some point. I wouldn't say right now that it's a commitment, but it's possible. . . .

When I was on the [local legislature], I didn't envision myself as a [state] legislator. And then there came a point where I said I was getting off [the local legislature], and there was the opportunity to be in the [state] legislature and move some of the issues that were frustrating me at the local office. . . .

I considered [running for the leadership] last year, and I pretty much decided that was inconsistent with my agenda or trying to actually do [a significant issue]. . . . You have to sort of give up your issues, those big issues, when you get into leadership, and think about other people's issues. . . . How to take care of other people—that's what you do.

This legislator's subsequent political life might have come as a surprise at the time of the interview: The legislator did indeed become a member of the party leadership and served two additional terms before losing a reelection bid, in large part due to his key role in successfully pushing through the big issue that he had referred to in the interview. He and some others were targeted for defeat by independent groups angry with the new policy. He had decided to pursue the leadership position for a complicated set of interrelated reasons, having to do with a felt sense that on the issue he cared about most, he could be more effective as a negotiator with the senate and the governor, and that there was a hole in the leadership in terms of knowledge of both broad policy goals and political savvy.

After his defeat, he rediscovered parts of his private life that he missed, went on an exercise regimen, and following a break, once again continued to work on political issues through other means—though he stayed involved with his signature issue even immediately after the defeat. The term before his defeat had been particularly demanding of his time as well as his intellectual and emotional energy, and it took a lot out of him. But he misses politics and considers from time to time trying again for elected office.

In a way, I felt [defeat] was a tremendous relief. There was just so much pressure those last 2 years. I had been in 10 years, it's a citizen legislature, you get paid [very little]. At some point, it was getting to be almost a full-time job, the way I was doing it. Being a leader, and being the key person, not only on [one important piece of legislation], but on this [other one] as well. People call you up, the chamber of commerce, they want a speech. You're constantly running around. . . . You know, you don't like to lose, but it was also a tremendous relief.

[Pursuing the leadership] was this thing about what issue I wanted to push, but I also felt like I had . . . I'm good at [sizing up political situations], so I also felt like [my party's] caucus, I don't see anybody stepping up to the plate that I think is better than me. If I had to size it up, it was 70 percent wanting to move my issue, 30 percent feeling like, I don't see that there's anybody else that's going to do this better than I could do it.

There's a lot of issues going in those years that I voted for that went through [my committee] that I was just kind of trusting other members—you know, "I can't think about that right now." It took a conscious decision on my part, and there's a cost to doing it. In fact, I think there was a cost to my district. I couldn't do constituent service the way I wanted to. You can't get that deep into an issue and still be following up on, trying to get someone's kid to be a page in the legislature, or somebody's got somebody in jail and needs some help, whatever it is. . . . It played a role [in my defeat]. It made me more distant from my constituents, the fact that I had gotten so deeply into these issues, I just couldn't be as responsive. I don't think people felt like I was unresponsive, but with an aggressive opposition campaign, with professionals—you know, they had some stuff to work with. And you know, my district won under [the legislation].

He describes in detail how his district fared better under the legislation.

So that's what I was working on, but that's a hard case to make because it's big picture, it's long-term, it's not about the immediate stuff. . . . It was a very calculated campaign. I knew the people who were doing it; I could watch it unfold. . . . They ran a smart campaign, there was no question. I could see it in the way the letters were coming in the paper and the way it was being done. It was very subtle, but very smart.

The longer I was out . . . it was certainly true for me, it may be true to a lesser extent for other people who don't allow themselves to get in as deeply as I did—but there's a way that I really felt like I lost myself. I lost my ability to sit down across the table from a friend and be present emotionally. . . . My mind was just going a mile a minute or [I was] just distracted. There was a way that I just couldn't be present. I also think that frankly, that affected my ability to campaign in [the last election], that I wasn't as good at the door as I was when I was first campaigned. It was harder for me to be present; too many things [were] going on in my mind.

As I got more and more to be able to sit across the table from somebody and be present, I had less and less desire to throw myself back into this political stuff. Unlike the first time I got into it—I didn't know what I was getting into really—now I know exactly what it's like. I have a harder time, willingly, subjecting myself to that. . . . Having said that . . . I haven't counted it out as a possibility. I do still feel some desire. A common question I get is, "Do you miss it?" The answer is, I miss having the power. I miss having the power when I get up in the morning, to actually be able to do something by noon. What I don't miss is all the other stuff, the personal costs of being in that environment. Which, like I said, I think I was good at. But there's a cost. So I don't know. . . . My typical response is that when I get angry enough about something, I'll probably throw myself back into it. But I don't see myself going back into the legislature; I think if I ran again for something, it would be for some statewide office. . . . Although anything's possible, I suppose.

I never thought I'd be there 10 years. I didn't go there with the intention of being there forever. I thought I might be there 5 or 6 years. But I just didn't think I could let it go. I kept thinking, we can do this [big issue]. We can push this over the top.

* * *

I realized that I'm not going to be retired from the legislature someday as the longest or the oldest serving member. And I think right now I am very much fueled by what is going on and the leadership aspect is more captivating. And I'm also seeing that at some point there is going to be an end, at least to this chapter—and that could be in another term, it could be another two terms.

But you know if I retire after 10 years, I'll be [young still]. There are other things calling to me. My wife and I expect maybe putting an offer in on a house later this week, and I think we would like to start working on a family. So I'll always be around the play in politics and maybe even come back someday. Or if there is another opportunity, but I know I'm going to have to leave.

So let's make the most of this while it's here. . . . Let's try and do something positive. I feel somewhat well regarded by the people that I serve with, which is very important too. And to be able to have people say, "Look, he cares, he worked hard, he did a good job." . . .

There is so much of it that is a matter of luck and timing. You could be the best person in the world and never get a chance. I believe that fate may play a hand someday. And I've been lucky, I've been able to make the most of the opportunity. I'm still a little bit out of my league, and that's good. I guess it's a little bit of a challenge. With each [term] there's been a little bit more to do and

I felt, oh my god, am I going to be able to do this? But the session went pretty well and I actually—this is the best session I've had....

When [a member of Congress] doesn't run again, it will be nice to be speculated about to possibly move into that seat. I hope to be able to say, "Well, I'm not going to play that game [even] a little bit." I mean, it's a nice recognition by this sprawling district. You've got to raise so much money and again, just the thought of being in Washington. If I wasn't married, or if [my wife] and I decided, let's both do this, we're not going to have any kids, we don't want to do other things, fine....

I'll probably plug away here for a while, and then hang up my cleats and do some other campaign-related work.

This legislator also might have surprised himself. He remained in the legislature for several additional terms, and by the time he left, he had indeed become one of the most senior members in his party and was a top leader. Other aspects went more according to his stated plans: he and his wife bought a house, and they had 3 children.

What finally pushed him out of the legislature was the prospect of a particularly enticing management job in the private sector that would require all of his attention. The position draws on the political skills he acquired during his legislative service, but his new efforts are directed out of state, so he does not have to lobby his former colleagues.

He openly misses politics, and given the right set of future circumstances, could imagine running again for elected office. One opportunity for higher office almost opened up for him, but in the end neither the timing nor the other political and personal factors came into proper alignment. Note that in the intervening years his metaphor moves from contact to noncontact sports: Cleats have been replaced by running shoes.

I had a very difficult decision, but I guess a very deliberative decision, as to whether this was something worth hanging up my running shoes and moving on professionally. The difficulty ... is that I really had two full-time jobs. My wife and I have 3 children.... I made the decision to make the break.... I'm into my second year [on this job].

It's great. I haven't looked back. I miss it terribly, and sometimes worse than others. But what I don't miss is that when I come home, there aren't five messages on the machine every night. I felt like I was kind of in between—like those old movies, with the cowboy riding in between 2 horses on a stage coach. I had a political career, on the one hand, and I had a professional career, on the other hand. It's nice to be able just to hop onto one horse. . . . But I still feel the pull.

I was a little longer in the tooth [in the legislature], but even then there was a sense of seeing it [the end] and not being able to cut through the fog, . . . and it was part of seeing whether there are other political opportunities that could come up.

He describes the details of the possible political situations created by potential vacancies in higher offices in the state and redistricting.

Just as this professional opportunity came through, a political opportunity did not. I think I probably could have won the nomination and I think I might even have been able to put together a winning campaign. But 2 years later, I would have been facing [another opponent] who would have probably clobbered me.

Even as recently as a couple of months ago [when another possible situation arose], my phone started ringing again. It's like your old girlfriend calling up—"Hello, don't I look great?"

Had political events transpired differently, we might be having a different discussion today.

Could you imagine getting back into politics sometime in the future?

Yes, which may be more candid than, "Well, you never say never." But I'm not sure how or when, or if that will ever take place. The governor asked me [to take on a position], which is not full-time, and I knew fairly quickly that I couldn't do that and do my job the way I think I need to do it. . . . I don't know, it's hard to say. But can I envision it? I can, and I know it because I miss it so much and in a certain way I think I got fairly capable at it. . . . I left loving it.

In an ironic twist on how personal and professional conflicts can work themselves out, one popular legislator, who is still serving in the legislature, spoke of his decision to forgo the pursuit of higher office due to the time demands that such an attempt would entail, combined with the fact that his legislative service up to that point had prevented him from saving enough money to afford the run.

There's a lot of people back home that ask me, "Are you going to run for statewide office?" I truthfully think I know enough people now to raise the money and I clearly think that my political skills are good enough for me to be able to know how to do that. But the kicker is, I couldn't go 10 months without a salary. I don't know what I'd do. I got a mortgage, I got a life. I don't know how I'd support myself.

The next excerpt, the final one presented in this section, weaves together many different strands of this decision: concerns about moving up within the chamber, political ambition more generally, financial and family affairs, political calculations, and psychological factors. Again, these concerns often lead to decisions to leave, and appear to be beginning to push this particular legislator in that direction, but for now he has decided to stay. His remarks demonstrate that the individual components of a set of widely shared concerns can combine in varying ways, depending on the individual legislator and his or her family.

It's kind of an economic as well as a—I'm getting older and I don't have to be as cautious because [my] kids are out of college, my mortgage will be paid next year, so if I get booted out. . . . Taking chances doesn't have the same implications economically that it used to have. Reality principles say, "I'm 53, am I going to be in the legislature forever?" That's something else, 13 years is the longest I've ever held a job. . . .

A lot of people tell you, "Be patient, be patient," which is true, there is a pretty substantial turnover here. The problem for [me] is that the real power is concentrated in the hands of the people [in a different geographic area]. . . . How am I going to make a mark?

What were your thoughts about this, say, 10 years ago?

Well, 10 years ago my desire was to line up to become a committee chair, get a chairmanship—see if I could do something in a specific area. I think I was partly frustrated then. I came from a position of substantial authority to a position with very little authority. I spent basically 6 years as a freshman before I got a committee chairmanship. . . . That made my job a little exciting, a new challenge. Now I've been committee chair for 7 years, I'm trying to do something else. In the legislature there aren't that many jobs that are better than being a committee chair. . . . I was offered a leadership position this year—I always call it the black hole of leadership, being made into [an] assistant [leader]. . . . No one's ever heard from again.

This legislator still serves in the legislature and has appeared to have avoided the "black hole." He has a high-profile committee assignment and leads an important legislative group within the legislature.

Leaving in Pursuit of Higher Office

In the interviews, many legislators expressed plans to pursue another office—sometimes these plans were concrete and tied to a decision to leave after that term; at other times the plans were more general and long-term. In the surveys, 25 percent of the respondents answered yes to the question: "Do you have plans to run for another office, or hope to be named to an appointed office, in the next 5 years?" Another 8 percent responded maybe, and 7 percent weren't sure. The survey also requested that the legislators name the other offices they planned to pursue. By far the most frequently listed offices were Congress and the state senate.

Predictably, within Vermont the planned pursuit of the state senate predominated (there is only one congressional seat in the state); in fact, only 1 person listed Congress. In Connecticut the two offices were listed equally frequently, while in New York, Congress was the more popular choice. Other offices listed more than once, though far less frequently, were governor, lieutenant governor, attorney general, secretary of state, the judiciary, and agency commissioner. Reflecting the lower level of legislative professionalization, the respondents in Vermont also listed the school and parole boards.

The survey also suggested that the relative political importance legislators placed on different geographic levels, or what are sometimes referred to as "areal roles," was not related to these plans.[7] Furthermore, the average levels of personal satisfaction with legislative service are actually slighter higher for those expressing a plan for another office than those denying such plans.[8] And though men and women differed in how and when they arrived in the state legislature, they do not seem to differ regarding plans to pursue other offices. Some nonstatistically significant differences do emerge when both sex and party affiliation are separated. Among Democrats, 18 percent of the women expressed these plans versus 24 percent of the men. Among Republicans, 44 percent of the women expressed these plans versus 28 percent of the men.

Other patterns in the survey responses reflect the influence of opportunities for advancement, both within and outside the chamber, on these decisions. Past research on political ambition, as well as common sense, suggest that the more opportunities there are for internal advancement, other things being equal, the less legislators would pursue outside office.[9] By the same token, the more opportunities there are for outside advancement, the more legislators would pursue those offices. Of course, political culture plays a role, but opportunity structure and political culture can influence each other.

Regarding opportunities within the chamber, note that Republicans, who were in the minority in all three chambers, were more likely than Democrats to express plans or hopes for another office. Thirty-one percent of Republicans expressed such plans versus 21 percent of Democrats. If responses are limited to either yes or no, a clearer pattern emerges, in which 38 percent of Republicans responded yes, versus 25 percent of Democrats.[10] But also note that the average number of terms actually served in the legislature by members of each party was strikingly similar: 3.7 for Democrats and 3.6 for Republicans. This similarity held up across the three states, though in New York Democrats served slightly longer than Republicans—a pattern that was reversed in Vermont.[11]

Although not statistically significant, the state-level pattern in expressed plans for another office suggests a similar effect to that of party. In New York, where there is less turnover of leadership and committee chairs, and therefore fewer opportunities for internal advancement, as well as a larger number of higher elected offices to pursue (particularly Congress), 37 percent of the respondents answered yes. In Vermont, where there is greater opportunity for internal advancement and far fewer outside offices, 26 percent responded yes. In Connecticut, which falls somewhere between the two on these dimensions, 32 percent responded yes. The fact that legislators in New York serve longer than legislators in the other two states also taps into the effects of other factors such as salary that are described elsewhere in this book.[12]

But the interviews reveal that at the individual level, ambition for higher office plays out in different ways. Sometimes it is fueled by the belief that upward mobility within the chamber has been too limited; other times this belief merely provides the spark that ignites an ambition already deeply held within, and in some cases burning brightly for a long period of time, as the final excerpt below demonstrates. This ambition can also be driven by the specific ideological and policy-oriented concerns that originally motivated service in the house, and a related desire to be more effective regarding them and thus have an even greater impact.

Actually acting on the ambition for another office, however, is another matter again. More often than not, the decision to leave the legislature in pursuit of another office is driven in part by family and outside professional concerns—a feeling that the time for taking a shot at a higher level is right regarding those concerns—and a belief that the current political state of the legislature is not conducive to their policy or personal goals. Once again, these factors are woven together in complicated ways. Note the paradox in the first excerpt, for example, of how the family and professional costs of serving in the legislature push the legislator to decide to embark on a pursuit that cuts even further into family life and professional career.

[I decided to run for Congress] in the late summer . . . halfway through my [leadership] service. I'd been [a] leader for one session.

. . . I felt as though my experience in the legislature had been great, but that spending more time in the legislature would not significantly add to my understanding of the process in a way or my ability in the process. I was also at the point where I could no longer justify the professional or economic disruption to my family and my career by spending more time in the legislature. I'd seen too many people give up, just sort of lose their capacity to have a career, and lose their economic base and lose their independence, by staying too long. And third, the U.S. Congress, I thought, would be a pretty exciting challenge and I did think that the federal government was the greatest threat to our children's future in America. I still think that. But I really felt as though, if you're going to sort of whipsaw your career and ask your kids to give up a lot of time, it better be goddamn important. And so I figured, why not?

. . . I think it was the right time for me. I think the chances of me going back to the legislature again were slim—in other words, it was kind of a situation where if I hadn't run for Congress, I probably would not have run for reelection.

. . . I could no longer do everything I had to do family wise and financially, and spend so much time in the legislature. And I also felt 8 years, it's a lot of time. That's a fair amount of time to be a legislator. And I didn't think that people that stayed around longer than that were necessarily better at it than the people that didn't. There were personal reasons to do it, and the practical political reason was that I felt there was an incumbent [member of Congress] that I thought was vulnerable, and I had a chance. It was worth taking the chance. . . . I lost in the primary, pretty hard, flat—big, expensive, tough primary.

...I just couldn't do the legislative thing longer. See, what happens to some people—there may be a few people that can be tremendously efficient, I suppose, in their time. But I didn't see a way how I could make a living and educate my kids—I had 3 young kids—and spend the time needed to do a good job in the legislature. You can do it for a while, but you can't do it for a really long time.

...I could be out to pasture permanently. That's a real possibility. I don't know....Because things can happen quickly and I didn't leave being a politician because I didn't like it. I personally found that having 3 young kids, practicing law full-time, being [a] leader, and running for Congress full tilt, all at the same time, was a lot of goddamn work. I burned out at some time—not sure when because I kept going—but I was pretty goddamned burned out.

Though hardly "out to pasture," this legislator never did run again for elected office and now has an active legal practice. Regarding formal political activities since the legislature, the now former legislator characterized its primary form as a "graduation from the donee status to the donor status." There are no active plans to reenter elective politics—"my political trail is pretty cold."

I know some people continue to practice law and remain in the legislature, and frankly after being out ... I'm amazed at the number of people that are still there. I don't know how they do it, but I was not so brilliant as a lawyer or so organized in my day-to-day life that I could manage to do both very well.

...But I tell you, I miss all the fascinating things that go on in a legislature. It was very, very interesting, all the time, I found. I thought it was intellectually like a banquet because they're so many things there that you have to deal with.

* * *

Well, you know, first of all you don't time opportunity. There was an incumbent [state] senator who was a good friend of mine....I knew very early in the session that [the senator] was probably not going to run again for that senate seat. So at that point, I kind of had to go through the head stuff to say, "You know, do I want to be in the senate?" As soon as I knew there was an opening I figured well, let's think about it.

If you want to know why I decided to do it, I will tell you that the chair of my committee I believe will continue to be there in the legislature for quite a while. That means I would be continuing to be [second]. I choose not to do that. I like being chair.

You were chair this year, right?

I was *acting* chair. . . . My public answer is that I have 4 to 6 more years to devote to the legislature, and I'd rather work in the smaller body where there is more personal impact. My private answer is that I don't want to be [second] in that committee forever. I've had a belly full of [the leadership], and the polarization of the party in [the lower house of] the legislature isn't going to end in 3 or 4 years. So for all those reasons I go for the senate race. . . . I've only been in the legislature 4 years. If I spend another 4 to 6 more years in politics, I could have a major leadership position in the senate.

This legislator was successful in the bid for the state senate and served there for several years, along the way becoming a real, "nonacting" committee chair, before recently retiring from legislative service.

* * *

My ultimate goal, whether I will get there or not, remains to be seen—and I don't tell many people this—my ultimate goal is to be a United States senator. And I don't know what path will take me there. . . . My ultimate goal has been to go through the elective process.

. . . I honestly felt for my style of leadership—I'd been uncomfortable many times with the way things have been done in the [state] house in dealing with the way the agenda was created—for me personally to function within the legislature I can function I think much more effectively . . . in the senate, than I could have—even though I feel I've done well for myself and for my constituency in the house. I think I can be much more effective. Plus it fits in with my plan to try to move [up]. . . . I suspect it's very possible that the path to be United States senator could be through Congress. I know that being one of 435 is got to be one damn tough row to hoe. . . . The ultimate goal to really have a chance to affect policy is in the Senate in Washington. You know, that's where I'd like to head.

. . . You think about how you grow and develop, and. how your goals change. . . . My goal then—and this was about 10 years ago—I felt then that if I could ever become [head of an agency] in the state . . . that would be just *it*— I would have reached it. I think, I don't know, I really honestly believe had I pursued it, and wanted to go that route, when [the governor] was elected to his first full term . . . and developed the coalition of [industry] support, that I might have been able to become [an agency head], but I didn't consciously go after it because I knew that [the state senator], or I thought that [the state senator], was finally going to retire. [He] was going to retire 2 years ago, but was convinced to run again. . . . So I consciously decided then not to run for the senate, but I also put people on notice that in 2 years when [he retired] I would be out of the chute and ready to run.

. . . I think I, as an individual, can be more effective [in the state senate] at finding that middle ground, being a moderate force, being a fiscal, responsible voice, with respect to [the] budget. . . . I want to be there as a Democratic businessman, I guess, that knows where the middle ground is. Quite frankly, I want to be out from under [the speaker's] influence in the legislature. I want to be one of [a smaller number] rather than one of 150. . . . If there's any validity to my long-range goal, running from the house to the senate is the next logical step. Some would say stay in the house, but . . . I think I've peaked in the house.

This legislator did not make it to the U.S. Senate but was successful in a bid for the state senate, and while there was named to head the agency alluded to here. The now former legislator currently occupies a prominent position in a business organization. In terms of elected office, the former legislator will not run again, at least before professional retirement, but does hope one day to secure a high-level position in a presidential administration.

Leaving to Leave

A few legislators decided to leave without any specific plans for other offices. For some of these legislators, it was not so much the "pull" of business and family as the "push" of certain aspects of legislative service that they found no longer tolerable. These aspects included experiencing repeated losses on important legislative matters, feeling shut out of the legislative process (especially a problem within the minority party), and dealing with the frustration of witnessing frequent compromise on key core principles, despite the recognition of the necessary place of compromise in the legislative process. The following excerpt, from one of the more ideologically extreme legislators, exemplifies these concerns.

My areas of interest, like property tax reform or health care, welfare reform, workfare—issues like that are much bigger than my committee and require coalition building. . . . I would have to say that most of the people, most of the 150 people in the legislature, are nice. And I get along with nice people; nice people get along with me. I can develop a relationship with people who have a respectful relationship with me. It's very difficult for me to maintain a respectful, cordial relationship with hypocrites. If you are a conservative Republican opposed to raising the minimum wage, I understand your ideology. You're being true to yourself, and we'll work on some other issues together. And I'm not going to burn my bridges with you over a minimum wage thing, where I understand where you are coming from.

But to have "friends," and I put that in quotes, because it is very difficult to maintain friendships with people who, on the one hand, share the same values with you but would betray those interests because the party said to do it, drove me nuts. Just drove me nuts. And yet these are the people I'm closest to in terms of values. And if I was going to have friendships with people, those are the people with whom I would kind of gravitate to. But that happened too many times, those kinds of betrayals. And they weren't personal betrayals to me; they were betrayals on an issue of importance to both of us. And they had their rationalizations—yeah, you're doing this for that reason over here.

Well, I just saw that too many times. And it seemed like in the end, the bottom line was their need to maintain a decent relationship with the speaker, to advance some other particular kind of interest. Not necessarily personal, but oftentimes there was an overlap. Committee assignment, getting a chairmanship, whatever. . . .

The struggle for me is to, on the one hand, be more tolerant of people with differences from me, and then at the same time be true to some goals about— that have to do with justice, human reparation, and dignity. It's hard. You can talk about how you want to be nonpartisan, that would be ideal. But when the two sides are being totally asshole, how do you do that?

This legislator returned to an educational career, and blended that work with continued political activism and community service, including a later stint in elected office at the city level. Service in a legislature at the more local level was more gratifying, in part "because you were involved in all the issues" instead of just a few, and because one's "voice" was relatively stronger. Party loyalty was a factor in the decision to run for a position at the city level—no one from the party was coming forward to run. Most recently, following a marital breakup, the now former legislator has relocated to another state and is occupied full-time with a teaching position, to the exclusion of more formal political activities.

More often, however, legislators who left without plans for other offices were primarily motivated by the financial and family concerns I have discussed previously, and at length. Yet it is important to note that these legislators are not rationalizing an exit that is in fact prompted by some kind of political defeat. In my cases here, they have been struggling with these tensions throughout their legislative service and are finally defeated, not by a political opponent, but by the structural incapacity to juggle too many things. Also note, as I reported earlier, that legislators and former legislators reflecting back on these tensions in the follow-up interviews agree that they have become more prominent in recent years.

[I left] because it got very difficult to live on $20,000 a year. And at [my] age, I realize that if I stayed in the legislature another 5 years and decided to make a career change . . . it was going to be even more difficult. As it is now, I hooked in with a good placement service, and you know we are moving forward and it looks good job wise. The money is not there, and the problem is the older you get, the harder it is to make a jump into another career. So it was financial. If I was making $70,000 as a legislator, the legislature would have more of a professional type of aspect to it, which would then allow you to transfer that into the private sector much more easily. The view of this legislature is that it's a part-time job.

. . . As far as any employer allowing you to really work, the problem was most employers—I mean watch TV or read the newspapers, and you'll know that this is not a part-time job like it used to be. This is full-time, and I'm going to be paying an employee to be in the legislature. And most employers don't see that benefit.

. . . Not only do I see a [financial] struggle, I see a lot of the good people leaving because of the time constraints. More and more of the really skilled legislators have left because of the time constraints, and because of the bull that they have to go through between their employers and the legislature.

This legislator subsequently found a well-paid position in banking soon after we spoke. But that was something he was not passionate about—it "was a way to make a living." He was recruited to run for elective public office a few years later, for an executive position with much higher pay than the state legislature. The trade-offs between legislative service and financial success seem no less stark to him, looking back on his experiences and observing current political life.

I'm not justifying when politicians go corrupt. When you're sitting there, like when I put a [development] deal together, the lawyers were making tens of thousands of dollars, the developer's going to make millions of dollars, and I'm cutting a check to go to a fund-raiser that they're going to, you kind of see when a developer—and I didn't do this, I want to make that clear—when the developer would turn to somebody and say, "You know that $500-a-plate dinner you got to cough up, let me take care of that for you." We've got to as a nation start realizing that if we want our politicians to stay honest, we've got to give them the financial means to do that.

People say if you can't afford to run, then don't run. OK, well then what you're saying is you just want people who are extremely wealthy to run the country. That's not a healthy democracy.

... I was talking to a bunch of people and they were like, "It's hard to get good people to run for the state legislature." I'm like, "Hello! Why would you?"

* * *

Taking my legislative pay, and with the other things I had, I was able to make it, but I was coming down, crashing down, real quick. ... When I got there, I realized that I probably could make a change, could have an impact. If there was any way possible to stay there I would, but I just didn't have a way. ... It's OK if you have a spouse at home, to keep up with the bills, whatever. I just can't do it and be serious about the job. ...

I could have said—I have three committees—I could have said, "Well, I'll take two committees and I'll only show up on committee, won't take on any work. And I'll just go to the session when it's in session—I could have done all those things, I suppose, and floated along.

* * *

The story of one legislator in particular best illustrates this struggle. He was known to his colleagues as being an exceptionally conscientious legislator and more generally as an exceptionally good person. When colleagues in his party discussed the difficult family and financial struggles involved in service, many invoked his case as a classic example of the problem. Here are two illustrations.

You know, [my colleague] is a perfect example. ... [He's] not running for re-election, and it just, it's gotten to be. ... He was on [an important committee], he was on the ... conference committee. Very bright, good with numbers. Politically, you never had to question whether—he would walk into the room and listen to the debate for 2 minutes and know what was going on. But then at the same time double-check to make sure that he knew what was going on was what was actually going on. Great member.

His kids are I think maybe the same age as mine, or maybe a year or two older. So if he's looking at college tuition in a year or two, he runs a small business that struggles. Its busy time is in the spring. Some guy's claiming he made a mistake and is suing him for $2,000. It's a hassle, and he's saying, "Wait a minute, I have to direct my life in a way that—I have to listen to my wife finally." And try to earn some money so he can put his kids through college. And that's the real problem getting people 35 to 40 in the legislature is if they're not particularly ambitious and have things start to fall their way, they start to say, "Well now, I have—that was fun, it was interesting and I think I contributed—but now I have to get back to real life."

* * *

[There's] terrible, terrible tension and stress for most people, living this very schizophrenic life.... [My colleague] is not running again this time. Why? He's got kids who are about ready to go to college. He's got to get a real job.... He's got to make money. [Another colleague] is running for reelection. I'm surprised because she suffers not only economic loss—she's a nurse—but also because she's lost her seniority. She now goes back as a per diem nurse.... What makes it possible for me is really two things. I work for the most wonderful boss I've ever worked for.... The other thing that I have is much of what I do in my job informs my legislative life, and much of my legislative life informs my job.

Despite having a good fit between legislative service and outside professional career, this legislator ultimately retired from her outside career in order to pursue legislative service full-time. By then, she was close enough to retirement to make this possible, but is now paying a price for her long run of legislative service: lower retirement income due to working so long at a partial salary.

The decision to retire from legislative service was in part driven by age, and the toll that the long drives and time spent away from home were exacting. "After 14 years that wears a little thin." Her current political activities consist mostly of "writing checks."

A little further on in the campaign season, I spoke with the particular legislator whom the other legislators had been invoking. He verified the descriptions offered by his colleagues, with one important difference: He had in fact decided to run again. Ironically, his decision to stay, not an easy one for him to make, was indeed based on these family and professional concerns, but given his particular life context, they ultimately pushed him toward running again. As a compromise with the other demands on his life, however, he determined not to actively campaign for the position. Nonetheless, he was reelected. Note how he speaks of a desire to join his political and policy interest with the ability to have a career that could better support his family. Happily for him, this desire was subsequently realized.

I just wish that I could do [legislative service] and send my kid to college, . . . have a retirement plan, you know? I go through—I guess it's guilt or anxiety— I think about all the time I spend thinking about some of the things I'm trying to do, and working on them, on the one hand, and that they're not producing income necessarily, on the other. And that's a tension there for me. I could really get drawn up in the issues. They're interesting, they're fascinating. I see some others who spend much more time in the off-session working on things—I wish I could do more of that.

. . . For me, it's time to do something different. [My] business is not really going to do a lot. I had thought that perhaps I could get in with the [governor's] administration and take a position . . . although the governor and I have some political differences. I said, "Look, I can work for a boss, no problem. I'll drop out of this legislature." It's time to get a career, it's time to get a job.

[My] business has been really slowed down with the economy. . . . There's a lot of problems with the business, so I just decided this is not going to work. I'm going to make a move here. After serving four terms—my goal was to serve three terms, initially—and I went for one more, this was kind of dragging on. I had to make my decision. . . . It just seemed to me, like it was exciting the first year, but after about three terms, that would be about enough. . . . By the end of my first year, I thought that three terms would be enough.

. . . Getting a position with the governor's staff didn't work. . . . He had several positions open in his office. . . . Then I tried to find somebody to recruit [from my party] for my seat. I spent about 3 weeks calling people. . . . Everybody said either, "Gee, I've thought about it, but I can't do it," or, "No way, Jose." Nobody could do it. . . . It was getting late. . . . So I thought, I might as well get my name on the ballot anyway. And here I am, ready to go. I'm still—I gave my résumé right now, sent it off today.

... It's just a matter of—here I've got kids who want to go to college. They're both in high school, my daughter's a senior. And when I look at my personal finances I'm just not doing it. I've got to get serious and get busy, and get a position, somewhere that's going to allow me to send my kids to college and have a retirement, that kind of thing. My wife teaches and she's good at her position, as far as health insurance and some benefits like that. But those are all declining, they're negotiating those down. And it's just time for me to do something.

... I'm going to go to a workshop tonight about getting an MBA degree at [a] university. I'm going to look into that. One of my problems with the governor's office is that I have a bachelor's degree in [a certain area] and I've got some experience, and I think I know the budget pretty well, but they want somebody that's got some credentials as well. That's one of my weaknesses.

... Politics aren't a career, I believe. And if you do have a career, then your career can withstand being in the legislature for a while, but I don't think there are too many that can tolerate it for a long period of time.... At some point you've got to decide if you're going back to your career, or go into politics and do something else, but I don't think you can keep doing both really well.

At the end of the term to which he was reelected, this legislator left the legislature to head a nonprofit organization in the educational field. He had already decided in that legislative term that he would not seek another. He was then presented with the opportunity to work in the state administration at the deputy commissioner level in a field of his legislative expertise—a position he still occupies. This position has allowed him to continue to be involved in the issues and the kind of work he enjoyed in the legislature. In terms of traditional political activity, his last legislative term "ended the chapter" of his active involvement. When informed that his colleagues often held him up as a prime example of the problematic trade-offs between legislative service and career, he noted with a laugh that "I did not hold back on my complaining."

I finished out my last term as chair of a [prominent] committee. And that was a fun term; I'm glad I did it. We did [a big bill], it was the governor's initiative then. We got that through and actually did some good.

... I [now] spend a lot of time in the legislature—my office is right across the street from the capitol. I go over there a lot; I testify to the committees.... There's always something going on in this [issue] area.

... I'm really, really glad I did [serve]. And maybe it's because I know I'm not in the position [to go back].... If my [lottery] ticket comes in—every once in a while I get angry about something and say, "I'll fix it, I'll run for the legislature again and I'll make a change there." ... It was great work.

I don't really miss it, though. . . . I'm just as happy doing what I'm doing here. I have the opportunity to be influential in a similar kind of way, but I don't get to vote on anything. . . . Although we always try to give [the legislature] the straight information, we get to tell them what we think.

. . . At one point, I toyed a few years back with running for [a statewide office]. I guess I just didn't take it real seriously because I never acted on it. I thought about it for a while and just didn't leap. . . . I'm not even toying with ideas at this point. . . . You never know, you're never going to say, "Absolutely." Really, what I'm thinking about—my retirement plan is that I've got to work until I drop. I think I can actually afford 1 year of retirement, so timing is going to be everything.

. . . I remember thinking about it at the time. I really did enjoy being [in the legislature]. And maybe I would have thought more seriously about where it leads to if I'd have been a bigger risk taker or had the financial end been different, but it just didn't work out that way for me. Once I understood that and made that decision, it just wasn't an issue for me anymore.

. . . I really like what I'm doing now because I get paid to eat, sleep, and drink the issues.

There are also subvariations in these patterns of exit. A few legislators on the political Left described how their service prevented them from working toward their most important political goals. An example follows.

One of the frustrations has been that as a legislator, I am not able to do any organizing. The time, and actually doing the legislative work, is so consuming, I can't get out there and beat the bushes, and pull people together. You know, you have the minimum wage. You would like to think that people would get organized, and come in and testify for the minimum wage. There is no long-term organizing. And so the partnership that I need to be successful is really compromised by that lack of a base. And one of the rationalizations when I'm leaving the legislature is to go back to my community and be part of doing some of that base building.

Looking back now on this trade-off, this former legislator saw it even more starkly.

Running for the legislature really had been preceded by 20 years of activism. And my orientation had always been that I was part of building a mass movement. It was really disillusioning to be in the capitol at what turns out to be the pinnacle of my personal political power and when it came time to push for a higher minimum wage, we couldn't get as many people in the capitol as used car dealers who were worried about air conditioners and Freon. There were more used car dealers in the balcony than we could get minimum wage workers. That was the most dramatic thing for me.

But there was a disconnect between my personal view of how political change occurs and my personal role. I was supposed to be operating in partnership with a mass movement; I wasn't supposed to be posturing—just kind of putting out the [ideological] line for public consumption. I wanted to have some muscle. And I didn't have much muscle at all—an example would have been, say, on housing, where we put forward a protenant piece of legislation . . . and it would come back a prolandlord piece of legislation. And we didn't have the tenant strength to reverse it. So here I go in with good intentions of helping tenants and it comes back undermining tenants. . . . That was the biggest thing for me [in deciding to leave].

There were also a couple of instances in which the legislators had been defeated, and for family and professional reasons had decided not to try to retake their seats, despite a personal desire to do so. These excerpts follow. The first is from someone who was defeated in a reelection bid, while the second is from someone who had tried for the senate and then was being encouraged to run again for the house. For the time being, he had not yet decided to run for the senate again, though he was considering it.

If it were me making a decision on my own, I would go after my seat. I would win my seat back. . . . I probably can't—I don't know that I'm going to be able to do that because now that I've lost the seat and have had discussions with my husband about how it impacted our personal life, and now to have to go back and say, "Well, gee, I know that it really took me away from home." So I have a whole other dynamic there that just changes it, it really changes it. I don't know if that's something that's unique to women who have families. Maybe we get our chance once, but then if you lose you don't get the second chance because now you've got to face the family again. I mean, that's something that I don't know how many other people would be affected like that, but I know that as a woman it's something that really makes it difficult.

. . . I think that if I had been reelected and was still being forced to juggle, you can make the accommodations. You could think about how I can make this better, how can I do this better in terms of the personal life. But once you're in a position where now she works and she's not there [in the legislature] anymore, and to try to convince everybody that it'll be all right if I do this, they're already saying, "No, it won't be all right because we already know what it's like when you're there."

... It was really the intrusion on your private life.... For me it really—they missed me. They didn't like not having me there, and I went home every night. I didn't even have to do it like many of the others do it.... It just was an intrusion. Your life is not your own. There's always a function that you have to attend. There's always somewhere that you have to go, and you can't ever get away from it. If you have a close family that depends on you and wants you to be—they just hated it.

This legislator returned to the kind of work—in state government—that she had done prior to her election. She remained extremely active in her community. On her death, several prominent female elected officeholders credited her for their careers.

* * *

The last month of the session, I had decided that if we didn't [pass an important issue], and that's why the session ran late, then I would run for the senate.... The problem is in the senate, so I'm going to run for the senate.

[After I lost], my pal, my chairman, and others said, "Run for the house next time; we need you back in the house." I said no. I'm not going back to do that. I made my decision to leave the house. I'm not going to go back and recoup the glory days of the past. I'll have a bunch of freshmen that don't know who I am, and I'll be up and have a bunch of people that were a little bit below me who are going to now go, "He's the guy that got beat and came back, and we've been here and he hasn't."

[My wife] has given me permission to run [again] for the senate. She asked me if I had been thinking about it. I said, "Yeah, I've been thinking about it." She said, "Look, I wasn't very supportive the last time. I want you to—if you're going to do this, I'll be behind you." She said, "Last summer, I didn't help you much.... I hadn't realized how much I resented you being in the legislature, and family wise, missing time with the kids, and if you ran for the senate, what would be different?" And I'm going to coach my little league and coach my basketball, and I kind of liked it.... She said, "I didn't realize that I resented it until after [you] had lost and [were] around, and then it—the difference was—it felt so different in how much I enjoyed it. I realized that, and I resented a lot of it." ... It was a hell of a lot of fun, though.

So you didn't burn out?

Oh no, I didn't.

This legislator did indeed try again for the state senate and won. He is still serving there. Along the way, he lost the seat in a close election, due to the political fallout from a particularly controversial law that he had supported. To win back the seat the following term, he did not change his views about the legislation; instead, according to him, his constituents had a couple of years to live with the law and work through their anger over it, and to reflect on the issues. In the end, after the 2 years, they "graduated" and elected him again. His most recent reelection was his first "easy victory."

The trade-offs with family time have remained, so his loss was in some respects a blessing for the additional family time it yielded him, and it came at an especially important time in his children's lives. Things have become easier in this regard lately, particularly regarding campaigning, because he has retired from his primary outside occupation.

Two years later [after the reelection defeat], I set out to take a look at whether or not I should run again. I made a list of—I think there were 39—people I knew who had told me to my face that they'd always voted for me, but because of [this issue] they weren't going to be there. I decided to go around and survey that group.

. . . The first one I went to, and I got out of the car, and I walked across the lawn. And I hadn't even got to the guy yet, and he goes, "My wife and I are going to vote for you this year." I was surprised and maybe a little flustered, and I said, "Well, *why?*" He poked me in the shoulder and said, "You served your time." I wasn't looking forward to the first of those walks across the lawns.

I had another one that was similar, almost virtually the same thing. "My wife and I are going to vote for you. I'm glad you're here." Then we chatted about whatever we chatted about. Then, as I was leaving, he said, "Oh, by the way, who are you running against?" And I said, "I'm running against the same fellow I ran against 2 years ago." And he said, "Who's that?" And I said, "What do you mean, who's that? You voted for the guy." And he said, "Ah, we didn't know who we were voting for, we were voting *against you.*"

. . . It was a textbook case where the legislature went through a very intense and rigorous education process on an issue that no one wanted to deal with. . . . The legislature went through an education process and surprised itself with what it had come up with. When the public was forced to go through an education process and live with the legislation that was passed, a year and a half later, they had graduated. . . . I was proud of my neighbors.

... [In the 2 years out of office] we went on some trips, my kids and I went [on a trip], I did coach some baseball, and I did a bunch of stuff that if I'd been in office, I wouldn't have done. All those things have fond memories and reaffirmed the reasons why I went into the legislature to begin with.... Losing was terrible, but life went on very well.... We did some things that you can't do when the kids are [older]. Because of that loss, we squeezed in some real neat stuff.... Things we never would have done—a glorious opportunity to do things with them at an age when it made a difference.

When my kids were young, I probably was not around for those months [of intense legislative work] when I should have been, in the evenings.... Now my kids [are older], and when I'm home, I don't see *them*.

Summary

Decisions about leaving the legislature are the product of many factors. Some reflect a natural life span on one's greatest effectiveness within the chamber, often in combination with the availability of other, usually higher offices; others reflect the tensions with outside careers and family described in detail in chapter 3. All the factors can interact. But regardless of the particular combination of factors and the ultimate outcome, many legislators agonize over the decision.

More specifically:

- A sense of investment, the joy of serving, and the belief that what they are doing is important keep many legislators in the job.
- The pull of other offices is a powerful attraction for many legislators, but in the actual decision to leave the legislature in pursuit of another office, other factors often come into alignment. Opportunity structures, both within and outside the chamber, exert a significant influence on the context of the decision. At the individual level, the mix of political, professional, and personal factors is complicated.
- Decisions to leave without pursuing another office are usually driven primarily by family and professional concerns, but dissatisfactions with certain aspects of legislative service are important to some.
- Legislators' ultimate political paths often differ dramatically from what they anticipate for themselves.

5

Falling Down and Standing Up

Obviously, not everything I saw and heard during the time I spent observing and interviewing the legislators inspired me. The legislatures and the people who serve in them are not without their flaws, and some of these flaws get in the way of the democratic process and forging the best possible public policy. There are five potential problems in particular that I wish to discuss in this final chapter: ambition and ego, partisanship, top-down leadership, incompetence, and prejudice. In each legislature, these problems are interconnected in some important respects and cannot be fully addressed through simple institutional reforms. They tended to reveal themselves in my observations and between the lines of interviews considered in their entirety rather than specific passages, so there are relatively fewer interview excerpts appearing here than in earlier chapters. I will also be more evaluative and speculative in my commentary. I conclude the chapter with some ruminations about the dilemmas involved in structuring a legislature.

Note at the outset, however, two key points regarding the legislatures' problems. First, at the individual level, these problems are outweighed by the amount of good that I encountered. Second, I saw only the merest indirect evidence of out-and-out corruption—the use of public power for narrowly private ends.[1] If the political process is broken, it is not because of the individual legislators. More likely, it is because of the multidimensional and multilayered ways in which moneyed interests have been able to leverage the political system writ large, especially in terms of biases in culture and information, the monopoly on "expert" opinion, the dominance in the financing of elections—particularly national-level and statewide elections—and the extended and sustained access to decision making at all levels and stages, from issue formation to implementation and litigation.[2] That problem cannot be fixed by term limits or any other supposed solution directed at the legislators themselves; reform efforts instead must be employed further upstream in the political process—campaign finance, for one—and probably need to recognize that the political process cannot be abstracted from the economic system. I will return briefly to these topics at the conclusion of this chapter, but they are really the subject for another book.

Ambition and Ego

Ambition is a complicated matter in politics. It is not per se a bad thing; indeed, the system runs on it in part, as James Madison understood and taught us so well. I did encounter some legislators, however, for whom a particular version of it occupied what I thought to be too large a portion of their motivations for service. Drawing on my earlier discussions of the emotional challenges of public service (see "Enduring Criticism and Attack" in chapter 3), I might call this the Lasswell danger. For a small handful of legislators, the idea that they could make themselves famous across the state or even beyond its boundaries appeared to threaten the centrality of their other, more civic motives for being involved in politics. That this could happen seems only natural, and in fact, I was surprised that such motivations did not surface more often given the frank nature of the conversations that I was able to have with the legislators. Furthermore, good public policy and effective leadership can result from these kinds of motivations. Nonetheless, in a few cases, it did trouble me. What accompanied this kind of consuming ambition was a tendency on the part of the legislators to discuss legislative matters in personal terms: things that were done to them as individuals; how they as individuals understood and accomplished things that few others did or even could; or how something they accomplished or won affected their individual standing. What seemed more in the background was a deeper interest in the policy outcome and the importance of that to others in the state. When these few legislators discussed their colleagues in the legislative process, they often framed their comments around individual-level gains and losses—whether someone had helped or hurt their standing and power in the legislature or the state. They often told stories about how they were right and others were wrong, or how they understood something that others did not. The legislative process often appeared to be, in their minds, primarily about individuals and their standing, and most particularly about themselves.

One legislator, who I would not include neatly into this category but who did perhaps bump up against it, was extremely open and thoughtful about this aspect of legislative service, both for himself and others. In his case, these tendencies were woven into a basic ideological commitment rooted in his sense of justice. In the following excerpt, he talks about his desire to become known throughout the state through his public service and the personal importance of the job to him.

There is a public recognition component to it, from getting deeply into one or two issues, specialization—public recognition can follow from that, getting known on an issue. Maybe this [issue] is a horse that I can ride. I can certainly ride it in this building, but if it's big enough, I can ride it across the state. Had that [issue] passed, that would be a great horse to ride.

How important is this job to you?

I ask myself that question. It's very important to me. It's what I think I want to do, and what I think I'd like to do, for the next 8 or 10 years. The older I get, the more I see that when things don't turn out the way I want to, that there's a silver lining. I think if I lost my race I would be *very* upset and hurting. I don't think it would cause me to come down with cancer, the way it might some people. But it would be a big loss, and I would be floating around for a while, trying to figure out what to do—whether to go into business, or to be retired, or get some legislative political job, whether it's lobbying, or the state, or advocacy. So it's pretty important to me. I haven't yet lived it out; I haven't lived out this dream, fantasy, curiosity, that I told you about. I want to live it out so that I know that for whatever reasons I've gone as far as I wanted to go, as far as I can. I think it's a younger person's dream. I wish I'd started 10 or 15 years, in that sense, earlier.

. . . I think politicians are needy people. People say they have big egos; I really think it's the opposite. They have a big appetite for ego gratification. But egos need stroking. Why do some people put themselves out, work, take a risk? I don't know. I think it has something to do with their mothers.

A few years later, this legislator succeeded in latching onto a second big issue, but his high-profile and effective work on it ended up swamping his political career. He was narrowly defeated in a subsequent reelection bid—a loss that was widely attributed to be the product of this involvement.

He originally didn't think he would lose the election, but he was targeted by some groups that were particularly opposed to the policy he had worked on, and his opponent was able to enlist the support of some extremely visible political figures in the state. In addition, several locally prominent people he had considered supporters and friends came out against his reelection, so that in the end, after the loss, he "was hurt and a little pissed." At the same time, the way he exited prompted an outpouring of thanks from those who appreciated the new policy, which immensely gratified him. As a way to go out, "it was like a dream come true."

Afterward, he worked behind the scenes to shore up the new public policy and ward off attacks on it. Professionally, he essentially retired. He considers reentering the political arena from time to time, but has in all likelihood run his last campaign.

These kinds of views were reinforced by another legislator who had just been defeated. Though he rejects ideology as the reason for his pursuit of political office, he was known as an ideological leader in his party and state.

You go [to the legislature] quite frankly because you want to be loved and accepted. Politics doesn't replace having a woman who loves you or a man who loves you, or children who love you, but it's the second-best thing to it. . . . It's an acclaim and a glamour that will satisfy my need to figure out why I'm here. It's a reaffirmation of love, to get elected. And it's the opposite, of course, when you get beat.

I was able to put it in perspective better than a lot of defeated pols, but there was withdrawal. It was pretty serious. I've never been divorced, but I can imagine that's what it's like. Suddenly, all the reinforcement that was taken for granted is no longer there, and you got to be the person you really are again. No more hiding behind "the honorable" and having doors opened for you. . . . Nobody in their right mind would put their name on a secret ballot if they didn't have to. That's scary. . . . Acceptance is total, rejection is total, whether it's by one vote or a thousand votes.

How did you decide to run in the first place?

I got bored. . . . It was a feeling that there's got to be more to life than this. There's nothing that's a higher high than getting yourself elected and being an "honorable." . . . [My ideology] had nothing to do with it at all—it was the middle-aged crisis. . . . People who end up in the legislature, they may say—claim to high heavens—that they're going there to get a job done. That's pretty egotistical, isn't it?

...I don't know what to say to a reporter who asks you that question, "Why did you run?" without sounding callous or dumb or brutally honest. "Me and the little lady didn't get along anymore, and she said it would be good if I get out, and what the hell, this isn't 12 months." ... I used to say, "Well, what do you want me to do, bowl on Wednesday night?" I got to have something to do. I don't refinish furniture, and I don't hang around in barrooms, and I don't think much of bowling. So I went into politics.

Another legislator, who more clearly fits the concern about problematic ego and ambition, offered the following revealing discussion of how he arrived at whether he was a Democrat or Republican.

At that point in time I started to think seriously about getting involved politically, whether or not I was a Republican or Democrat.... Within 6 months or so I joined the [local] Democratic [Party] ... because that was the [party] to be involved in. The Republican Party is still not as strong here. That's where the game was being played.

None of the three states was entirely free of legislators who exhibited these tendencies, but in one state, Vermont, there was a related version of the problem that was more widespread and also more diluted in intensity. In that state, there was a tendency among some of the more liberal members, who were often also the most extensively educated and well-off financially, to be somewhat arrogant toward the other members. I encountered this both in the interviews and my observations. These members also tended to live in and around Burlington, Vermont's largest city. There was a second, less salient version of this problem, and of a conservative type: There were some more educated and wealthier members who were somewhat abrasive in their behavior in the legislature, relative to the dominant political culture in the state. In both instances, these conflicts tracked onto a broader political tension between later arrivals to the state and the more "native" Vermonters.

In Vermont, native is a term whose meaning is constantly both evolving and contested. During the time I observed the legislators, it included on the loosest end, someone who had been living in the state for as little as 10 years, to on the strictest end, only someone whose parents had grown up in the state. Similar tensions exist in other states that combine a rich tradition of hardscrabble pioneering or farming families that go back several generations with a more recent influx of immigrants, usually more politically liberal, who are often in search of a new way of life thought to be more balanced, natural, and aesthetic. The immediate examples that come to mind are Maine, New Mexico, and Oregon. Political issues that often divide old-timers and relative newcomers include social issues like gay rights, the tension between environmental preservation and land development, and anything that encroaches on the political autonomy of the town, such as reform in the financing of public education. And although conservatism as a national political force has arguably become more aggressive over the past 20 years, in Vermont the phenomenon also possessed this native versus nonnative element.[3] Having a less professionalized legislature probably helps to feature these tensions within the statehouse.

The antipathy toward some of these members was palpable, and it was not limited to those who sat on the other side of an ideological divide from the offenders. "Flatlanders," "library liberals," "limousine liberals," and "trust-fund revolutionaries" were some of the disparaging labels I heard during my visits. During the interviews, one legislator on the Left, a relatively recent arrival to the state who was sensitive to the problem and had been accepted by his native colleagues (and lived life without the aid of a trust fund), spoke of the dynamic at length. Here is part of what he said:

The person I'm actually closest to in the legislature . . . is a Republican from [the north of the state]. He comes from a labor background, but he's one of these wild and crazy Republicans. Sort of libertarian, and he's a wonderful guy. . . . And we spend a lot of time together. And then moving away from that would be people who were not liberal Democrats. They were people who did have a really good sense of regular people's needs and tended to be good on issues. And we would disagree on gay rights, for instance. These friends were not with me on gay rights, but they would tolerate me on some goofy thing like that. And I would be with them on some issues that yuppie, down-country representers, the liberal Dems, couldn't understand, like moose or fishing. . . . Yeah, I was an out-of-stater, but I was with them on issues that they thought were important, that liberals sometimes laughed at, not understanding their importance.

There's a kind of elitism among some of the down-country Democrats.

They don't see or respect the progressive side of native Vermonters. And because they don't see it, they can't respect it—and a lot of representatives felt that. I mean, the native Vermonters could feel that disrespect and feel the distance. And so when it came to something like gay rights, they could blow it off.

A longtime Republican legislator-farmer and a native of the state by any definition offered a similar assessment of this group. He pointed to what he experienced as their arrogance and smugness, their overly ideological approach, and their privileged background.

[They] approach the world one-up. And one of the reasons they're not more effective than they are, given the amount of energy they put into it, is because people get the idea that they think they're better than everybody else and they look down on them. Which they do. There's an arrogance there—just like in the well-trained champion horse.

Partisanship

The value of party discipline and even in some instances strict party control is one of the least appreciated aspects of a well-functioning democratic legislative process, at least in the United States. Theoretically, parties can provide efficient ways of organizing political behavior into intelligible and easily graspable dimensions, and supply a clear mechanism for political accountability. Nevertheless, how many times does one hear a fellow citizen proudly proclaim that he or she votes "for the man or woman, not the party"? At the same time, that citizen often knows almost nothing about the policy positions of that man or woman. We know from political science that despite the ways in which the parties have declined over the years as people-based vehicles for encouraging political participation, party identification is still the single-best predictor of a citizen's vote. Still, it is not unusual to read a newspaper editorial endorsement for a candidate that does not take into account the party record of the candidate running but only the individual candidate's positions. And of course, candidates are often loath to fully embrace a party mantle when they run for office.

Political scientists studying the foibles of the American political system over the past 40 years have consistently beaten the drum for more party-based politics and government as a way to improve it. But more recently, both political scientists and media pundits have also voiced concerns over too much partisanship (which is different from party-based politics per se). I do not mean here to discredit a strong party system, and indeed, it is my impression that media and public views about the nature of party government in each of the three states, and particularly in New York, are overly jaundiced (see my discussion appearing below, for instance). It was nonetheless also my impression during the interviews and observations that there were some members of the majority party—Democrats—who were overly keen to exclude the minority members—Republicans—from the process.[4] By the same token, there were several Republicans who looked at the entire process through a cynical lens and saw nothing but strict partisanship. In other words, this latter group of Republican legislators shared some of the same negative thinking about their own legislatures that I am trying to counter in this book.

Not surprisingly, these tendencies were the strongest in New York, which arguably has the strongest system of party discipline within the legislature among the three states. But I am describing individual-level views that were taken too far. On both parties' counts, these tendencies led to rigid, unconstructive political thinking and strategy. Legislators who viewed the legislature this way also tended to personalize the process, in ways similar to what I have described in the section on ego.

Here is one example of some comments made by this type of legislator, who happens to be a Republican.

We had our [prison] bill that we brought out this past year. It wasn't a Republican issue; it was very similar to the three strikes and you're out bill that was making its ways through Washington. And there were a lot of us that had a real problem with the language.... So I offered an amendment in [committee] when that bill came through there that said, if a person commits a second dangerous felony offense [after] being released from prison within 3 years of his first conviction, it's life in prison with no parole. It was defeated. And I told them, "I don't understand how you do this." Law enforcement people are telling us what is happening to these guys, and in the same stretch of the imagination what you're saying is, we don't care about the victims anymore.

Do you think that particular proposal was heard and considered, and simply more people disagreed than agreed with you?

No, because what was interesting was that what a lot of people told me after the vote was over, that it was a caucus decision. And I said, "But you sat there when I interviewed . . . the chief district attorney." . . . I think the problem here is that the Democrats in the state have been in power so long that they don't care what we think. I really believe that.

Is there an alternative method or venue where you can make some headway with your Democratic colleagues?

I don't think so. I think today's hearing was a perfect example of showmanship. For what? For show. . . . Right now, I think there's a real sense of arrogance here that whatever they want to do they can do; the voters aren't going to hold them accountable. So why should we mess anything up? Who cares?

So you don't really see any avenue to become involved?

It's going to be in a very limited nature, and it will only be something that they totally believe in. I don't see much of an opportunity to really change their mind on major policy issues, which really shapes where [the state] goes. I mean, you may win some little bitty battles here and there, but on major issues they are going to be driven to do whatever they want as long as they have a majority.

Top-Down Control

Related to partisanship is the nature and extent of the control exerted by top party leaders, and in particular the speaker, the majority leader, and the minority leader. In New York, the extent of control by the leadership has long been considered by the media and the public to be a shortcoming of the state's political system. "Three men in a room"—meaning the governor, the speaker of the assembly, and the majority leader of the senate—is the phrase commonly invoked to describe the state's budget-making process and the deliberation and decision-making on the most important policy matters. In the same vein, party caucuses in the New York assembly are tightly guarded affairs, almost exclusively reserved for members only. In Connecticut and Vermont, in contrast, outsiders can usually sit in on the discussions, though they are sometimes questioned about their affiliation and purpose. The more open caucus systems in those states also mean that more important conversations often happen outside and prior to the party caucus meetings. Within committees, party caucuses and general discussions are also more open, exchange-oriented events in Connecticut and Vermont than they are in New York—and particularly so in Vermont. In New York, during the time of my observations, a rank-and-file member scheduling a meeting with the speaker had the feel of arranging an audience with the pope—one member with whom I spent some time often joked about "kissing the ring." Conversely, in Vermont members flowed in and out of the speaker's office throughout the day, without appointments. Proposals to reform the political system in New York have long called for more openness to the media and the public, and increased formal opportunities for rank-and-file participation in state legislative proceedings and decision making.

I thus expected to hear frequent grumblings from legislators in New York about the tight grip of leadership, but this was not the case. Though there were such grumblings, much more prevalent was the view that although party leadership ran a tight ship in the legislative battle, the opportunity for input also existed, and that the leadership did respond to the accumulated preferences of its members. This squared with my own impressions and added to my sense, based on my observations of the committee process, that there was generally a greater division of legislative labor in New York, at the level of the individual legislator, and that the reflective, discursive work on policy was more often done outside the formal meetings and with the greater assistance of staff. But I should also note that based on impressions from the follow-up interviews, in more recent years the collective dissatisfaction with this aspect of the process has increased, on both sides of the aisle. In all three states, the party leadership tended to exert a tighter grip on the process in the majority party than it did in the minority party—a feature that has been widely documented for legislatures more generally, and that is entirely consistent with the demands of party governance.

Ralph Wright

There is one particular leader, however, whom I want to discuss at greater length and with identification.[5] Ralph Wright served as house speaker in Vermont during most of the time of my observations and interviews. He was a fascinating character to me, even before I ever actually met him, because he served as a lightning rod for his colleagues' observations, concerns, and complaints about the legislature in a way that I've never encountered before or since, and indeed, in a way that I've never encountered in any institution larger than a family. It is partly for those reasons that I consider him here. But I also want to give him an extended treatment as an early look forward to the conclusion of this chapter and book, where I consider Vermont and the idea of a citizen legislature more generally. Institutionally, citizen legislatures provide more space for the emergence and influence of people like Wright. As I repeat at the end of the account, I am left unsure whether or not this is good for the state's political life.

Ralph Wright was awed, feared, disliked, liked, respected, and resented, all at the same time. Many of his colleagues seemed fixated on him in discussing not only the legislative process generally but their own experiences in it. He was a man known to be many things: a savvy street-fighting politician, who knew when to fight and when to bide his time; a zealous ideological jungle fighter on behalf of liberal and progressive concerns, specifically economic ones; a skilled and manipulative amateur psychologist, who knew how to read people quickly and accurately, and in particular who could infer what they most wanted and feared, both in the legislature and life; a reassuring uncle figure who knew the right compliment for the right situation; and finally, an abrasive, insecure man, a bully who carried grudges and possessed a long memory.

In Vermont, the speaker enjoys a wide range of formal powers over the process.[6] But formal powers cannot begin to explain the stranglehold that Wright exerted on the collective imagination of his colleagues. I had to explore him. The more his colleagues discussed him, the more interesting he became. Fortunately, it was not long thereafter that on one of my observation trips, the legislator I was following around took me into the speaker's office. There were 5 or 6 other legislators in the room, and they were having a brainstorming session to work out a problem with a piece of legislation. After the introductions were made, Wright looked me over and casually asked, in front of everyone, "So, what does a professor at a place like Syracuse make for a salary?" I went on to have periodic access to the speaker's office during my trips.

Though I kept with my project as originally conceived, I was sometimes tempted to set it aside and simply work on Wright's political biography. Alas, he beat me to it. In the aftermath of his defeat for reelection to the legislature, he immediately began writing his own political memoirs and subsequently published *All Politics Is Personal*. I got the chance to read through and comment on the work before it was published, and also had several conversations with Wright during its writing. I would stop in when I was in the state and see him in his small office in Bennington. He would talk about his experiences, and ask me (in vain) about what other legislators were saying about the legislative process and, of course, him. He would then go on to speculate about their comments, usually correctly. Although I believed he was being honest with me in our conversations, I did sometimes feel like I was being probed or worked in some way, and he would at times hypothesize, in the third person, about my own desires and wants—again, usually correctly. In 1996, the same year his memoirs appeared in print, he was named by President Clinton as a special assistant in the U.S. Department of Education, a position he held until 2000.

Wright was a transplanted working-class Bostonian, a former Marine who came to elective politics somewhat later in life, during a teaching career working with behavioral "problem" children in the Bennington school system. He was originally elected to the speakership as a minority party legislator. The commonly told story there is that he made promises to several Republican members of the legislature in order to get their support and also won their good favor by taking them to a Boston Bruins game. A picture of the group at the game found its way into the Vermont papers, and the group of Republicans was thenceforth known, even by Wright himself, as "Ralph's hockey team." Wright was the state's longest-serving speaker, holding the office for 10 years. He helped to put Democrats solidly in the majority in part by his tireless recruiting and training of candidates in the off-session—an activity that also helped to secure his re-election as speaker in each new legislature, as the first-term Democrats felt loyalty toward him even before they arrived. In summer 1994, he appeared to have survived an attempted "coup" of his speakership from one of his own assistants, who had become disenchanted with Wright's leadership style, but that fall, he was indeed deposed—not by a rival Democratic leader but rather by the constituents in his own district. He attributed the loss to a more ideologically focused and well-backed opponent, his concentration on the other legislative races in the state, and a lack of enthusiasm about his own local campaign.

I am not sure exactly how to evaluate Ralph Wright's leadership, and neither, apparently, are his colleagues. If one takes on the perspective of someone committed to liberal or progressive political causes, it would be easy to make a powerful argument that the state was fortunate to have had him at the helm of the house for that many years. And it is almost certainly the case that he made the house a more forceful and independent body than it would have been without him. In addition, I often saw him responding to the wishes of his caucus and constantly saying, publicly and privately, that he needed to check in with "my members" before going forward with anything significant. On the other hand, some of the greatest strengths of Vermont's citizen legislature were compromised by Wright's interpersonal and political style. He certainly had a negative psychological effect on many legislators who I considered to be both wise and effective. They felt constricted, constrained, and were less satisfied with their experiences than they would have been otherwise. Day to day, fear of him was palpable among certain members.

Interview conversations in Vermont always at least touched on Wright, whether or not I brought him up as a topic. In order to control for the effects of partisanship in evaluating his leadership, I have quoted no Republicans in the excerpts that appear below. Perhaps the single-best overall discussion of him came from one of the few legislators who was located to Wright's left politically. This legislator struggled with how he felt about the man, and mixed great respect with deep criticism.

I have a great deal of respect for the speaker and what he accomplished. He just did some great things. But at the same time he's a son of a bitch. And that was another contradiction—[to] see and feel as close as I did to a guy who has done a lot for the people that I care about, the people he cares about, and at the same time, create a process that is so intimidating. [W]hen you have a process based almost on coercion, you can't have constructive dialogue.

In this last biennium we had 90-plus Democrats [out of 150], and with that, with those numbers, he was able to stack important committees who would then generate bills, bring them out on the floor, and just push them right through. And the people on those committees, who were very competent— there's some very strong Democrats whose heart is in public policy and who really want to do the right thing. But there's no question that a good debate with all sides being aired makes for a better piece of legislation. And we lost that. We lost the ability for dialogue. And I don't mean dialogue two ways, I mean just having a discussion, a community, or a community discussion. Just being able to get all the pieces here, being honest and trying to understand each other's take on things. He created a process where that couldn't happen.

I feel very sad that a man who has the heart he does, did not have the personal tools to maintain a forum that in the long-term would be best for [the process] and the people that the two of us care most about.

I feel really bad for him because it's one of those Greek tragedy kinds of things. You know, to get to the position of speaker, at least in today's Vermont, you have to be very calculating. And you have to be full of yourself—and he is. And as he accumulated more power, he just wasn't able to balance his ego with his policy base. There's some contradictions created within him that were then reflected in the house as a whole, that were not in the end helpful for any-body—for him as a speaker or for the policies that we cared most about. It's really a shame to me; he's a great guy.

You just talked about contradictions reflected in the house, and it's an interesting per-spective. I would like to hear a little more about that.

Well, on the issue of the statewide contract for teachers, he comes from Ben-nington, and Bennington got caught in a teachers' strike. And they didn't han-dle it well, and he was pretty pissed at the way they handled it. And he's a pro-labor guy. But they really screwed up, was his view. And so then he had this idea, and I give the guy credit for being creative and being bold. I mean, he has power—by god, he's going to use it, right? And I like that, but the direction he went on the statewide contract was pretty antilabor.

And then the teachers misplayed it and chose to go head-on with the speaker publicly. Rather than send a couple of emissaries in and talk behind closed doors with people he trusts, and try to work out something, they went public head-on. Well, this is where the ego comes in. Forget the public policy piece. He was, "I've got all these hotsy-totsy teachers," who are making good money compared to his own background historically. And so it was a fight. This was a real fight, and it was a personal fight. It really clouded the whole picture. And it undermined what was his most important goal of the session because he couldn't separate that.

I mean, the teachers blew it, but he's a responsible person. . . . He can say, "Listen . . . there are some differences here, let's try to work it out." He could have done that. That kind of thing would be replicated over and over again. He would personalize things, and then when he would personalize, he would lose sight of his own policy interests.

Reevaluating Wright's leadership with the benefit of hindsight, this legislator saw fewer contradictions and was left with a more positive overall appraisal of his effectiveness.

I think it's important to couch his weaknesses in his tactical strengths. He got a lot done. In looking at his leadership style . . . he gave [talented party members] a lot of power. He was very much the generalist—he didn't want to know the details. He picked people he trusted and he gave them a considerable amount of responsibility. And then he really knew how to engineer timing and debate. The guy was brilliant from that kind of perspective, lawmaking and those details.

. . . The other piece that was very real is that he had this incredible power of intimidation because he used personal insults in such an incisive way; he just really knew how to hit people's weak spots. And he knew how to buy votes— not with money, but with favors.

. . . He was really good at that. I really loved the guy—he was so real. The reason I got along with him as well as I did is that I understood him. I really understood the guy. And he hurt me—he hurt me publicly. But that was the way he did business. I didn't take it personally. . . . A couple of instances, in small groups, he'd make fun of me. . . . He'd just be reminding me of who's got the power and he just really nailed me. . . . He comes from a working-class background; I come from a more or less working-class background. He knows my vulnerabilities. He gets expensive suits, and I'd get discount store clothes—and he knew it and he fucked with my head. Just using tools of trade.

Other colleagues noted similar personality traits, but did not perceive the same balance with positive characteristics.

There was actually a fear factor there. People got afraid of the man. . . . Afraid of bad committee assignments, afraid of his explosions of temper—he could be brutal. I've spent a number of years in the military and I've seen people chew people out, and he did a good job of it. There were folks I knew who got on his bad side, and the word went out from him to the committee chairs that their bills were not to move. They lost all influence. Plus, it was psychological. . . . My committee chair, who has since left the house, said, "You know, I left that house and I realized that for 6 years I was afraid, and I was in the 'in' group." It was a strange psychology; it was a total dictatorship.

How much of all this was ideological versus simply personal control? Was it Lenin or Stalin?

It was a fear of being purged. More Stalin than Lenin. It was less the substance, than "by god, I got [the senate leader]."

* * *

I guess we have to talk about Ralph when we get to that point. I have a great deal of respect for Ralph as an individual, as a person, as a leader. The one thing that concerns me about him and the way he conducted himself was that he did not have much use for, or much respect for, difference of opinion. . . . It was very difficult—honestly I'm not proud to say this—I was intimidated by him. And no one should ever be intimidated by anyone in that process. And I'm not intimidated by many people.

. . . I can't tell you how much I didn't know—I can't imagine how much I didn't know and how naive I was when I went to Montpelier as to how things got done. If you wanted to get something done, you really had to do it. There was a lot of window dressing and showcasing that goes on, you learn those things as you go on, and some of that I learned the hard way.

I guess that one of the things that used to concern me as a freshman, maybe even a second-term legislator, I would see the quote, unquote, "Ralph's lieutenants" running around—the bright, upstart, two- and three-term Democrats that were on the appropriations committee, ways and means, maybe part of the leadership team. Quite unapproachable, a lot of them. I always said to myself, if I could get in that position. . . . I would be helpful to people, open to people. That's the way I conducted myself, and I think as a result of that, I have as much or more respect as a person that's achieved a certain amount of seniority in the Democratic Party in the legislature. Probably have more Republican friends and respect from key Republican people than a lot of the Democrats do. I've worked with them openly, and they come to me. I've tried to put the partisan bullshit behind us.

. . . There are times when it's probably beneficial on behalf of your constituency, on behalf of the party, on behalf of the issue that you're working for, to be tough and not flexible, . . . but it doesn't have to be the norm. I saw that as being the norm, more than I would have liked it to be. . . . I feel like I'm in a little bit of a unique situation because—and this is where it starts to get a little touchy for me, but I feel strongly enough about it to tell you about it—I honestly think the only reason that I, as [a] Democrat who was not part of the lieutenant, part of the inner circle of the speaker, the only reason that I ended up on [a high-profile committee] was that I took the initiative as a second-term member, on my own, to run for [a leadership] position. I came within one vote of beating the favored candidate.

. . . Ralph controls his committee chairs, there's no question about it. If there's a piece of legislation that he doesn't want passed out, 9 times out of 10, he can tell that committee chair to hold it. . . . Conversely, if there's a bill that he wants and that's important to him or his constituency or the Democratic leadership, tell them to move it. Even though the chairperson may not want to. That's one of the prices of being a chair. If you feel strongly enough that what he's asking of you is not right or you don't believe in it, or whatever, it's your obligation, it's your opportunity to go to him and try to convince him of that. And I've seen many people do that.

* * *

As much as I respected Ralph's political skills and I agree with him on a vast majority of issues, I thought that after 10 years in power, accumulating power in a particular way . . . at the risk of slipping into psychospeak, which I try to avoid at all costs, I do think that legislatures, and this one during last term, can dysfunction like a dysfunctional family. Everybody knew what was going on, but nobody was going to say it. . . . [T]hey didn't say them out loud, but they said them in The Thrush [a Montpelier bar] and they said them in their rented abodes during the wintertime, but the real rule breaker was saying them out loud.

Wright also had a fair number of defenders—this is obviously true at some level since he had put together an unprecedented number of successful bids for speaker. He was seen as an effective leader, and also as someone who responded to and reflected the views of his caucus, if with a left slant, and then fought hard for the party's position. Here are examples of the more positive view, from 3 longtime legislators who were relatively close to him in different ways—Wright's critics in the legislature would have perhaps considered them to be members of the inner circle or lieutenants that the other legislator mentioned earlier.

Ralph Wright has made a hell of a difference in the house. The Republicans gave him shit and criticized his personal style, but that didn't bother them at all; what bothered them was that he was getting things done. Since they couldn't take him out on the issues, they took him on personality and all this other nonsense. He as speaker gave people their lead: Do your homework and make your case, and we'll bring it up for a vote. . . . [He] let the committees, encouraged committees, to study the issues and do what's best.

If there was a political hot potato, he would call people in from different committees and ask, "How do we deal with this? This is what my gut says. You can't do this, you can do this. How do we get through this?" And then he would usually ask everybody a bunch of questions. We would have to show them why their ideas are crazy. And then come back—and it had to be in private—he'd ask you a few more questions, and it sort of depended on the issue. . . . The speaker would ask the chair and vice chair, or 2 people from this committee or 2 from that committee, and say, "This is what these people are working on; when it comes to your committee, what's going to happen?" Well, these people are not going to go along with it, so the speaker might say, "You people keep talking—I'm leaving because unless you work out something between the two committees that will get through, you don't have anything."

. . . I always got a kick out of people who talked about, "Well, this is Ralph Wright's bill or Ralph Wright's proposal." I'd go, "Gee, you know, that's Ed's proposal or Bill's proposal. Ed pitched it in front of Ralph and these 3 or these 2 women, and I said that makes sense, if we can." Ralph would say, "Well, if you can all hang together, then that's what we'll do." And then suddenly, it's Ralph Wright's proposal.

I want to ask you two questions about that. The first one is, it sounds pretty inclusive and democratic in a lot of ways, on the part of leadership. Was it?

Ralph had a gut for what was politically—how to do it, when to do it, and how to let people back themselves into a corner or play themselves out. He understood the politics of the floor and the house and that, but didn't understand numbers. He didn't understand the technical aspects of legislation. He would have people get in there and argue in front of him. You know, "If you can't convince me, you're not going to convince them."

So it doesn't sound like, then, that the party leadership was exercising this kind of puppet control over what people would do, which is what you hear sometimes.

Oh, that's horseshit. I said earlier that the Republicans, that line was: Ralph Wright, Massachusetts-style politician, that rewards his friends and punishes his enemies, and he's an arm-twister. And that's through them because they don't want to say: Ralph Wright, the guy who got through the clean water bill or who protected mobile home residents. The same Republicans who would bitch about Ralph Wright would go back to their districts and say, "I voted for these six bills," which basically were the ones that he facilitated, supported. He probably got some of them to vote for it because they didn't have—by the time he was done, they probably didn't have a choice.

Recently reflecting back on this issue in a follow-up interview, this legislator added a class component to his analysis of the anti-Wright rhetoric. He recalled that Wright encouraged and rewarded effectiveness for anyone, regardless of whether the legislator was a woman or blue-collar, and that this threatened some of the "old boy network" from more elite backgrounds. He also noted that one of the speakers who followed Wright proved to be more closed and one-sided than Wright had been known to be.

* * *

Ralph Wright would go to you and say, "I really need your vote." And he may even be abrasive. He's likely to be abrasive sometimes. But if you go to Ralph and say, "Look, Ralph, I just can't do it, I just can't do it. I don't like it," or "it's all wrong," or "my mother-in-law will leave me out of her will," or whatever it is. "On this one, I can't even consider it." He'll say, "Fine, I understand that. If I get in a real bind, can I come and talk to you again?" And he'll walk away.

Yeah, he won't give up. But if you keep saying no and you have what he thinks is a—whether it be conscience or constituency reasons—he'll never ask you, he'll never challenge you to go against those. But he's very obvious about that when he gets going on that. Where he did, I think, twist arms perhaps—and I think he would be proud of it—it was on the so-called gay rights issue. [I think he would say], "Absolutely, you're damn right I did. I went out in those halls; nobody else could do it." . . .

Ralph can be abrasive, he will get in people's face. I know Ralph and I know he will do anything for you on a personal basis, but he sometimes forgets about people's sensitivities, and that I think can get him into trouble.

* * *

My experience has been, he's used [power] for good things. And so I'm willing to say he's aggressive and he plays hardball, and that's OK with me . . . for my causes. If I was on the other side, I would say, "This is an outrage! How can we tolerate this?" He has no more power than we give him, ultimately. He's a man who doesn't blink very often, doesn't bluff. He's ready to pull the trigger if he has to. . . . To come up against him, you've got to be ready because he's going to go all the way. Most people back down.

Now he's got this aura about him. It's bigger than he is. . . . [But] if you believe in what you're going to do and you don't back down, you can work with him. . . . It's all how you go about it. If you go up against him and you do it the right way, you'll be OK. If you try to double-cross him, if you try to play a game, then you're liable to end up on the bad side of him. You're liable to end up banished in a nasty committee. . . . I believe, though, that he just doesn't sit back there and tell people what to do without listening to people—you just have to know how to do that.

What does the man himself say? There are some things I'd like to include below, but despite Wright's repeated protestations that I could quote him on everything he said during our conversations unless he specifically informed me otherwise, I will restrain myself. Including them would violate the spirit of the context for our conversations, if not his exact instructions. Nonetheless, here are some excerpts that shed some light on how he saw his leadership, and provide support for both the pro- and anti-Wright views. Readers interested in his speakership might also consult his memoirs.

I could read people. I knew where their hot buttons were. That wasn't so much that it would benefit me, which it did, as it was that I was interested in people. I like people. . . . So I would listen to people. Some people were motivated by pretty ordinary things. They just wanted to do a good job. They didn't want to be embarrassed. They liked the heat of battle. There were people who had a trauma about speaking on the floor. . . . I hate to say this, but more than once, I reread Machiavelli.

. . . I believe in confrontation. I believe in knowing who's sitting in front of you, even if they're in the back of the room. If you had people who were fervent on issues, you had to have an agenda that included some of them. If you had people who were absolute nos, you had to at least be willing to take them on. If you're going to have a fight, if you're going out in the alley, get your goddamn hands out of your pockets. Don't go out there thinking you're going to be able to talk the guy out of administering a beating. You're going to take a beating and you might as well put up the best fight you can.

In the middle group, you found out what turned them on. If it wasn't issues, maybe it was a conference you could send them to. Maybe it was the Red Sox. I won the speakership by one vote, when I was in the minority. I don't know whether that's ever been done before. . . . And they were for the most part very conservative Republicans, the 8 or so that came over and voted for me. Why did they do that? I know why, because I paid attention to them. I would stop and chat with them. Not talk about issues—we'd just get in a fight over that.

But maybe talk about the Red Sox or about my car battery. . . . That was no different than being a teacher and liking the smell of the classroom.

. . . I've always had an agenda. I've always been a liberal. . . . For instance, nobody had to explain to me why we should change the health system. I know why universal health care is a must for America. . . . From the moment it got thought of or I was in a position to be able to think about these things, I wanted to reform how we paid for schools—the unfairest tax known to man is the property tax. It's got nothing to do with your wealth.

. . . Now where did I get the agenda? With health care it came from the governor. With property tax reform it came from me, this time.

. . . There are three ways you vote in a legislature. The highest level of vote is the conscience vote. You got to be careful with that; you can't make everything a conscience issue. If you're the rep from Istanbul, and you come to me and say, "We got to have a bridge. Can you help me on this, Ralph?" Yeah, sure. We'll build two hundred bridges this year, you might as well have one. Make sure it goes over a river. . . . Conscience votes, there's not a lot of them.

. . . Then there's the constituent vote, if you can ever figure out what the hell your constituents want. I didn't have money to send a poll out three times a week, saying, "What do you think about these ten issues?" . . . I guess if I was forced, I'd say I come from a fairly liberal district and I would probably be pretty safe voting the liberal way, which I was, obviously. But it's not a guarantee.

There's a third way of voting, and that's what I call your seatmate voting. If you turn to me and say, "Ralph, will you help me? I need this bridge." Yeah sure, what the hell, no problem. I don't care about them. And the bulk of those bills you don't care about. So that's where the horse-trading comes in. I don't know how many times I gave a lecture to new members—and sometimes veteran members who never got it—saying, "Why are you such a hard-ass?" Almost like you take greater pride in standing up to somebody than saying sure, let me help you. Don't you understand that that's how coalitions are put together, that someday you are going to need *them*? People will forgive, but they never forget, in politics.

. . . So there were three groups of people and there were three ways of motivations to vote, and you just had to understand them. I don't think, again, it took a rocket scientist to figure this out. I had an agenda. I believed in it.

. . . The caucus guides you too. . . . They were going to be conservative, liberal, lots in the middle. And you had to go down to the caucus, and try and decipher what the caucus wanted to do because they had to have a sense of empowerment. We used to, behind the scenes—up front, we'd go down there and say, "OK, what are your priorities?" And hope they list your priorities. But even if they didn't, it was so difficult in caucus, with the dichotomy of personalities and philosophies, that they'd never agree on anything. When I left there we had 88 members—if you got 35 members to agree on the second coming of Christ, it was a miracle. So you could always leave the caucus and say, "Well, the caucus is undecided, so we'll take our own lead." I was pretty good [at] knowing what I wanted, and going down and steering the caucus—getting them to believe that this is what they want.

With the liberals, I didn't have any problems. . . . With the middle group, you probably had to have three good reasons. . . . With the conservatives, you had to work at them. You might have to call them and say, "Hey, stay with me on this one. I'd really appreciate it. I need your help on this."

. . . What did [vote counting] amount to? It wasn't anything secret. . . . It was just hard work. It was keep talking to them. They say they have trouble with this bill. Leave them alone. Go back to them, say, "You know, I've been thinking about that. What if I change this section? I listened to what you said yesterday. You were having trouble, section 7108. What if we can change that? Would you be all right with the bill?" They might say, "Yeah, I think I can help." *If* you can change it. If it changes the whole temper of the bill, you have to try to get to them some other way.

You have to know where they're coming from. . . . Now if they really just want a junket to San Francisco and they're playing a game with you—"Well, I just don't think I can support this vote back home." They were testing me. They were seeing how committed I am. And if they could get away voting the easy way and not displeasing the speaker, who had done all these things for them, put them on the committee of their choice, etc. I had done these things. I had given and given and given and given. If they could have got away with that, they would have. But my answer was pretty conclusive: "Goddamn you, this is friendship now. I don't need you when I'm right." They knew I was serious. . . . I had other members who would just hold out; they always wanted to be the last ones on board. I'd say to them, "Boy, it's a good thing this isn't a lifeboat." They were always hard to get. Some just wanted the attention.

. . . You had to be patient with that. People used to say, "Jeez, Mr. Speaker, you're a big, powerful guy." And I'd say, "You know, I've never groveled and humbled myself anywhere near, in all of my life, what I do in a week here." And it was the truth. I took crap from people I would have punched in the nose 20 years earlier. I wouldn't have thought of listening to that crap. And now I'm sitting there saying, "Interesting. Gee, you got a point." Ugh.

. . . You just had to be aware what was driving the member you were speaking to. Was it the junket to San Francisco? Was it just attention? Or was it that he or she was really concerned about this, really had problems, and just would-n't feel right voting for it?

Incompetence

Although I was truly impressed and sometimes even awed by the breadth and depth of the policy and political knowledge that the legislators, taken as a group, possessed, and was actually intimidated by what they were ex-pected to know, there were nonetheless times when I thought that a given legislator was not quite up on the issues being discussed in committee or on the floor. A few of the legislators I met also struck me as somewhat lacking in intellectual curiosity. I do not presume to have the knowledge and expertise to evaluate in detail the intelligence of the legislators, par-ticularly based on my inherently limited experiences of what they know and how their minds work, and of course my own inherent limitations. Furthermore, having a range of intellects in the house is necessarily one hallmark of a citizen legislature. In addition, there are many legitimate forms of division of labor in a legislature, and having a subset of legisla-tors who are most interested and active in developing policy for the state is certainly one of them.

But the subject still needs discussing. I thought that there was room for improvement among some of the legislators I observed. They approached policy-related information on the strictest need-to-know basis, and were far more interested in making interpersonal connections with notable po-litical figures at the capitol and in their districts. It is important to note in this regard that the phenomenon was not apparently related to the state; indeed, in some respects, which I will discuss below, the legislators in the least professionalized legislature were the most competent on an individ-ual basis and considered absent the backing of staff. Neither did it have all that much to do simply with age; the "faceless 40" factor I have de-scribed in chapter 2 had more to do with a general level of activity in en-gaging and pushing policy initiatives, not necessarily levels of knowledge. Legislators who one might place into a faceless 40 category often quietly did their homework in committee and on the floor, and those who were retired obviously had more time for all the reading required.

I did not introduce the topic of competence in our interview conversa-tions, but sometimes the legislators brought it up themselves. Here are some illustrative examples from those who perceived a problem.

There are legislators who don't have the intellect to be up there. They don't—they cannot grasp the issues. I'm not saying they are stupid people but they don't have the intellect to be in the legislature because they cannot grasp the issues. . . . Some of [the legislators] just create problems because they are so out and off the wall, and you look at them and you—when they get up to discuss their point and sit down, the chamber is almost giggling because they've made an absolute fool out of themselves on the floor of the house.

I mean, there was a representative who my district borders, and we were getting into this issue on the radio. We were debating on the casino bill, and I didn't think the casino was good for [a city]. I was like, "Your district is coming back." And he said, "I don't even have a movie theater in my district." I said, "Yes, you do. You have 14 movie theaters in your district." I said, "Yes, you *do*." I even named the street it was located on, that they just opened up about 3 months ago. He said, "There's a movie theater there?" You worry about somebody like that. We're not talking about a little store that opened up. We're talking about Showcase Cinema opened up a new major movie house.

* * *

[There are legislators who] are not very knowledgeable; they're not involved and they generally don't read the bills. They sort of float along and they're there, and it's a prestige kind of thing. And their votes are almost predictable on issues. They're generally old; they've generally been there awhile; they're generally not well educated; they're generally all male. They're what I picture the way the legislature probably was 40 years ago. They used to say in Vermont—each town had one vote—that they sent the dumbest guy in town or the one that they wanted to get out of town, they made him the legislator. . . . You hear that a lot from old Vermonters. . . . They're not folks who stand for anything. Many of them, you wonder how they ever got elected.

Prejudice

Any institution in the United States is going to be marked, to some degree, by prejudice, racism, and sexism. The state legislature is no different. My strong impression, however, is that it is indeed different from most other institutions in the degree to which it has overcome these problems. This claim may strike readers as particularly hard to believe, even compared with some of my other claims. Nonetheless, I believe that relative to most other realms in the professional world, particularly in the private sector, the legislature is remarkably free of prejudice and bias. Note that I am writing here of the way the legislature operates and not about the content of the policies that are passed. I leave that analysis to others. But in the legislature, women and minorities have immediately visible and legitimate claims to positions of leadership, and both groups are needed to pass legislation and conduct the work of the body, and are relied on to do so. Especially at the level of the committee, I did not detect any fundamental exclusion of women or minorities from the process. There are many reasons for this, but one of the primary ones is also the simplest: legislators are people who necessarily mix with a great variety of other people in their day-to-day lives. They learn about and learn to be comfortable with others.

Was there evidence of stereotype-motivated thinking and behavior in my observations of the legislature? Of course there was—and the legislators also recognized it in the interview conversations. Not surprisingly, the problem tended to be identified by minority and female legislators. In all three states, I would occasionally hear the phrase "old boys club." An illustrative example of the experience of the problem is provided by the following excerpt, in which an African American legislator expresses surprise at encountering the problem, given the nature of the legislative position.

I thought that people, once they reached a certain point in life, that even if they had the attitude, that it might be handled in a different manner. . . . Not hiding it but handling it. . . . It's not going away, but you would think people, once they became elected officials, because they are politic and all that stuff to get there—I was really surprised when people reached a level of a state legislator, attempting to make policy decisions for the state, having not arrived at a degree of sophistication to be able to deal with all people.

The Citizen Legislature

With the growing professionalism in state legislatures, candidates facing greater challenges for election (at least when a seat is being contested), the increased sophistication and expense of campaigns, and the growing demands on state government in general, a genuine "citizen legislature" appears to be an endangered species, if it is not already extinct. For many years—at least since the early 1970s—political scientists have called for greater professionalism in state legislatures, so much of this development may be a good thing for democratic representative governance.

Among the three legislatures I studied, Vermont's is certainly the closest to a citizen legislature. Members serving in Vermont come from many walks of life, and on other dimensions, like gender and income, more closely resemble the state's population. Even without the fascination with Ralph Wright, my observations there were in many respects the most interesting of the three states, and set me thinking in particular about the advantages and disadvantages of a less professionalized legislature. I wish to conclude this chapter, and also this book, with some musings and experiences related to this topic.

Absent spending extended periods of time in other equally less professionalized legislatures, it may well be the case that the positive things I am about to describe have more to do with the specific culture of Vermont's legislature or Vermont's political culture more generally. Indeed, having a small state, with a relatively small budget, a relatively small gap between the rich and the poor, and the absence for the most part of seemingly intractable inner-city urban problems may have fueled much of what I relate. Like so many people who have driven through the state's mountains and valleys on a sparkling summer afternoon or a crisp fall morning with the trees ablaze, I too may have been charmed, but by the state's political life. Nonetheless, these impressions remain some of my most powerful experiences from the time I spent working on this project.

I knew something interesting was afoot on my first trip to the state. The legislator I was going to follow around for a couple of days had invited me to stay in the guest room of her home, rather than have me stay at a hotel in her district. That had never happened before. I enjoyed breakfast in the morning with her family, which included a one-legged bird. She referred to Governor Howard Dean simply as "Howard," and took me up to meet him at a health care policy conference that first morning. Later in the trip, at my first opportunity to watch the entire house in action, I sat in the house gallery, which on the first floor of the chamber consisted of a long upholstered bench rimming the wall, separated from the legislators by a simple knee-high wooden railing. Vermont's legislature usually does not get a lot of academic attention beyond the mailed survey, so I was somewhat of a novelty there. As I was sitting and watching, several legislators introduced themselves to me, including someone in the leadership, and we then sat together while they commented on what was going on and the personalities involved. To talk with me, they simply stepped over the railing and joined me on the bench. In most other capitols, legislators must leave the chamber room in order to speak to gallery visitors (a fact many Vermont legislators were surprised to learn).

Suddenly, I noticed that a Republican was standing up reporting a bill to the house—a bill that was apparently going to be backed by the Democrats. This was not a symbolic resolution or a recognition of a high school wrestling team but rather a substantive piece of legislation. I said to no one in particular, "Isn't that a *Republican*? What's he doing reporting the bill? How was *that* allowed?" The leader smiled and replied, "Oh that's right, you're from *New York*." The other bookend on those kinds of experiences came later, on a longer trip to the capital during the height of the legislative session. There is a tradition during the session of a Tuesday "Farmer's Night" in the legislature, when the house chamber is opened in the evening to the entire Montpelier community to attend performances by local artists. Many of the legislators attend as well. People sit where they like. This particular evening a chamber orchestra was playing, and as I was sitting enjoying the music and people watching from a balcony, I was joined by a Republican leader I had come to know. He proceeded to identify for me various state political notables who were sprinkled throughout the audience, including 2 in particular who were beginning a romantic attachment that he was happy to see. There they all were, sharing the experience with their constituents. With a smile, I turned to him and repeated a phrase that he liked to use when talking about the interpersonal aspects of the legislative process: "It's a small state."

In the follow-up interviews, one longtime legislator reflected on the political culture of the state by noting a group of the Vermont National Guard that had been sent to Mississippi to prepare for duty in Iraq.

We're still small enough where those people are people—they're not a number, and they talk about their families. It just drills into me, even up in Burlington, which to some of us is another world because of its urbanization [he laughs], they still have that community spirit and community heart. To me, it's amazing.

Politics and policy in the Vermont legislature took place on a human scale. This was in evidence and reinforced everywhere, from the design and layout of the statehouse to the fact that almost all the legislators ate lunch together in small groups in a cafeteria that was open to anyone. They also conducted much of their individual work and negotiations in the cafeteria. As one former legislator recently observed in a follow-up interview, there were only three or four rooms where it was really possible to close the door and shut others out. Because the legislators had just one committee assignment, and because staff assistance was thin, I found that they tended to know the details of their committee's bills much better than legislators in other states. They listened to each other in committee meetings, in part because they had to rely on each other to do the difficult work of legislating. Committee meetings were authentic work sessions. All of this is mirrored by the fact that Vermont legislators much more frequently chose committee work as "the most important thing" they do as legislators than did the legislators in the other two states.[7] In committees in particular, but also more generally, there was the cultural, physical, temporal, and emotional space to have real conversations, and deliberate openly and honestly, and across party lines. Even in the inner sanctum of the speaker's office, among the so-called lieutenants, there was the feel of a collegial working group, problem solving tough political issues.

The political process at the statehouse was both graspable and inspiring at the same time. It was easy to think, watching the Vermont legislators go about their business, that the citizen legislature "works." It was also easy to conclude that if the legislators were willing to return, and their constituents were willing to return them, they should not be barred from doing so by term limits.

There is another side to the story, of course. As I have mentioned earlier, not all the legislators were up to the task, and in Vermont they did not have the same high backstop of professional staff to keep bad ideas from flying out of the place. It was encouraging, but disturbing too, to see the opinion of the body moved by speeches made on the floor just prior to a bill being voted out, even if the ultimate outcome was seldom in doubt. Thus one Vermont legislator, who had completed a long and successful career in government service at the national level prior to his election to the house, offered the following critical observation of his own chamber:

We're just on the edge of being ineffective, given the kinds of problems, and the detail and the complexity of things we have to deal with. Between people being part-time and not having any staff, and not getting any expense money, for telephones and things like that. . . . The reading, if you do it diligently and conscientiously—I have a hard time keeping up with it.

And given the salary structure of the Vermont legislature, there is another danger: that it attracts certain people who can most afford to serve under those circumstances. Even though Vermont's legislators, on average, live in families with lower incomes than do legislators in either Connecticut or New York, there is nonetheless a tangible sense in the state, related to the resentment toward some of the liberal legislators in the state that I described earlier, of legislative service being in some cases a realm for the well-to-do who are looking for something to do. One former legislator, who though not wealthy, was easily able to accommodate the financial trade-off of service, focused in on this in the follow-up interviews and voiced a concern that the phenomenon was growing.

I do see the body changing—I sound like a curmudgeon here—but I see it changing for the worse because of economics. If you look at the present legislature, you have young people who are in jobs that they get paid while they're away, you have an awful lot of retired people, for whom this is a pleasant second income, and you've got a lot of people who don't need to work anyway. And I don't think that's a citizen legislature that truly represents Vermont. And I see that growing every year—the preponderance of consultants, . . . a lot of trust fund kids.

Another legislator, viewing the same dynamic from closer to the bottom of the economic distribution, revealed a similar frustration during the original interviews.

It's been a nightmare. I went to the legislature and thought, I'll run for the legislature, I'll get myself a good résumé, and I'll apply to law school. . . . Because farming isn't really the place where you can make money, and it's gotten worse. . . . It's a pretty hectic life, where there's not a lot for me. . . .

Even in a small state like this, politics—as much as I hate to admit it, and I hate to admit it more than anybody—politics is easier for people with money. . . . I've made up for lack of money with just plain sheer grit.

Another downside to the citizen legislature as it is currently constituted is that its decisions can often be heavily influenced by the governor's office, with its more fully developed administrative and technical expertise. Indeed, increasing the independence of legislatures was one of the goals behind the movement to professionalize them. A former Vermont house member who went on to serve in the senate and then the governor's administration described how he became much more aware, by experiencing the governing process from both sides, of just how thorough this influence can be.

When I was in the house, . . . we were in a Democratic majority of the house working with a Democratic administration. There were times when I, either personally . . . or as part of our party caucus, would sometimes run head-on into the administration and serious opposition, and not get things done that you think you should have been able to get done.

Conversely, when I became part of the administration, . . . I learned very quickly why the administration gets 90 or 95 percent of what it wants. That's something that I would never thought of, or believed, when I first went into the legislature. It has a great deal to do with knowledge and information . . . and control of information. I think there are an awful lot of positive aspects to having a citizen legislature—one of the downfalls is that I think by default, we defer a lot more power and authority to the administration. . . . I'm not suggesting it's good or bad, it just is. The administration just has so much influence and authority.

. . . We would start the beginning of a legislative session, . . . and we would start with a legislative agenda and initiatives, budget initiatives, financially related issues, fees, taxes, and would end up, almost without exception at the end of the year—we'd have to go around the barn three or four times to get there—but we'd end up with almost 100 percent of what we asked for and started with. I was pleased by it when I was a member of the administration, but frustrated by it when I was a legislator.

He speculates that this dynamic might be different in the upcoming biennium, with a Democratic legislature and a Republican governor.

Another former Vermont legislator, who had not served in the administration but who had been an integral part of a legislative team that had passed a significant reform of the state's educational finance system, echoed this view in describing how unusual the experience surrounding the reform was.

The lobbyists in the statehouse commented on this passage, having watched it, that they had never seen anything like that, where an issue really came out of the legislature. The governor did not provide any leadership on this. The governor was actually pulling in the other direction in some ways. So we actually developed a bill, got it passed, got it onto the governor's desk, signed it into law, and it actually worked. The details had been worked out, in the legislature, by citizen-legislators. Which is not how the system is supposed to work; it's supposed to be, the citizen-legislature is there to review the administration's initiatives.

And then there is the question of just how much of what works well in Vermont can be exported to another state with greater diversity, more urbanization, and a much larger population. How much could be changed without sacrificing the benefits of a more professionalized legislature? Certainly, it is possible to adopt the Vermont model of committee assignments and committee work—there is nothing in a large, diverse state that precludes that. It may also be possible for the leaders in another state to observe some of the benefits of having a more cooperative political culture, and then use that knowledge as an inspiration to change their own culture. But beyond that, stiff limits may set in.

My final thought returns me to where I started this book. In order to work well, the citizen legislature asks a lot from its members. Making the professional and emotional commitment to the demands of legislative service, and scrambling to assemble the money and time to pursue reelection, while at the same time maintaining a happy, healthy, and financially secure family, is probably asking too much.

Before anything else, these legislators need to be paid a good professional wage that reflects the importance and responsibility of their work. In Connecticut and New York, $100,000 per year is not extravagant, and from the standpoint of the states' budgets or a comparison with the corporate world, it is cheap. In Vermont, recognizing that the budget is much smaller and the legislative job can be less than full-time throughout the year, something like $30,000 would be appropriate. But given recent public views about political life and politicians, pay raises for legislators are not likely to be popular proposals. Legislators are not earning the money they are currently getting, so the complaint will go. That view is widely shared across the nation, and many state legislatures have essentially given up on raises in recent years—indeed, only twenty-four states have raised their legislative pay since 1999, including cost-of-living adjustments.[8]

Of course, raising the pay levels as I am suggesting runs the risk of placing into service a permanent class of politicians, thereby threatening some of the most significant benefits of a citizen legislature. In reflecting back on his service, one legislative leader who decided to retire in large part because of the financial trade-offs involved in public service nonetheless held onto the view that the comings and goings of legislators who struggle with the tension is a good thing.

I think it's important to maintain both feet in a real-life, nonpolitical situation, if you can, at the same time you serve in office. . . . It's not a lifetime thing—it shouldn't be. It shouldn't be a career. It should be a stage in your life when you provide some public service. . . . It's good to have the change in faces too. I think the process benefits from people who go in, do a good job and leave, and let new people with new ideas, and maybe a little more initiative at the time, more optimistic, try it again, pull the oar. . . . I like the renewal aspect of it—it refreshes itself all the time, which is I think very healthy.

On the other hand, as many current and former legislators observed, the financial tensions are only growing with each passing year, so that a genuine citizen legislature might be threatened as much or more by salaries that are too low as it is by salaries that are too high.

The way campaigns are currently financed probably has as much to do with keeping a wider variety of people out of legislative service, and causing a burden for those who do serve, as does the stingy legislative pay scale. Setting aside for a moment concerns about the effects of private money on the governing process and policy outcomes, the current private financing system privileges wealthy and well-connected potential candidates. Furthermore, raising the money necessary for a run can take an enormous amount of effort, and greatly adds to the time required both to seek and retain an elected office. For these reasons, instituting some system of public financing of campaigns is as critical as paying the legislators a good wage.

Arizona's "clean elections" system is a good place to start. It is voluntary, but it also provides matching funds for candidates who accept the public financing yet are being outspent by a privately financed opponent or who are targeted for defeat by interest groups making independent expenditures.[9] Thus, candidates hoping to outspend publicly financed opponents through private contributions must decide early on in the process whether they want to risk coming up short. The data from the 2002 and 2004 election cycles suggest that the system attracts a greater number of candidates, increases small donations by a greater number of people, evens out the effects of money on electoral outcomes, and has a positive effect on overall political participation.

But large increases in legislative pay and significant reforms of campaign financing are distant prospects in most states. Thus, as it is currently constituted, there is a perverse irony in the citizen legislature: What may be good for the political process and the civic life of the state may be bad for the individual legislators. That is an irony the Romans would have found rich.

Appendix
Methods and Contexts

One of the advantages of choosing to study state legislatures is that it is possible to observe and interview the legislators themselves rather than members of their staffs.[1] This difference was critical in a study like this one, which required extended access in order to gather and tell the legislators' stories. But there are good reasons to study state legislators, beyond simply enhanced access.

Why Study State Legislators?

State-level governments have always been important elements in the nation's political system, and for that reason alone their legislatures are worthy subjects of study. But during the past 30 years, state legislatures have changed dramatically. In particular, they have become increasingly professional; that is, they have increased their institutional independence, become more productive and competent, and retained a higher percentage of their principal workforce—legislators. Consequently, their significance as policymaking institutions has increased.

But along with this increased professionalization and influence has come a fragmentation of power within legislatures.[2] Individual legislators run their own sophisticated and increasingly costly campaigns, draw on pools of competent, professionally trained staff, if not their own individually assigned staffers, and forge their own individual relations with members of the media. As collections of these individuals, legislatures are thus harder to lead than they used to be. Legislatures are becoming more egalitarian internally; they are more open to the influence of individual legislators. As Alan Ehrenhalt notes: "The only way to win [in the legislature] is to traffic in the commodities that make a difference in any open political system at any level—talent, enthusiasm, and time."[3] It is also becoming harder just to *be* a state legislator as well as to *become* one. One must work hard at it and must really want it. One must be a talented entrepreneur.

In light of these changes, knowledge about why state legislators pursue office, how they experience their service, and how they wrestle with decisions to leave or stay becomes even more timely and relevant than it was before. As state legislatures become more powerful externally and more egalitarian internally, the individuals who are able, willing, and predisposed to make a long-term commitment to the legislative process will have even more impact on the state's policies.

In addition, with the "devolution" of much political authority and policy responsibility from the federal level to the states during the past 25 years, the state legislature's prominence as an important locus of policymaking is heightened even further.[4] Granted, there is much concern that the states will not be up to the task of responsibly taking over significant national programs, in particular that they do not possess sufficient legislative and administrative capacity. But regardless of whether states embark on a desperate "race to the bottom"—unraveling the set of social programs that had previously existed at the national level—or engage in a new era of innovation and experimentation—evoking the cherished notion of fifty separate "laboratories of democracy"—they will have a central importance in understanding the nature of U.S. politics.

Methods

This study employs the traditional methods used to research legislatures: collection of official record data, administration of surveys, engaging in observation, and conducting interviews.

Granted, the conclusions that we might draw from this study are obviously limited to some extent by the attention to three houses during one 2-year time period, with follow-up interviews occurring several years later. It is possible that the particular types of issues considered by a legislature in a given session or the particular political dynamics existing in a state at that time will influence the patterns found within that chamber. Such effects could distort not only our notion of recruitment into, service in, and exit from the specific chamber or legislatures more generally but also our notion of the different patterns found across different kinds of legislatures. In this regard, a sustained longitudinal study with a larger number of chambers would be preferred. But there is clearly a trade-off between breadth and depth involved here, and for my purposes of trying to understand the totality of recruitment, service, and exit at the individual level, I have decided to emphasize depth.

There are good reasons, however, to think that this study is likely to uncover generally valid patterns within and among the chambers (assuming such patterns exist). First, although each state's legislature is different from the next, the legislatures I have chosen are reflective in some key respects of the mix across the nation. Second, the time period in which I conducted my examination was for the most part not remarkably different from other periods in the recent history of the three states (with the exception of Vermont's consideration in 1994 of a major health care reform proposal). It was in most respects a time of "politics as usual." As Robert Putnam argues, this is an important consideration in studying legislatures.[5] Third, the use of in-depth interviews and selected follow-up conversations taps into a longer-term perspective, and allows some feel for potential period and generational influences.

I mailed surveys in 1994 to all the house members. Two hundred and thirty-three legislators returned completed surveys, for an overall response rate of 52 percent—49 percent in Connecticut, 44 percent in New York, and 63 percent in Vermont. These rates either match or are higher than those of many comparable state-level studies.[6] Survey respondents were representative of the chamber populations on the following dimensions: gender, race, party identification, age, seniority, activity levels, margin of victory, number of bill introductions, number of speeches made on the chamber floor, and ideology as measured by interest group ratings of voting behavior.[7] The survey contains questions concerning various aspects of legislative activity, attitudes toward service in the legislature, general areas and levels of legislative interest, views of the process of representation, ideology, views of the district, and plans for the future. Many of the questions were originally developed for a separate study.

The most noteworthy parts of the study, however, are the interviews and observations. During 1994 and 1995, I interviewed 77 legislators— 21 in Connecticut, 30 in New York, and 26 in Vermont. The interviews ranged in length from 50 minutes to 4 hours, and averaged approximately 2 hours. The longer interviews were usually spread out over two meetings. They took place at the capitol, and in district offices, business offices, homes, diners, and restaurants—in a small number of cases they were conducted over the telephone. Interview subjects were chosen to reflect the population of the entire chamber in each state in terms of age, gender, party, seniority, prior legislative service, occupation, education, length of residence in state, marital and children status, race, and type of district (readily available information on these items varied somewhat with each state).

The interview covered the topics that are the primary concern of this book: recruitment, attitudes about service, and decisions to leave or stay. I asked the legislators to talk about their own experience and also to comment on their colleagues. In addition, the interview contained questions about an assortment of legislative activities.

In constructing the interview, I attempted to leave it open enough to allow the legislators to formulate their views as they wished, yet structured enough to allow for a systematic though almost at all times qualitative analysis. My strategy here was similar to Putnam's: to create an interview that would "suggest certain topics for discussion, striving for a formulation as constant as possible across interviews, but striving also to maintain the tone of a genuine conversation."[8] Following Robert Merton, I also attempted to achieve a *range* regarding the subject matter that was wide enough to allow for the emergence of as many relevant elements and patterns as possible; a degree of *specificity* that was sufficient to compare legislators' responses at certain points; a *depth* that allowed for the emergence of the affective and cognitive meanings of the expressions and experiences they chose to relate; and a sense of the personal *contexts* that gave their present situations and expressions meaning.[9]

My observations largely preceded the time period in which I conducted the interviews, but also extended through it. The process was often, but not exclusively, organized around spending a legislative workday with an individual legislator, and included the observation of floor sessions, committee meetings, and party caucuses (the last in Vermont only); interactions in hallways, lounges, and cafeterias; receptions held by lobbyists; and various district activities. In following the legislators around, I cannot claim to have seen the world as they see it but I can claim, at least in a limited sense, to have seen their world. In general I was successful in my efforts; most legislators made efforts to include me in everything they did during the day (or tell me about it immediately afterward) and to explain to me what they were doing while they were doing it. In several instances, I was able to see things normally not open to the public; my ticket of "he's with me" gave me admission to some "backroom" scenes I had not planned on seeing.[10]

Finally, although I draw on interviews I conducted with all 77 legislators from the three states, in writing the book I concentrate greater attention on some legislators' comments in order to illustrate the more general points. It is with many of these legislators (and now former legislators) that I conducted the twenty-three follow-up interviews in winter 2004–2005. The interviews were conducted by telephone and averaged approximately 40 minutes in length.

Granted, the information provided by the observations and interviews is far from perfect, but in combination with the other data it offers a substantially more complete portrait of legislative attitudes about service than what we have seen thus far. And from a selfish standpoint, the legislators were simply fascinating people to talk to and spend time with.

Institutional Contexts and the Three Chambers

The comparative aspect of my study will allow me to speculate on whether legislators in one chamber vary systematically from those in another, and if so why. Studying different chambers, and more important studying different *kinds* of chambers, will allow me to examine what institutional factors might be related to different intrachamber patterns. Nonetheless, the primary focus of my work is to understand individual legislators in general.

In this regard, there also must be a clear attention to the institutional context within which the behavior occurs, for it may be the case that the activities that are most meaningful to legislators will vary somewhat from state to state. In my analysis of both the interview and participant observation-based data as well as the official record data, I look for evidence of these differences. Indeed, the significance of context is a crucial reason for using in-depth interviews with legislators as the basis for much of the analysis, for it is through such interviews that the researcher can gain a more nuanced understanding of how these kinds of contextual factors might operate.

I chose the lower houses of Connecticut, New York, and Vermont in order to provide variation on several dimensions that I thought might be important for understanding legislators. To some extent, they were also chosen because they were relatively accessible to me, given my desire to spend substantial amounts of time with the legislators in each state.

Perhaps the most important dimension on which the three houses differ is professionalization. Legislative scholars have consistently emphasized the significance of professionalization in understanding a legislature's political life and the behavior of the members within it. Levels of professionalization have been thought to influence, among other things, the incentives and goals of individual members, the capacity of the institution and its members to fulfill those goals, and the type of person drawn to the legislature in the first place.

The legislatures examined here represent profoundly different levels of professionalization. The legislative scholar Peverill Squire has developed an overall index of professionalization of the state legislatures based on recent data on salary, staff, and time in session, and using the U.S. Congress as a benchmark.[11] In his index, New York's legislature ranked third, Connecticut's legislature ranked twentieth, and Vermont's legislature ranked thirty-third. Similarly, the National Conference of State Legislatures grouped the fifty state legislatures into three categories of professionalization based on the same three factors.[12] Under this scheme, New York's legislature was placed in the most professionalized category (full time, high pay, large staff), Connecticut's legislature was placed in the middle category (a hybrid), and Vermont's legislature was placed in the least professionalized category (part time, low pay, small staff).

Discussions of personal finances come up repeatedly in my book. Note that at the time of the interviews, New York's legislators earned $57,500, along with per diem allowances for session days and travel, and a mileage allowance. In addition, most legislators also qualified for extra stipends in lieu of salary for committee and leadership duties, commonly known as "lulu," which at that time could be as high as $30,000. Connecticut's legislators earned $16,160, supplemented only by a mileage allowance. A small number of leadership positions qualified for additional compensation, as much as $6,400. Vermont's legislators earned $8,160, with a per diem allowance for session days and a mileage allowance. Only the speaker earned an additional compensation of $8,160.

Other potentially important dimensions on which the states differ include the historical context of party control and competition, the sheer quantity of legislative output, the influence of outside forces such as interest groups, and the type of legislative district (many of these are no doubt related to professionalism). At the time of the interviews, all three of the chambers I examined were operating under a comfortable Democratic majority. But regarding party control and competition more generally, both Connecticut and New York had strong competitive party systems with strong state party leaders within the legislature, while Vermont had a relatively weaker party system that had recently been growing in strength.[13]

In a recent study of electoral competitiveness in all fifty states that placed each state into one of five categories based on the percentage of seats won by less than 60 percent of the vote during the mid-1990s, New York was placed in the most competitive category (more than 50 percent), Vermont in the second most competitive category (40 to 40 percent), and Connecticut in the middle category (30 to 39 percent).[14] The *average* margin of victory for legislators in each state for the election immediately preceding the administration of the interviews and surveys, however, was 44.8 percent in New York, 30.6 percent in Connecticut, and 21.8 percent in Vermont. These apparently inconsistent findings are explained by the number of legislators running completely unopposed, which was highest in New York.[15]

Regarding legislative turnover, a recent study examined turnover in all fifty states during the 1990s and placed each state in one of six categories based on the average yearly turnover. New York was in the most stable category (less than 15 percent), while Connecticut and Vermont were in the middle two categories (20 to 24 percent and 25 to 29 percent, respectively).[16]

Regarding legislative output in terms of introductions and enactments, New York's output has tended to be among the highest (14,600 and 720 enacted in 1993, for example), Vermont's among the lowest (800 and 115), and Connecticut's somewhere around the mean (3,400 and 477).[17]

Interest groups have had a relatively strong influence in Connecticut, and a weaker but growing one in New York and Vermont.[18]

In terms of district type, the three states collectively exhibit a wide variety. In the cases of Connecticut and New York, there is much diversity within the states as well. Regarding district size, a legislator in Vermont obviously represents just a sliver, at around 4,000, of the constituents represented by a legislator in New York, at around 120,000, with Connecticut falling in between, at around 20,000.

In addition, there are differences in institutional norms and mores among the three states. For example, in Vermont, where house members serve on only one committee, formal committee meetings tend to be long working sessions with much discussion and collective deliberation, while in New York, where assembly members often serve on as many as six committees, committee meetings tend to be perfunctory affairs, with only brief discussions and symbolic protests. In Connecticut, where house members usually serve on two or three committees, the meetings are somewhere in between. In the same vein, the overall legislative agendas in New York and Vermont appeared to be more tightly controlled by the leadership than in Connecticut (in Vermont's case, this may have been due to the strength and prowess of the speaker during the time period studied).

I should note, though, that in three potentially important respects the states do not differ that much: political ideology, political culture—at least as rendered by the work of Daniel Elazar—and term limits. Based on a study of liberalism in policy output and state public opinion, the three states are among the top thirteen for policy liberalism and the top eleven for public opinion liberalism.[19] In terms of Elazar's political cultures, the three states are either of the "moralistic" or "individualistic-moralistic" culture.[20] Here, there is good reason to suspect that this does not present a significant problem. Although there is wide acceptance of the importance of state political culture for understanding a state's political dynamics, research suggests that since the 1970s, particularly as legislatures have generally become more professional and populations have become more mobile, this specific notion of culture type by itself may not tell us that much about the kinds of individual legislators found within each state.[21] Finally, also note that none of the three states limits the number of terms a legislator can serve.

Notes

Notes to Chapter 1

1. For more on this aspect of the in-depth interview as I have constructed it, see Reeher 1996.

2. A recent exhaustive review of the literature on recruitment and retention in U.S. legislatures observes that little work has been done at the state level on how and why people pursue legislative office, and there is no mention at all of any research directly examining why legislators stay in service—this research is generally inferential, using ambition theory (Moncrief 1999). Two recent books do explore aspects of the recruitment process in state legislatures, but they do not examine the legislative experience in the same depth or from the same perspective as I am doing here (see Moncrief, Squire, and Jewell 2001; Gaddie 2004).

3. For arguments and evidence to this effect, see Reeher 1996; Volgy 2001. Also note that at the time of the interviews, about half of the members of the U.S. Congress had previously served in a state legislature (Berkman 1994).

4. In four states, the limits were repealed by state supreme courts; in two others (Idaho and Utah), they were repealed by the legislature.

5. Based on a recent poll of cable and satellite television subscribers conducted by Peter D. Hart Research Associates (2004). Another poll of Utah citizens during the time that term limits were being repealed there by the legislature showed that 76 percent did not favor repeal (Spangler and Bernick 2003).

6. See Rosenthal 2004, 5.

7. See, for example, Egan 2002; Broder 2001.

8. More realistically, such bodies of citizens could have an important advisory role or inform the public debate. See, for example, Fishkin 1995; Dahl 1989. From the standpoint of actually crafting legislation, this kind of deliberation among the general public is next to impossible given the patterns in media coverage of political matters, the political economy of information flows, and the time and attention for politics available to the average citizen, but an extended argument to this effect would occupy another book. For good overall points on the issue, see Dahl 1989.

9. The figures in this paragraph and the next one are reported in Rosenthal et al. 2003, 15–17; Patterson 2000; Morin 1999. Similar figures are found in a

more recent poll by Peter D. Hart Research Associates (2004) conducted for C-SPAN. Rosenthal et al. also supply a useful reading list on the general topic. Another helpful summary of public views is found in Bok 2001. For public views of state legislatures in particular, see A. Rosenthal 1998, 2; Rosenthal et al. 2001, 4; Rosenthal et al. 2003, 15–17. One study of public views toward state legislatures indicates that disapproval goes up with the level of legislative professionalism and constituency size (Hamman 2001). This finding is consistent with my argument—discussed later in this chapter—regarding the effects of increased political complexity.

10. For a useful summary, see Putnam 2000.

11. For some other examples, see Mahtesian 1998.

12. Volgy 2001, 22.

13. McDonough 2000, 19.

14. See Patterson 2000, 13.

15. For useful summaries, see Patterson 2001; Putnam 2000.

16. See Rosenthal et al. 2003, 17.

17. The poem is reproduced here with Castro's permission. I briefly spoke with her about both her poem and future, and she told me that she plans on studying political science in college, with the ultimate goal of becoming a politician. I take this as a hopeful sign.

18. While trust in national government shot up in the wake of the attacks, it is not known whether opinions about elected politicians changed dramatically (Putnam 2002). It is also not clear whether the change in attitude about national government extended beyond foreign policy, or if it will be permanent. Early returns suggest that the answer is no on all accounts. Summarizing a Roper Center poll designed to plumb the true nature of the apparent spike in government trust, Gary Langer (2002, 9) concluded "what mainly changed after September 11 was the subject—not so much the level of trust, but the focus of that trust. Before the attacks, people were chiefly expressing their low trust in government's ability to handle social issues. After September 11, they were referring primarily to their high trust in its ability to fight terrorism." Even that trust may be waning, as suggested by more recent public opinion polls on the wisdom of undertaking the war in Iraq.

19. This observation has been widely made in several different ways. For various statements, see Hartz 1955; King 1997; Lipset 1996; Reeher 1996.

20. Norman Jacobson ([1963] 1993) has written a fascinating essay exploring this theme and what it has meant for the academic study of political science.

21. Ibid., 269.

22. Ibid.

23. Ibid., 267.

24. Arthur Schlesinger Jr., commencement speech at Middlebury College, Middlebury, Vermont, May 29, 1994, as reprinted in the *Rutland Herald*, June 1, 1994.

25. Here I mean the entire system of campaigning, including but not limited to the financing of campaigns. Consider Britain's regulation of the use of television in campaigns, for example, under which candidates and parties are forbidden from buying television or radio advertisements.

26. For summaries of the data demonstrating this trend in income and wealth, see Danziger and Gottschalk 1995; Keister 2000; Sutcliffe 2001; Vleminckx and Smeeding 2001; the most recent edition of *The Green Book*, published by the U.S. House of Representatives.

Note also that I am making a distinctively relative argument here. Given the nature of politics—a set of persons laboring in a collective decision-making process (either working together or competing) for the purposes of hopefully self-governance—the relative spread of resources is what most matters, not the absolute levels in comparison with points in the past. Having said that, note nonetheless that even in absolute terms, the real incomes of the bottom 40 percent of the nation have fallen in recent years. Between 1977 and 1999, for example, the real after-tax incomes of U.S. households in the bottom fifth of the income distribution fell by 12 percent, while their share of the total income dropped from 5.7 to 4.2 percent. The next lowest fifth in the distribution saw its real income fall by 9.5 percent, and its share of the total income drop from 11.5 to 9.7 percent. On the other hand, households in the highest fifth of the distribution saw their real incomes increase by 38.2 percent, while their share of the total increased from 44.2 to 50.4 percent. Households in the top 1 percent of the distribution enjoyed the steepest ride upward, which is perhaps most relevant to the point I am making about the changing appearance, from a bottom-up perspective, of the campaign finance system. Their real incomes rose 119.7 percent, while their share of the total rose from 7.3 to 12.9 percent (representing more than a 50 percent increase in their proportion of the whole). Their share of the total income was approaching the entire share of the bottom 40 percent. These figures are from the Congressional Budget Office, as reported in the *New York Times*, September 5, 1999.

27. Francia et al. 1999.

28. Phillips 2002, 328. More generally, Phillips supplies a detailed historical overview of how wealth has influenced politics (and vice versa) and argues that the United States is currently approaching a democratic crisis in this regard.

29. Lewis 2004, 4.

30. Among many others, see Patterson 1993, 2000.

31. See, for example, Ginsberg and Shefter 2002.

32. "Isn't it one great precaution not to let them taste of arguments while they are young? I suppose you aren't unaware that when lads get their first taste of them, they misuse them as though it were play, always using them to contradict; and imitating those men by whom they are refuted, they themselves refute others, like puppies enjoying pulling and tearing with argument at those who happen to be near" (*Republic*, Book VII, 539b [Bloom trans.]).

33. See Matthews 1985, 32.

34. For a useful and critical overview, see Green and Shapiro 1994, 98–146. Many of the rational choice theorists respond to these criticisms in Friedman 1996. Although the models have been applied to state legislatures, Congress has received the lion's share of the theory's applications.

35. Note that Green and Shapiro argue that the empirical payoff of this approach has been meager so far. One upshot of their critique is that legislators are "a varied lot," not one-dimensional in the way that rational choice theory would posit (1994, 139). This adds further support to my assertion that legislators need more study as human beings—an argument I make later in this chapter.

36. Dionne 1993.

37. "Greenspan's Sharp Tongue" 2003.

38. "Officials Find Snow Is Problem" 2003; "A Treasure" 2003.

39. Breidenbach and Weaver 2003.

40. See Patterson 2002; Kovach and Rosenstiel 2001; McChesney 2000.

41. See Kriss 2003b.

42. A broader context, however, suggests a somewhat different view of the legislature's spending on its own operations. According to the National Conference of State Legislatures, and using U.S. Census Bureau figures from 2001, the latest available for all 50 states, New York ranks third in the nation in total expenditures on its legislative branch (California and Pennsylvania spend more). The high ranking is not surprising since New York is a big state, with a large budget and a professionalized legislature. But in terms of legislative spending per capita, New York ranks seventeenth, and in terms of legislative spending as a percentage of general state government expenditures, New York ranks twenty-seventh.

43. "Shameful Spenders" 2004.

44. "Populist vs. Demagogue" 2003; "Don't Let Dream Die" 2003. It was left to the city's more progressive alternative paper to provide the opportunity for the senator to explain his reasoning and actions; see Schwartz 2003.

45. "Come Together" 2003; "Desperate for Jobs" 2003.

46. "Walsh and Destiny" 2003.

47. Creelan and Moulton 2004. Though widely heralded, the report often demonstrates a fairly mechanical and formal understanding of the legislative process, and focuses its attention on the legislature, to the exclusion of the electoral process and the governor. It quickly became a truncheon that was swung in almost every newspaper story on the state's political process.

48. Case 2005; "Objection" 2005.

49. See Rosenthal et al. 2003, 21.

50. See Moncrief, Squire, and Jewell 2001; King 1997; Ehrenhalt 1992.

51. For some examples, see King 1997.

52. See Mahtesian 1997, 1998; A. Rosenthal 1998.

53. A. Rosenthal 1998, 72. Note that overall, however, at least in states with-

out term limits, turnover has been in a long-term decline. See Moncrief, Niemi, and Powell 2004.

54. Moncrief, Squire, and Jewell 2001, 1. It should be noted that much of this proportion reflects incumbent legislators crafting safe electoral districts through redistricting.

55. See Hanson 1989, 233–34; Rosenthal et al. 2003, 6.

56. See, for example, A. Rosenthal 1998; Hanson 1989; Mahtesian 1997; Thompson, Kurtz, and Moncrief 1996.

57. Reeher 1996.

58. A recent, notable theoretical and empirical treatment of political office-holder ethics that advances a similar view is Andrew Sabl's *Ruling Passions: Political Offices and Democratic Ethics* (2002). Sabl argues for something he calls "democratic constancy."

59. One of the most concise, pointed, and powerful critiques of individual politicians I have read in recent years, which illustrates the exceptions to the rule, is Bill Keller's (2002) farewell to Senators Strom Thurmond, Phil Gramm, and Jesse Helms. At the state level, see Renzulli 2002. In addition to individual-level exceptions to the rule, there are also, I would concede, certain local political structures in the United States that are problematic for a variety of reasons. City politics in Albany, New York, comes to my mind as a prime and relatively nearby example.

60. Schattschneider 1942, 37.

61. See Gaventa 1980; Greider 1992; King 1997; Phillips 2002; Renzulli 2002. Gaventa might want to correct my characterization of him to an "activist," but since he holds a PhD and has published academic works, I list him here as a political scientist.

62. See Reeher 1996.

63. Regarding this idea, and my way of expressing it, I am following Stainton 1999—and by extension Lorca. Although it stretches the comparison beyond the breaking point, I might have called my book something like *Legislative Ballads*. Here are Stainton's words: "In drafting *Poem of the Deep Song*, Lorca sought to capture the Gypsy world not from the outside, as his predecessors had done, but from within, to suggest rather than to explain. He aimed to create a body of work that Gypsies themselves would find authentic" (99).

64. Reeher 1996, 30 (quoting Bruner 1986, 52).

NOTES TO CHAPTER 2

1. This was a multiseat district.

2. These figures are derived from my survey. For additional figures from other states on number of years lived within a legislative district, see Rosenthal 2004, 20; Moncrief, Squire, and Jewell 2001, 35.

3. These figures are derived from my survey. I believe the lower figure in New York is ultimately due to political geography, in particular the prevalence of county and larger city legislatures, as opposed to smaller town councils. Thus, on a per capita basis there are more opportunities for lower level legislative experience in Connecticut and Vermont.

4. I am including in the category of "four or more" responses like "too many to list" and "a lot." In a recent survey of state legislative candidates in 8 states, 23 percent had run for the state legislature in the past, 25 percent *currently* held an elective office, and 10 percent currently held an appointive office. Sixty percent had significant prior political experience working on a campaign or for a party (Moncrief, Squire, and Jewell 2001, 35–37).

5. In lower house races in recent years, candidates in New York raised (or gave to their own campaigns) on average about $50,000 each and about $70,000 if the seat was open. In Connecticut, these averages were about $14,000 and $16,000, respectively. In Vermont, they were about $1,800 and $2,000, respectively. The figures are based on information reported by the Institute on Money in State Politics, and listed on its Web site.

6. For supporting evidence from a multistate study of candidates, see Moncrief, Squire, and Jewell 2001, 30.

7. In particular, see Reeher 1996, 29–30, 238–39. In making this argument, I am also drawing on the work of John Kingdon and Fred Greenstein, cited in Reeher 1996.

8. This interview took place at about the same time as Robert Putnam's first article on the topic of social capital was published in the *Journal of Democracy*; it is not clear whether he is consciously borrowing the term from that publication or earlier publications by other authors, and I did not think to ask.

9. On the role of family, see Moncrief, Squire, and Jewell 2001, 40.

10. On women's challenges as candidates, see Moncrief, Squire, and Jewell 2001, 97.

11. On female success rates, see Seltzer, Newman, and Leighton 1997; Darcy, Welch, and Clark 1994. On women coming to the legislature at a comparatively older age and their different paths taken to the legislature, see C. S. Rosenthal 1998.

12. p = .03.

13. p = .02. The differences are consistent across the three states. The largest relative gap is in New York.

14. See Squire 1992. This relationship has been taken as fact for many years in legislative research, but the time has probably come to reexamine it critically. Changes in the assumptions and decision making of state party leaders, who often recruit candidates, as well as more general social changes prompt this observation. See also Nechemias 1987; Sanbonmatsu 2000.

15. Likewise, in Moncrief, Squire, and Jewell's study (2001, 37) proportionately more candidates who currently held political office ran for open seats, which suggests more strategic behavior on their part. This finding is also consistent with those on congressional and U.S. Senate candidates (see Berkman 1994; Francis 1993).

16. On the change more generally, see Ehrenhalt 1992.

Notes to Chapter 3

1. The story of the Connecticut income tax can be found later in this chapter.

2. One question concerned the relative importance of being a legislator compared with other significant life activities (Pearson correlation coefficient = 0.25; Sig. < 0.01), and the other concerned the relative influence of the respondent on the entire house chamber (Pearson correlation coefficient = 0.26; Sig. < 0.01).

3. Lascher 1993, 29, 34.

4. These findings are based on an independent samples t-test analysis of the relation between these variables and whether or not the respondents selected an 8 or a 9 on the 9-point scale.

5. Ideology was measured by the answer to the following question: "Relative to your colleagues in both parties in the house [assembly in New York], what are your political beliefs?" The respondents located themselves on a 9-point scale from "conservative" to "liberal." Distance from the ideological center of the house was derived by taking the difference between a legislator's own response and the median response of the entire house—in other words, running the legislator's own sense of self relative to his or her colleagues up against the median of the colleagues' relative senses of themselves. The mean ideological self-location for the respondents who selected either an 8 or a 9 on the 9-point job satisfaction scale was 4.7; the mean ideological self-location for the other respondents was 5.6 (Sig. < 0.01). The mean ideological distance from the chamber median for the respondents who selected either an 8 or a 9 was 1.5; the distance for the other respondents was 2.0 (Sig. < 0.01). For how these ideological measures match up with interest group ratings based on voting behavior, see Reeher 2001.

6. Pearson chi-square = 11.64; Sig. < 0.01.

7. In conducting an earlier set of observations in Connecticut, I witnessed a particularly dramatic example of this exclusion occurring within an appropriations committee meeting (Reeher 1996, 309). Here is how I reported it then: "Toward the end of the meeting, a Republican legislator offered an amendment concerning drunk driving. In a passionate argument in its favor, he referred to the practice of making a record against the Democrats [by offering politically popular amendments at a late date, knowing that they would fail, and then turning their failures into press releases], but swore that this was not part of that

strategy. He emphasized that the amendment spent no more money than the provisions it was designed to replace, only that it spent the money earlier. Democratic leaders then argued against the amendment, out of fiscal considerations. This was somewhat ironic, as the committee had just spent most of the previous two hours approving, on party votes, provisions recognized by members of both parties as 'pork-barrel' items for the Democratic legislators. The drunk driving amendment was defeated, again on a party vote. Some members of an organization called Remove Intoxicated Drivers (RID), who had been invited to the meeting by the Republican legislator, openly wept over the decision."

8. For a striking contrast, see the story of my first spate of observations in Vermont's capitol, related in the final section of chapter 5.

9. Rosenthal 2004, 22.

10. They also received compensation for travel and living expenses, which varied by state. See the appendix. In Vermont, the legislators were eligible for additional pay when meeting beyond the scheduled adjournment date, but they sometimes felt politically constrained not to accept this pay. They also received a per diem rate of compensation to offset expenses associated with living at the capital during the session.

11. See, for example, Kriss 2003a.

12. $p = .02$.

13. Pearson chi-square = 16.41; $p < .01$. These figures are derived from information in the surveys and official biographies.

14. Note that I spent a bit of time observing this particular legislator and came away with the clear impression that contrary to her self-description, she worked extremely hard and put a great amount of time into the legislative job.

15. Pearson chi-square = 57.68; $p < .01$. These figures are derived from information in the surveys and official biographies. Most state legislators have outside careers. A recent five-state study placed the figure at about 70 percent (Rosenthal 2004, 23).

16. Median ages in Vermont, Connecticut, and New York are 51, 45, and 49, respectively.

17. U.S. Bureau of the Census 1996, 465.

18. See the appendix for more information on the electoral competitiveness in the three states.

19. For a different set of statistics on electoral competition, see the appendix.

20. Kennedy 1956, 9. I was originally directed to this letter by Mack Mariani.

21. Lasswell 1948, 39. See also Lasswell 1960. For a similar discussion of these issues, see Reeher 1996, 20.

22. See Rutherford 1971.

23. Barber 1965.

24. The following description relies in part on previously published material; see Reeher 1996.

25. Note that the new tax system including an income tax was not dramatically more progressive than the old system based almost exclusively on property and sales taxes. In the version that was ultimately passed, families earning between $60,000 and $90,000 (a large group in Connecticut) still paid a higher percentage of their income in overall taxes than families earning higher incomes.

Notes to Chapter 4

1. Pearson chi-square = 7.68; Sig. < .01.

2. See, for example, Lascher 1993; Francis and Baker 1986; Blair and Henry 1981.

3. p = .07. Satisfaction could also increase as a *product* of service, but the combination of the relationship between terms served and satisfaction as well as the relationship between stated intentions to pursue additional terms and satisfaction suggests at least that causality runs the other way as well.

4. These factors are consistent with traditional "ambition theory" in legislative research, but they also drill deeper into specific reasons to leave. While the factors involved in deciding to leave have been studied to some degree regarding the U.S. Congress, they have received scant attention in state legislatures. For an overview, see Moncrief 1999. Generally consistent with my interview-based findings are those from a survey of Indiana and Missouri state legislators conducted several years previously (Francis and Baker 1986).

5. This finding is in contrast with a previous study of Arkansas state legislators, which found that family concerns constituted the single most important factor in decisions to leave, above political and financial concerns (Blair and Henry 1981). The study's findings, however, based as they are on a relatively unprofessionalized legislature, are consistent with my state-based pattern in the relative strength of the personal factors, with Vermont's legislature featuring them most prominently.

6. Council of State Governments Various years; see also Rosenthal et al. 2001, 36.

7. The survey question asked the respondents to rank the "following five arenas of government, policy, and politics in order of their interest to you as a legislator: district affairs; region/city affairs; state affairs; national affairs; international affairs."

8. p = 0.14.

9. The classic statement on political ambition is Schlesinger 1966. One problem with ambition theory, at least as it is often applied, is that it tends to confuse possible futures and orientations toward those futures with types of people. As the interviews here demonstrate, however, at the individual level reality is much more contingent and changeable with circumstance and situation.

10. Pearson chi-square = 3.37; Sig. = .07.

11. Only in Vermont was the difference close to being statistically significant (Sig. = .08).

12. New York legislators averaged 4.6 terms, Connecticut legislators averaged 3.1, and Vermont legislators averaged 3.4.

NOTES TO CHAPTER 5

1. One of the legislators I interviewed, however, was later tainted by a scandal associated with an appointed political position; another was tainted by a personal scandal.

2. Still one of the best analytic primers on how this occurs is John Gaventa's *Power and Powerlessness* (1980); one of the best empirical accounts of how this occurs in the national political arena is William Greider's extended investigative report of politics in the mid- to late 1980s, *Who Will Tell the People* (1992).

3. One recent issue in which these tensions were revealed in all their complexity was the reform in the financing of public education. The legislation was complicated, but in its essence it made the funding of education more of a statewide effort that involved a limited amount of wealth sharing among the towns. In addition to the obvious lines of conflict between property-rich towns with relatively fewer school-age children (due to the prevalence of vacation homes) and poorer towns, according to several legislators, the issue also pitted some of these poorer and more "native" towns *against* a reform that would actually serve their own economic interests because it threatened their local control over school funding.

4. For a more detailed qualitative treatment of party leadership, partisanship, and the party caucus as they played out in Connecticut a few years earlier, see Reeher 1996, 215–23.

5. I am breaking with anonymity here for two reasons: First, it is impossible to discuss this case of leadership otherwise; and second, Wright repeatedly stated in our conversations that he did not mind being quoted by name and otherwise being identified, and in fact encouraged me to do so.

6. A recent study of the institutional powers of the speaker's office in the forty-nine states with lower houses (Nebraska's legislature is unicameral), based on information from 1995–1996, placed New York tenth, Vermont twenty-third, and Connecticut thirty-fourth. New York and Vermont were only separated by 2 points on a scale with a 16-point range in scores. See Clucas 2001.

7. See the table in chapter 3. My observations are also consistent with a multistate study of leadership styles in committees that found a positive relationship between both the number of women in a legislature and less professionalization, and collaborative leadership (C. S. Rosenthal 1998).

8. These figures were derived from information taken from the National Conference of State Legislatures' Web site, and the Council of State Governments's *The Book of the States*, various years.

9. To qualify, legislative candidates must raise 210 $5 contributions from registered voters in their district. They are then provided with approximately $11,000 for a primary election and $17,000 for the general election. The matching funds top out at three times the original allotment. The information on Arizona's system reported here is from various publications of the Clean Elections Institute, a nonprofit organization based in Phoenix. Vermont has a similar system, but it only applies to campaigns for governor and lieutenant governor. Vermont's elections for the legislature are still pretty inexpensive compared with most other states, but they have been getting more costly in recent years. The other state with an extensive system of public financing for legislative elections is Maine.

Notes to the Appendix

1. For more elaborate discussions of the advantages of this kind of access at the state level, see Rosenthal 1988; Loomis 1992; Reeher 1996. Also note that some studies of Congress have made valid *theoretical* arguments for concentrating on staff. See, for example, Burgin 1991; Hall 1996.

2. See Ehrenhalt 1992; Rosenthal 1998; Jewell and Whicker 1994; Moncrief, Thompson, and Kurtz 1996.

3. Ehrenhalt 1992, 165.

4. There is some controversy over how much of this devolution has actually occurred, and whether any such trends were effectively reversed since 9-11 or were simply an artifact of national-level belt-tightening in certain policy areas.

5. Putnam 1973, 12.

6. See, for example, Thomas 1994; Hedge, Button, and Spear 1996, 87; Rosenthal 2004, 14.

7. See Reeher and Sowards 2000; Reeher 2001.

8. Putnam 1973, 19.

9. See Merton, Fiske, and Kendall 1956.

10. For more on this aspect of state legislative research, see Reeher 1996.

11. Squire 2000.

12. Verhovek 1995. See also Gierzynski and Ressmeyer 1991; King 2000.

13. Mayhew 1986; Hrebenar and Thomas 1993.

14. See Rosenthal et al. 2001, 10.

15. The margin of victory was calculated based on the difference, as a percentage of the total vote, between the winner and the best loser. This figure represents the difference between winning and losing for any legislator, and accom-

modates the fact that in Vermont, there are many multimember districts in which the closest runner-up may be from the same party as a winner.

16. Rosenthal et al. 2001, 36.

17. Council of State Governments Various years.

18. Hrebenar and Thomas 1993.

19. Wright, Erikson, and McIver 1987.

20. Elazar 1972.

21. See Freeman and Lyons 1992; Baker 1990; Thomas 1991. See also Ehrenhalt 1992.

References

"A Treasure Waits for a Candidate." 2003. *The Syracuse Post-Standard*, January 25.

Baker, John R. 1990. "Exploring the 'Missing Link': Political Culture as an Explanation of the Occupational Status and Diversity of State Legislators in Thirty States." *Western Political Quarterly* 43:597–611.

Barber, James David. 1965. *The Lawmakers: Recruitment and Adaptation to Legislative Life*. New Haven, CT: Yale University Press.

Berkman, Michael P. 1994. "State Legislators in Congress: Strategic Politicians, Professional Legislatures, and the Party Nexus." *American Journal of Political Science* 38:1025–55.

Blair, Diane Kincaid, and Ann R. Henry. 1981. "The Family Factor in State Legislative Turnover." *Legislative Studies Quarterly* 6:55–68.

Bok, Derek. 2001. *The Trouble with Government*. Cambridge: Harvard University Press.

Breidenbach, Michelle, and Teri Weaver. 2003. "Office Seekers Not Always Voters." *The Syracuse Post-Standard*, November 1.

Broder, David S. 2001. *Democracy Derailed: Initiative Campaigns and the Power of Money*. New York: Harvest.

Bruner, Jerome. 1986. *Actual Minds, Possible Worlds*. Cambridge: Harvard University Press.

Burgin, Eileen. 1991. "Representatives' Decisions on Participation in Foreign Policy Issues." *Legislative Studies Quarterly* 16:521–46.

Case, Dick. 2005. "Same State of Affairs Makes Arnold Look Good." *The Syracuse Post-Standard*, January 8.

Clucas, Richard A. 2001. "Principal-Agent Theory and the Power of State House Speakers." *Legislative Studies Quarterly* 26:319–38.

"Come Together: Don't Let Destiny Fall Because Elected Leaders Couldn't Find Their Way." 2003. *The Syracuse Post-Standard*, July 13.

Council of State Governments. Various years. *The Book of the States*. Lexington, KY.

Creelan, Jeremy M., and Laura M. Moulton. 2004. *The New York State Legisla-*

tive Process: An Evaluation and Blueprint for Reform. New York: New York University Brennan Center for Justice.

Dahl, Robert A. 1989. *Democracy and Its Critics*. New Haven, CT: Yale University Press.

Danziger, Sheldon, and Peter Gottschalk. 1995. *America Unequal*. New York: Russell Sage Foundation.

Darcy, R., Susan Welch, and Janet Clark. 1994. *Women, Elections, and Representation*. Lincoln: University of Nebraska Press.

"Desperate for Jobs." 2003. *The Syracuse Post-Standard*, July 6.

Dionne, E. J., Jr. 1993. "The High Cost of Cynicism." *The Washington Post National Weekly Edition*, May 24–30.

"Don't Let Dream Die." 2003. *The Syracuse Post-Standard*, June 26.

Egan, Timothy. 2002. "They Give, but They Also Take: Voters Muddle States' Finances." *The New York Times*, March 2.

Ehrenhalt, Alan. 1992. *The United States of Ambition: Politicians, Power, and the Pursuit of Office*. New York: Times Books.

Elazar, Daniel J. 1972. *American Federalism: A View from the States*. 2nd ed. New York: Thomas Crowell.

Fishkin, James S. 1995. *The Voice of the People: Public Opinion and Democracy*. New Haven, CT: Yale University Press.

Francia, Peter L., et al. 1999. "Individual Donors in the 1996 Federal Elections." In *Financing the 1996 Election*, ed. John Clifford Green. Armonk, NY: M. E. Sharpe.

Francis, Wayne L. 1993. "House to Senate Career Movement in the U.S. States: The Significance of Selectivity." *Legislative Studies Quarterly* 18:309–20.

Francis, Wayne L., and John R. Baker. 1986. "Why Do U.S. State Legislators Vacate Their Seats?" *Legislative Studies Quarterly* 11: 119–26.

Freeman, Patricia, and William Lyons. 1992. "Female Legislators: Is There a New Type of Woman in Office?" In *Changing Patterns in State Legislative Careers*, ed. Gary F. Moncrief and Joel A. Thompson. Ann Arbor: University of Michigan Press.

Friedman, Jeffrey, ed. 1996. *The Rational Choice Controversy: Economic Models of Politics Reconsidered*. New Haven, CT: Yale University Press.

Gaddie, Ronald Keith. 2004. *Born to Run: Origins of the Political Career*. Lanham, MD: Rowman and Littlefield.

Gaventa, John. 1980. *Power and Powerlessness: Quiescence and Rebellion in an Appalachian Valley*. Urbana: University of Illinois Press.

Gierzynski, Anthony, and Timothy J. Ressmeyer. 1991. "Professionalism and State Legislators." Paper presented at the annual meeting of the Southern Political Science Association, Tampa, Florida.

Ginsberg, Benjamin, and Martin Shefter. 2002. *Politics by Other Means*. 3rd ed. New York: W. W. Norton.

Green, Donald P., and Ian Shapiro. 1994. *Pathologies of Rational Choice Theory*. New Haven, CT: Yale University Press.

"Greenspan's Sharp Tongue May Have Cost Him His Fed Chair." 2003. *The Syracuse Post-Standard* (Associated Press), February 17.

Greider, William. 1992. *Who Will Tell the People: The Betrayal of American Democracy*. New York: Simon and Schuster.

Hall, Richard L. 1996. *Participation in Congress*. New Haven, CT: Yale University Press.

Hamman, John A. 2001. "Professionalism, Representation, and Public Assessment of State Legislative Performance." Paper presented at the annual meeting of the Midwest Political Science Association, Chicago.

Hanson, Royce. 1989. *Tribune of the People: The Minnesota Legislature and Its Leadership*. Minneapolis: University of Minnesota Press.

Hartz, Louis. 1955. *The Liberal Tradition in America*. New York: Harcourt Brace Jovanovich.

Hedge, David, James Button, and Mary Spear. 1996. "Accounting for the Quality of Black Legislative Life: The View from the States." *American Journal of Political Science* 40:82–98.

Hrebenar, Ronald J., and Clive S. Thomas. 1993. *Interest Group Politics in the Northeastern States*. University Park: Pennsylvania State University Press.

Jacobson, Norman. [1963] 1993. "Political Science and Political Education." In *Discipline and History: Political Science in the United States*, ed. James Farr and Raymond Seidelman. Ann Arbor: University of Michigan Press.

Jewell, Malcolm E., and Marcia Lynn Whicker. 1994. *Legislative Leadership in the American States*. Ann Arbor: University of Michigan Press.

Keister, Lisa A. 2000. *Wealth in America: Trends in Wealth Inequality*. New York: Cambridge University Press.

Keller, Bill. 2002. "Mr. T., Mr. G., and Mr. H." *The New York Times*, January 12.

Kennedy, John F. 1956. *Profiles in Courage*. New York: Harper and Brothers.

King, Anthony. 1997. *Running Scared: Why America's Politicians Campaign Too Much and Govern Too Little*. New York: Free Press.

King, James D. 2000. "Changes in Professionalism in U.S. State Legislatures." *Legislative Studies Quarterly* 25:327–43.

Kovach, Bill, and Tom Rosenstiel. 2001. *The Elements of Journalism: What Newspeople Should Know and the Public Should Expect*. New York: Three Rivers Press.

Kriss, Erik. 2003a. "The Priciest CNY Lawmakers: Hoffmann and Nozzolio." *The Syracuse Post-Standard*, August 3.

Kriss, Erik. 2003b. "Statehouse Spending Freeze Doesn't Add Up." *The Syracuse Post-Standard*, December 29.

Langer, Gary. 2002. "Trust in Government . . . to Do What?" *Public Perspective* (July/August): 7–10.

Lascher, Edward L., Jr. 1993. "Explaining the Appeal of Local Legislative Office." *State and Local Government Review* 25, no. 1:28–38.

Lasswell, Harold D. 1948. *Power and Personality.* New York: W. W. Norton.

Lasswell, Harold D. 1960. *Psychopathology and Politics.* New York: Viking.

Lewis, Charles. 2004. *The Buying of the President 2004: Who's Really Bankrolling Bush and His Challengers—and What They Expect in Return.* New York: Perennial.

Lipset, Seymour Martin. 1996. *American Exceptionalism: A Double-Edged Sword.* New York: W. W. Norton.

Loomis, Burdett. 1992. "Being There: Research in a State Legislature." In "Extension of Remarks," *American Political Science Association Legislative Studies Newsletter* 15:9–10.

Mahtesian, Charles. 1997. "The Sick Legislature Syndrome: And How to Avoid It." *Governing* (February).

Mahtesian, Charles. 1998. "The Politics of Ugliness." *Governing* (July).

Matthews, Donald R. 1985. "Legislative Recruitment and Legislative Careers." In *Handbook of Legislative Research*, ed. Gerhard Loewenburg, Samuel C. Patterson, and Malcolm E. Jewell. Cambridge: Harvard University Press.

Mayhew, David R. 1974. *Congress: The Electoral Connection.* New Haven, CT: Yale University Press.

Mayhew, David R. 1986. *Placing Parties in American Politics.* Princeton, NJ: Princeton University Press.

McChesney, Robert W. 2000. *Rich Media, Poor Democracy: Communication Politics in Dubious Times.* New York: New Press.

McDonough, John E. 2000. *Experiencing Politics: A Legislator's Stories of Government and Health Care.* Berkeley: University of California Press.

Merton, Robert K., Marjorie Fiske, and Patricia L. Kendall. 1956. *The Focused Interview.* Glencoe, IL: Free Press.

Moncrief, Gary F. 1999. "Recruitment and Retention in U.S. Legislatures." *Legislative Studies Quarterly* 24:173–208.

Moncrief, Gary F., Richard G. Niemi, and Lynda W. Powell. 2004. "Time, Term Limits, and Turnover: Trends in Membership Stability in U.S. State Legislatures." *Legislative Studies Quarterly* 29:357–81.

Moncrief, Gary F., Peverill Squire, and Malcolm E. Jewell. 2001. *Who Runs for the Legislature?* Upper Saddle River, NJ: Prentice Hall.

Moncrief, Gary F., Joel A. Thompson, and Karl T. Kurtz. 1996. "The Old Statehouse, It Ain't What It Used to Be." *Legislative Studies Quarterly* 21:57–72.

Morin, Richard. 1999. "Have the People Lost Their Voice?" *The Washington Post National Weekly Edition*, June 28.

Nechemias, Carol. 1987. "Changes in the Election of Women to U.S. Legislative Seats." *Legislative Studies Quarterly* 12:125–42.

"Objection: Lawmakers, Education Officials Should Fight for Students." 2005. *The Syracuse Post-Standard*, January 13.

"Officials Find Snow Is Problem Here at Home." 2003. *The Syracuse Post-Standard*, January 26.

Patterson, Thomas E. 1993. *Out of Order*. New York: Knopf.

Patterson, Thomas E. 2000. "Doing Well and Doing Good: How Soft News and Critical Journalism Are Shrinking the News Audience and Weakening Democracy—and What News Outlets Can Do about It." Typescript. Harvard University.

Patterson, Thomas E. 2001. *The American Democracy*. 5th ed. New York: Mc-Graw-Hill.

Patterson, Thomas E. 2002. *The Vanishing Voter: Public Involvement in an Age of Uncertainty*. New York: Knopf.

Peter D. Hart Research Associates, Inc. 2004. "C-SPAN and the American People 25 Years Later." Washington, DC.

Phillips, Kevin. 2002. *Wealth and Democracy: A Political History of the American Rich*. New York: Random House.

"Populist vs. Demagogue." 2003. *The Syracuse Post-Standard*, June 18.

Putnam, Robert D. 1973. *The Beliefs of Politicians: Ideology, Conflict, and Democracy in Britain and Italy*. New Haven, CT: Yale University Press.

Putnam, Robert D. 2000. *Bowling Alone: The Collapse and Revival of American Community*. New York: Simon and Schuster.

Putnam, Robert D. 2002. "Bowling Together: The United State of America." *American Prospect* (February 11).

Reeher, Grant. 1996. *Narratives of Justice: Legislators' Beliefs about Distributive Fairness*. Ann Arbor: University of Michigan Press.

Reeher, Grant. 2001. "Self-Reported Legislator Ideology versus Interest Group Ratings." *Polity* 34:231–40.

Reeher, Grant, and Kathryn Sowards. 2000. "Representing Reality? On the Accuracy of Legislators' Self-Reported Activity: An Examination of Legislators in Three States." Paper presented at the annual meeting of the Midwest Political Science Association, Chicago.

Renzulli, Diane. 2002. *Capitol Offenders: How Private Interests Govern Our States*. Washington, DC: The Center for Public Integrity.

Rosenthal, Alan. 1988. "State Legislatures—Where It's At." *The Political Science Teacher* 1:1–5.

Rosenthal, Alan. 1998. *The Decline of Representative Democracy: Process, Participation, and Power in State Legislatures*. Washington, DC: Congressional Quarterly Press.

Rosenthal, Alan. 2004. *Heavy Lifting: The Job of the American Legislature*. Washington, DC: Congressional Quarterly Press.

Rosenthal, Alan, John R. Hibbing, Burdett A. Loomis, and Karl T. Kurtz. 2003. *Republic on Trial*. Washington, DC: Congressional Quarterly Press.

Rosenthal, Alan, Karl T. Kurtz, John R. Hibbing, and Burdett A. Loomis. 2001. *The Case for Representative Democracy*. Washington, DC: National Conference of State Legislatures.

Rosenthal, Cindy Simon. 1998. "Determinants of Collaborative Leadership: Civic Engagement, Gender, or Organizational Norms?" *Political Research Quarterly* 51:847–68.

Rutherford, Brent M. 1971. "Psychopathology, Decision-Making, and Political Involvement." In *A Source Book for the Study of Personality and Politics*, ed. Fred I. Greenstein and Michael Lerner. Chicago: Markham.

Sabl, Andrew. 2002. *Ruling Passions: Political Offices and Democratic Ethics*. Princeton, NJ: Princeton University Press.

Sanbonmatsu, Kira. 2000. "Party Differences in the Recruitment of Women State Legislators." Paper presented at the annual meeting of the Midwest Political Science Association, Chicago.

Schattschneider, E. E. 1942. *Party Government*. New York: Farrar and Rinehart.

Schlesinger, Arthur, Jr. 1994. "In Defense of Politics." *Rutland Herald*, June 1.

Schlesinger, Joseph A. 1966. *Ambition and Politics: Political Careers in the United States*. New York: Rand McNally.

Schwartz, Eric. 2003. "Big Bad John." *Syracuse New Times*, July 23–30.

Seltzer, Richard A., Jody Newman, and Melissa Voorhees Leighton. 1997. *Sex as a Political Variable: Women as Candidates and Voters in U.S. Elections*. Boulder, CO: Lynne Rienner.

"Shameful Spenders." 2004. *The Syracuse Post-Standard*, January 2.

Spangler, Jerry D., and Bob Bernick Jr. 2003. "Are Lawmakers out of Touch?" *Deseret Morning News*, March 2.

Squire, Peverill. 1992. "Legislative Professionalization and Membership Diversity in State Legislatures." *Legislative Studies Quarterly* 17:69–79.

Squire, Peverill. 2000. "Uncontested Seats in State Legislative Elections." *Legislative Studies Quarterly* 25:131–46.

Stainton, Leslie. 1999. *Lorca: A Dream of Life*. New York: Farrar, Straus and Giroux.

Sutcliffe, Bob. 2001. *100 Ways of Seeing an Unequal World*. New York: Palgrave.

Thomas, Sue. 1991. "The Impact of Women on State Legislative Policies." *Journal of Politics* 53:958–76.

Thomas, Sue. 1994. *How Women Legislate*. New York: Oxford University Press.

Thompson, Joel A., Karl Kurtz, and Gary F. Moncrief. 1996. "We've Lost That Family Feeling: The Changing Norms of the New Breed of State Legislators." *Social Science Quarterly* 77:344–62.

U.S. Bureau of the Census. 1996. *Statistical Abstract of the United States: 1996.* 116th ed. Washington, DC.

Verhovek, Sam Howe. 1995. "With Power Shift, State Lawmakers See New Demands." *The New York Times*, September 24.

Vleminckx, Koen, and Timothy M. Smeeding, eds. 2001. *Child Well-Being, Child Poverty and Child Policy in Modern Nations.* Bristol, UK: Policy Press.

Volgy, Thomas J. 2001. *Politics in the Trenches: Citizens, Politicians, and the Fate of Democracy.* Tucson: University of Arizona Press.

"Walsh and Destiny." 2003. *The Syracuse Post-Standard*, August 17.

Wright, Gerald C., Jr., Robert S. Erikson, and John P. McIver. 1987. "Public Opinion and Policy Liberalism in the American States." *American Journal of Political Science* 31:980–1001.

Wright, Ralph. 1996. *All Politics Is Personal.* Manchester Center, VT: Marshall Jones Company.

Index

About the Author

Grant Reeher is an associate professor of political science at Syracuse University's Maxwell School of Citizenship and Public Affairs. He is the coauthor of *Click on Democracy: The Internet's Power to Change Political Apathy into Civic Action*, and coeditor of *The Insider's Guide to Political Internships: What to Do Once You're in the Door* and *Education for Citizenship: Ideas and Innovations in Political Learning*. He is also the author of *Narratives of Justice: Legislators' Beliefs about Distributive Fairness*.